OZ: ROAD TO OZ. Contains material originally published in magazine form as ROAD TO OZ #1-6. First printing 2013. ISBN# 978-0-7851-6404-3. Published by MARVEL WORLDWIDE, INC., a subsidiary of MARVEL ENTERTAINMENT, LLC. OFFICE OF PUBLICATION: 135 West 50th Street, New York, NY 10020. Copyright © 2012 and 2013 Marvel Characters, Inc. All rights reserved. All characters featured in this issue and the distinctive names and likenesses thereof, and all related indicia are trademarks of Marvel Characters, Inc. No similarity between any of the names, characters, persons, and/or institutions in this magazine with those of any living or dead person or institution is intended, and any such similarity which may exist is purely coincidental. **Printed in the U.S.A.** , and any such similarity which may exist is purely coincidental. Printed in the U.S.A. ALAN FINE, EVP - Office of the President, Marvel Worldwide, Inc. and EVP & CMO Marvel Characters B.V.; DAN BUCKLEY, Publisher & President - Print, Animation & Digital Divisions; JOE QUESADA, Chief Creative Officer; TOM BREVOORT, SVP of Publishing; DAVID BOGART, SVP of Operations & Procurement, Publishing; RUWAN JAYATILLEKE, SVP & Associate Publisher, Publishing; C.B. CEBULSKI, SVP of Creator & Content Development; DAVID GABRIEL, SVP of Print & Digital Publishing Sales; JIM O'KEEFE, VP of Operations & Logistics; DAN CARR, Executive Director of Publishing Technology; SUSAN CRESPI, Editorial Operations Manager; ALEX MORALES, Publishing Operations Manager; STAN LEE, Chairman Emeritus. For information regarding advertising in Marvel Comics or on Marvel.com, please contact Niza Disla, Director of Marvel Partnerships, at ndisla@marvel.com. For Marvel subscription inquiries, please call 800-217-9158. **Manufactured between 2/11/2013 and 3/15/2013 by R.R. DONNELLEY, INC., SALEM, VA, USA.**

10 9 8 7 6 5 4 3 2 1

ADAPTED FROM
THE BOOK BY
L. FRANK BAUM

Writer: **ERIC SHANOWER**
Artist: **SKOTTIE YOUNG**
Colorist: **JEAN-FRANCOIS BEAULIEU**
Letterer: **JEFF ECKLEBERRY**

Assistant Editor: **ELLIE PYLE**
Editor: **SANA AMANAT**

Collection Editor: **MARK D. BEAZLEY**
Assistant Editors: **NELSON RIBEIRO & ALEX STARBUCK**
Editor, Special Projects: **JENNIFER GRÜNWALD**
Senior Editor, Special Projects: **JEFF YOUNGQUIST**
SVP of Print & Digital Publishing Sales: **DAVID GABRIEL**

Editor in Chief: **AXEL ALONSO**
Chief Creative Officer: **JOE QUESADA**
Publisher: **DAN BUCKLEY**
Executive Producer: **ALAN FINE**

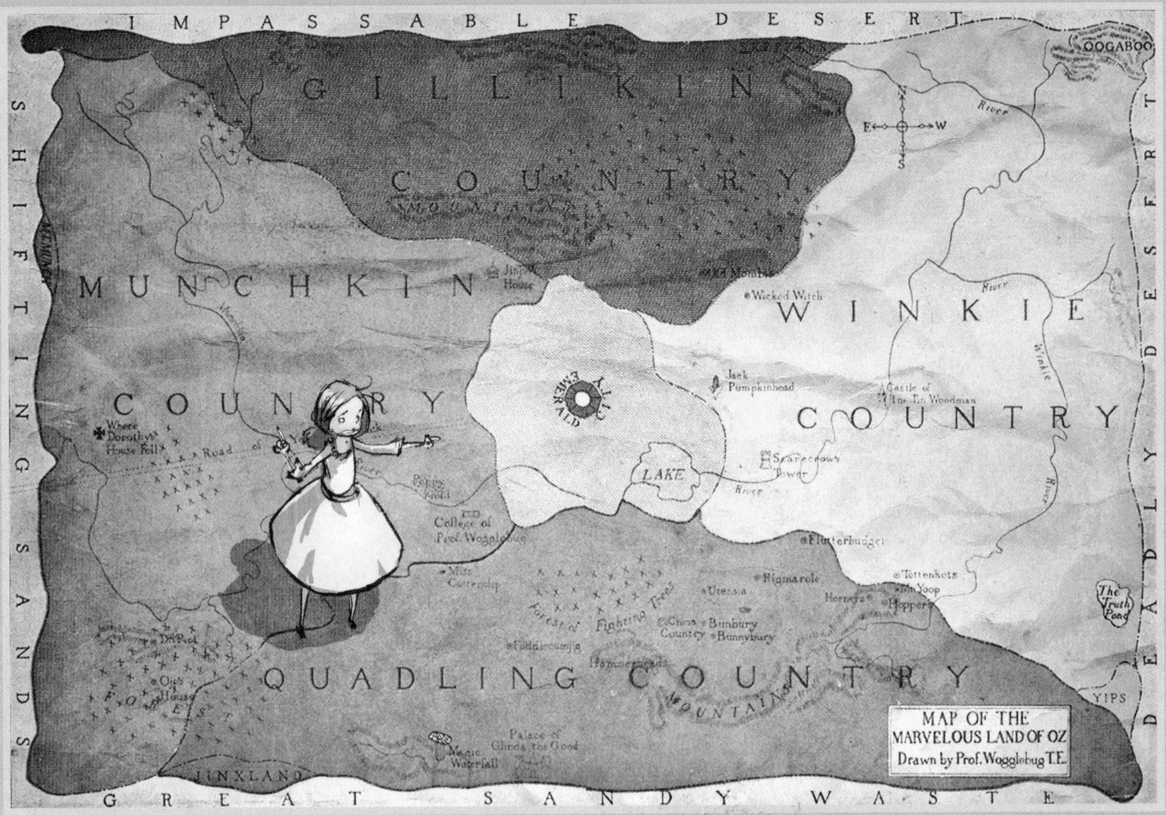
IMPASSABLE DESERT
OOGABOO
GILLIKIN COUNTRY
MOUNTAINS
SHIFTING SANDS
MUNCHKIN COUNTRY
Jinjur House
Wicked Witch
WINKIE COUNTRY
River
Winkie River
DEADLY DESERT
EMERALD CITY
Jack Pumpkinhead
Castle of The Tin Woodman
Where Dorothy's House Fell
Road of
Poppy Field
LAKE
Scarecrow's Tower
College of Prof. Wogglebug
Miss Cuttenclip
Flutterbudget
Rigmarole
Tottenhots
Utensia
Horners
Hoppers
The Truth Pond
Forest of Fighting Trees
China Country
Bunbury
Bunnybury
Fuddlecumjig
Dr. Pipt
Ojo's House
FOREST
QUADLING COUNTRY
MOUNTAINS
YIPS
Palace of Glinda the Good
Magic Waterfall
JINXLAND
MAP OF THE
MARVELOUS LAND OF OZ
Drawn by Prof. Wogglebug T.E.
GREAT SANDY WASTE

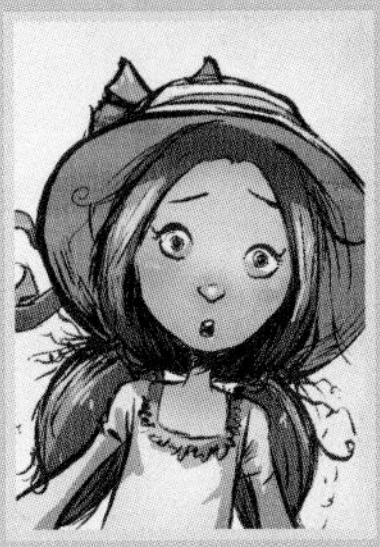

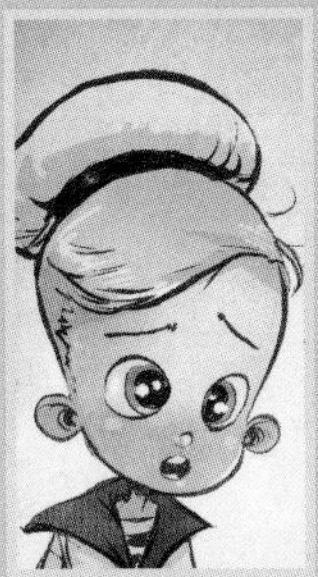

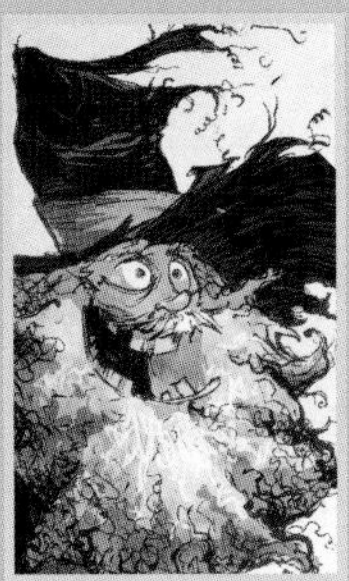

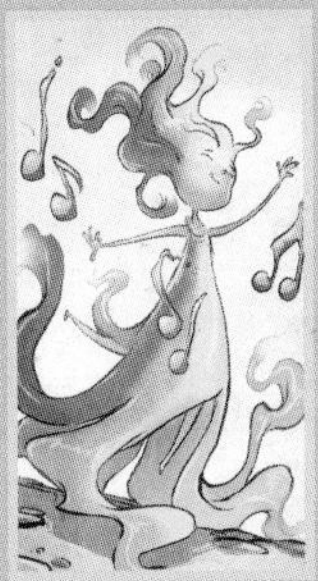

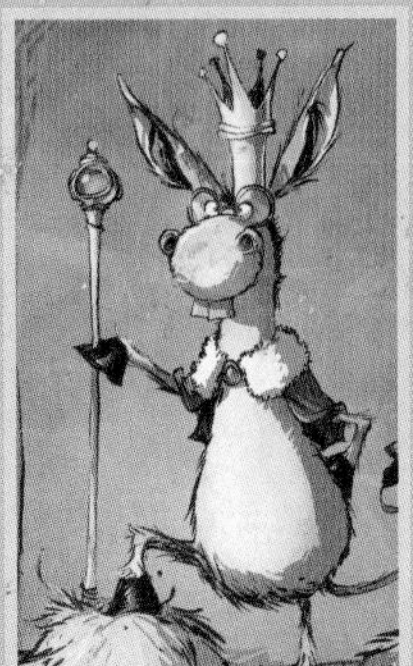

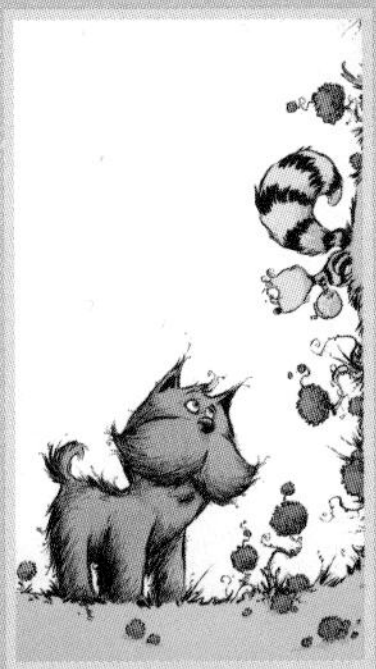

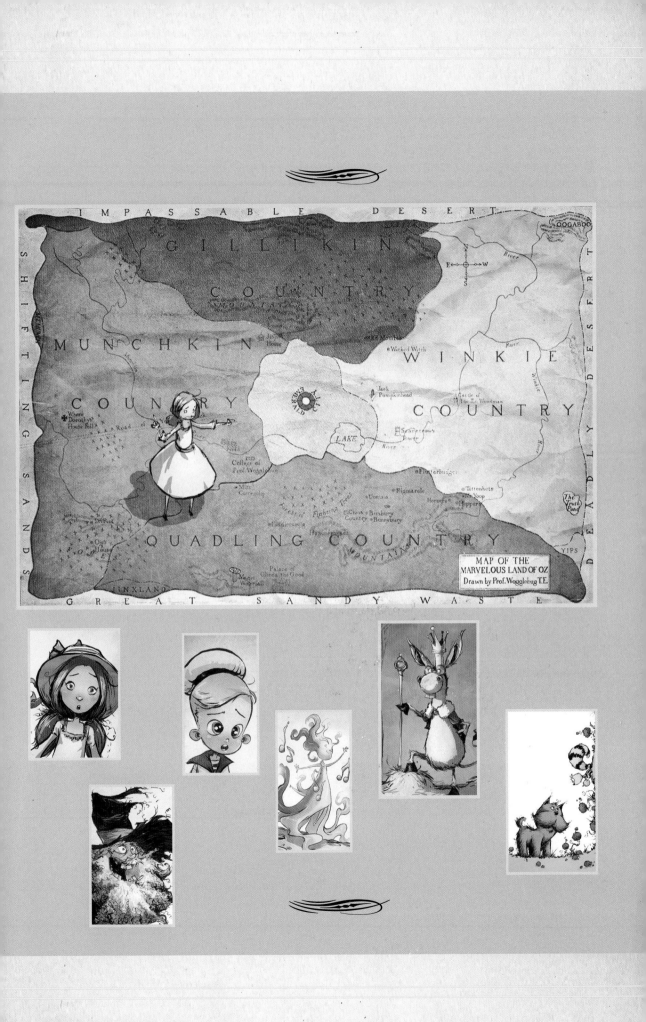

ROAD TRIP

We've arrived at *The Road to Oz*, the fifth comics adaptation of L. Frank Baum's Oz books. Several years ago when I started down this path with the first book, *The Wonderful Wizard of Oz*, traveling this far seemed barely a possibility. No other attempt to bring the Oz books to life in comics has lasted as long. But here we are. I hope you've enjoyed the journey this far as much as I have.

My personal road to Oz began farther back. I started along the road when I was six. *The Road to Oz* was the first full-length Oz book I ever read. Actually, I didn't read it myself. I was still learning to read, so my parents read *The Road to Oz* aloud to me a chapter a night.

I remember my terror as I listened to my father read the chapter about the fight with the Scoodlers. That evening my mother was away and I was in bed by the time she returned home. My father met her with the news that I was still wakeful, lying in darkness with the nightlight on, scared that the Scoodlers would get me.

Despite the Scoodlers—or maybe partly because of them—*The Road to Oz* catalyzed my subsequent love of the Oz books, so it retains a special place in my heart. Other readers of the Oz books have different reactions to *The Road to Oz*. Many consider it one of L. Frank Baum's weakest books. And I must admit that the plot isn't the most compelling. No exciting disaster propels Dorothy Gale and her companions into their adventures—no cyclone, no storm at sea, no earthquake as in previous Oz books.

Instead, as the title implies, they walk along a road. And as they walk, they encounter other characters in distinct episodes. It's very picaresque. If you haven't yet had a high school English class— or if it's been so long that you don't remember your high school English class—picaresque means an episodic story about roguish vagabonds. It's the roguish vagabonds, not the plot, that are the heart of *The Road to Oz*. They give the story its enduring power.

The most roguish of the vagabonds that join Dorothy is the first one, the Shaggy Man. He's a tramp who lives outside the structure of society and disdains the use of money. The Shaggy Man doesn't think the way other people do. His first conversation with Dorothy results in her exasperation. Yet he's the most practical and clear-headed character in the story. As an outsider who likes being an outsider, he's immediately appealing.

But the Shaggy Man has a dark side. In turning his back on society, he's turned his back on society's moral compass. In his first scene he "steals" Toto. This foreshadows a major revelation later on in the story, a memorable moment that becomes the single instance of character growth in *The Road to Oz*.

Speaking of Toto, he's the one major character from *The Wonderful Wizard of Oz* who had not yet returned to the Oz series. I'm happy to say that he's back in these pages, once more Dorothy's faithful companion.

The boy Button-Bright might not be the first thing one thinks of as a roguish vagabond. But if you define the category broadly, this lost, seemingly homeless wanderer qualifies as a vagabond. And the way he continually spouts his single comeback is a little roguish. How he got himself on the road to Oz and where he goes afterward is a mystery that L. Frank Baum leaves unsolved at the end of this story. It's not until a later book, *Sky Island*—not an Oz book, but in the top five of Baum's best— that readers learn some of the answers to the questions surrounding Button-Bright. But his hallmark habit of turning up unexpectedly and disappearing without explanation is on display right from his introduction in *The Road to Oz*.

Dorothy's remaining companion on the road is another girl: Polychrome, the daughter of the rainbow. But Polychrome's nature is different from Dorothy's in almost every way. Dorothy is a mortal human; Polychrome is a fairy. Dorothy is assured and robust; Polychrome is tentative and timid. Dorothy's always ready to face danger and pull through; Polychrome just likes to dance. Polychrome would probably be pretty annoying on her own, but her interaction with her companions provides gentle humor and her otherworldliness is intriguing. Skottie Young's insightful design and Jean-François Beaulieu's inspired coloring emphasize Polychrome's otherworldly qualities and bring new dimension to the character.

In fact, Skottie Young's vision of Oz goes on a field day with *The Road to Oz*. John R. Neill's illustrations for the original book rank with the best work of the early twentieth-century golden age of illustration. Skottie doesn't try to outdo Neill, he simply does what he does best—he gives us his new and vibrant view of Oz.

In this story Dorothy meets some pretty odd eccentrics—Johnny Dooit—the Musicker—the Queen of the Scoodlers. Skottie's designs nail each one. Readers of Baum's original book are in for a surprise when they see Skottie's rendition of Foxville. And when Dorothy greets the parade of bizarre and fascinating new characters in the Emerald City, I think you'll find it a challenge to pick out a favorite.

Who are all those new characters, anyway? You say you don't recognize them from the previous Oz books? That's because they're not from the Oz books, they're from some of L. Frank Baum's other fantasy stories. He introduced these folks into *The Road to Oz* in what seems to have been an early attempt at cross-promotion. By putting the main characters from his non-Oz books on display here, Baum was encouraging his readers to seek out the other books.

Before you rush out to find those other books, relax. You don't have to read those other books to enjoy meeting any of those characters here. I'll introduce them all by name and you can depend on Skottie Young's art to bring each one to life.

But if you want to find those books, their titles are *Queen Zixi of Ix*, *The Life and Adventures of Santa Claus*, *John Dough and the Cherub*, and *Dot and Tot of Merryland*. I recommend *Queen Zixi of Ix* as being among Baum's best works. Its illustrations by Frederick Richardson are beautiful. Lots of people like *The Life and Adventures of Santa Claus*. I loved *John Dough and the Cherub* when I was ten years old, and it has the advantage of John R. Neill illustrations. But *Dot and Tot of Merryland*? Well, just consider that title. "Twee" is putting it mildly. But if you like reading about dolls and toys and candy and pussycats and lots and lots of babies, then go for it.

I want to thank all the readers of these comics adaptations of the Oz books. You've welcomed Skottie Young's and my work more enthusiastically than I dared to hope when we began. So thank you. By the time you read this, I'll have begun work on the next book, *The Emerald City of Oz*. Hope to see you there!

Eric Shanower
San Diego, January 2013

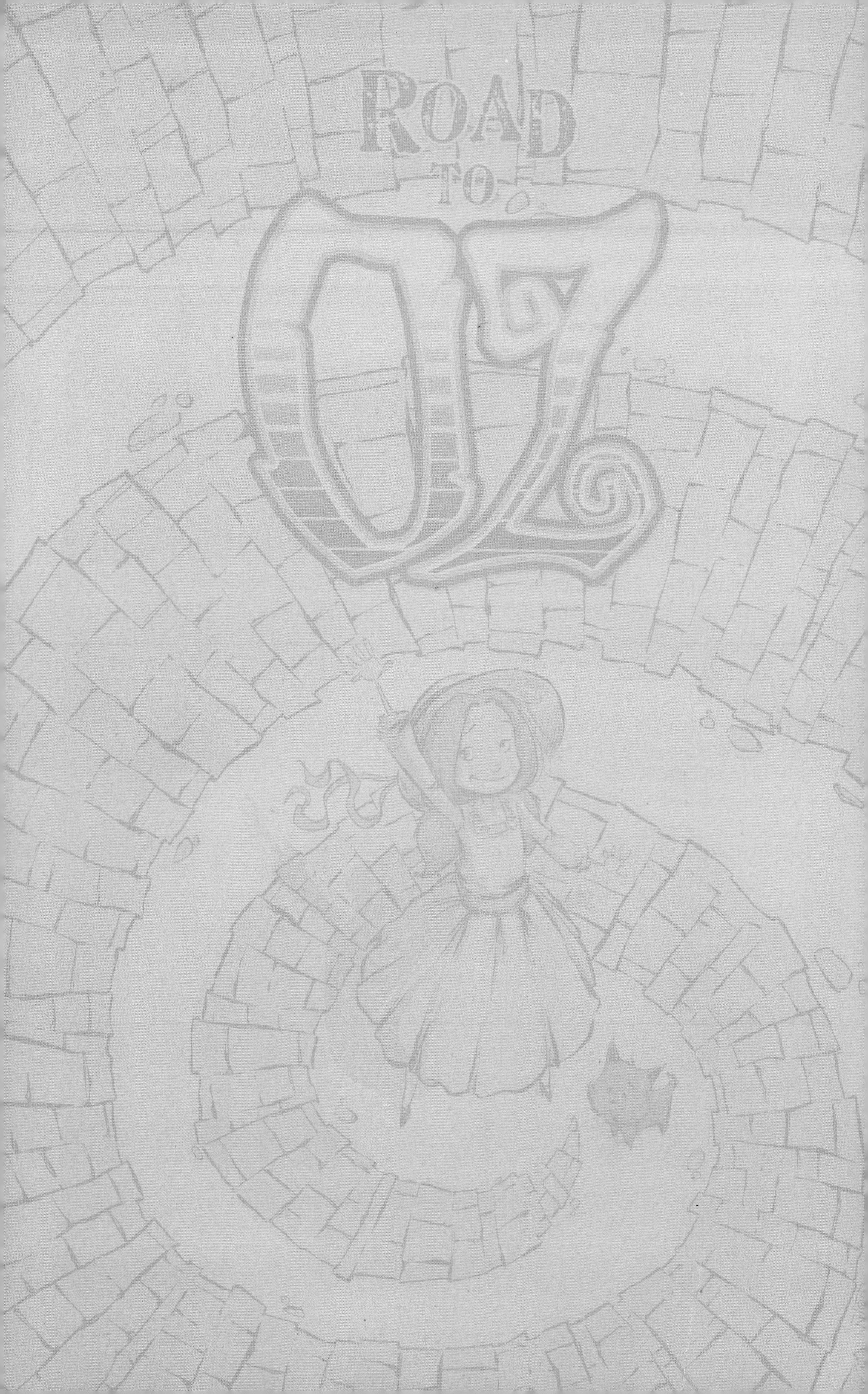
ROAD TO OZ

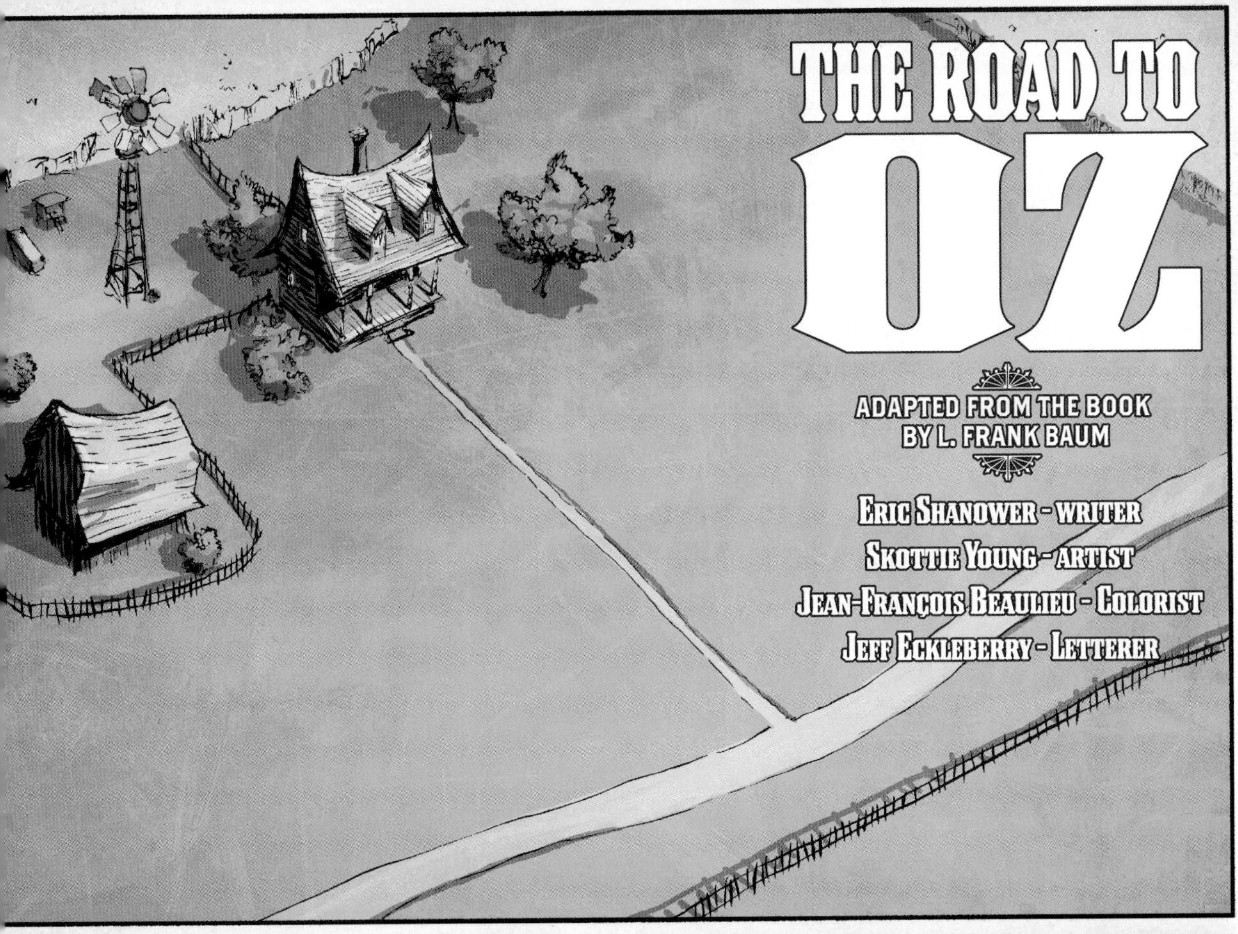
THE ROAD TO
OZ
ADAPTED FROM THE BOOK
BY L. FRANK BAUM
ERIC SHANOWER - WRITER
SKOTTIE YOUNG - ARTIST
JEAN-FRANÇOIS BEAULIEU - COLORIST
JEFF ECKLEBERRY - LETTERER

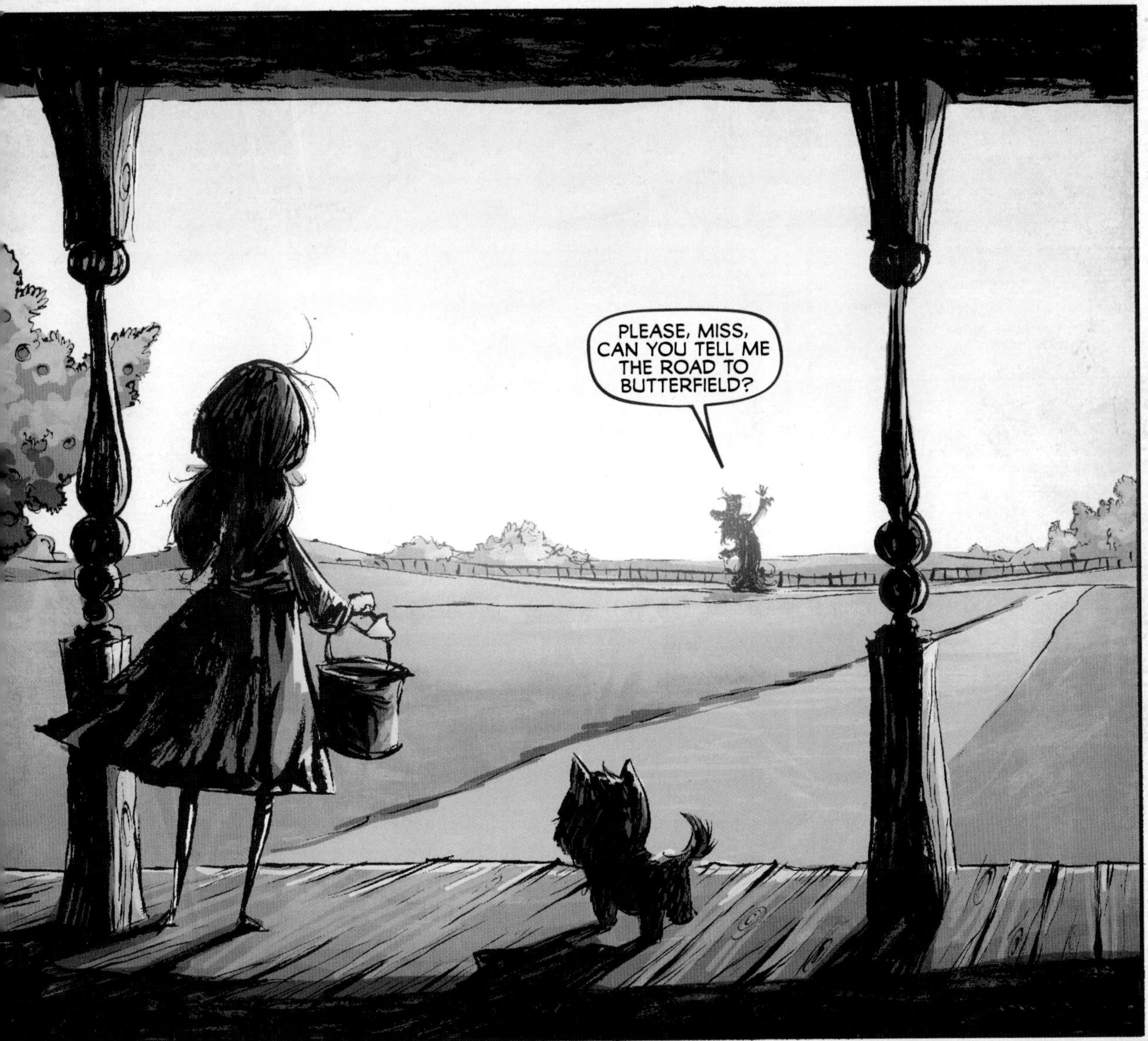
PLEASE, MISS, CAN YOU TELL ME THE ROAD TO BUTTERFIELD?

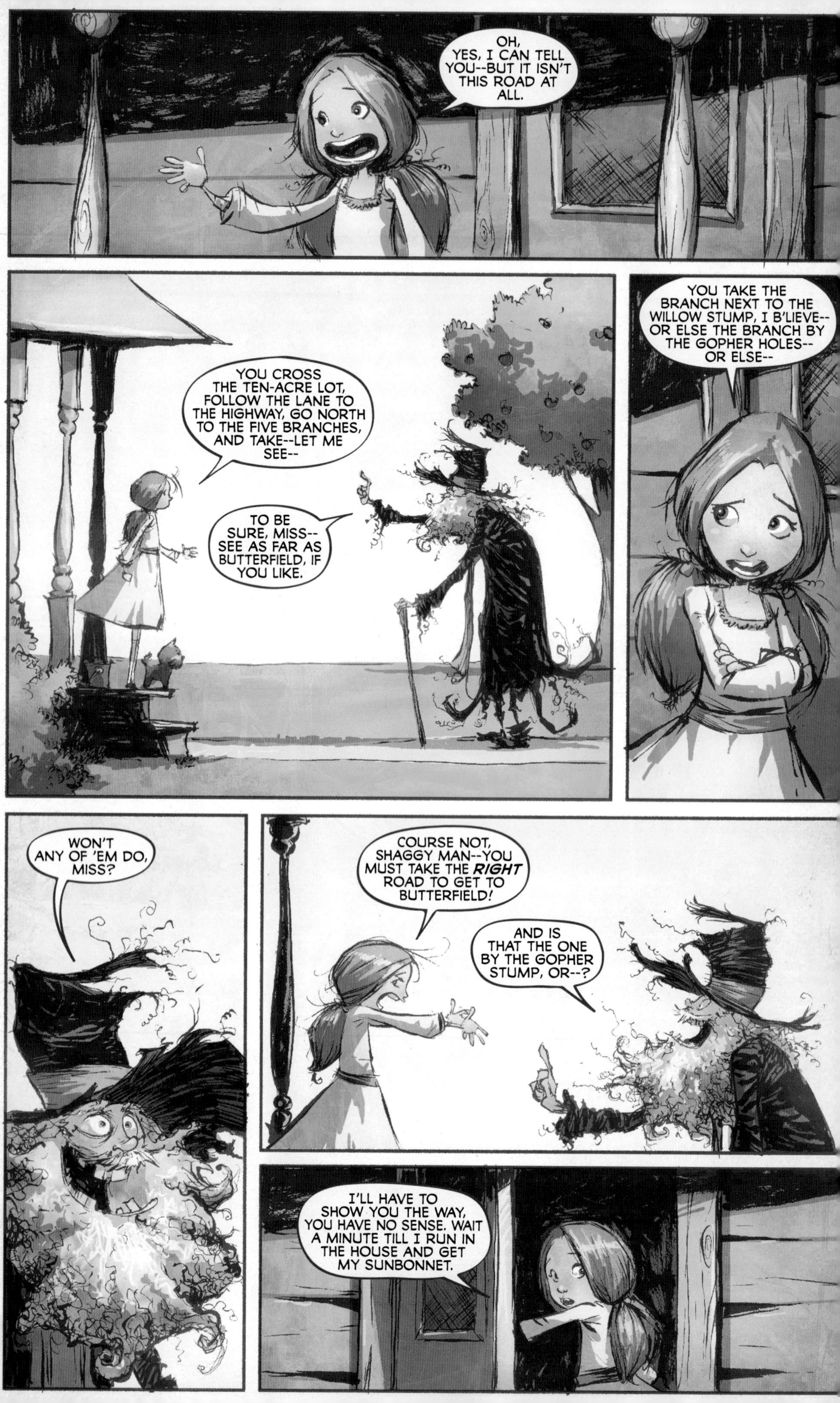
OH, YES, I CAN TELL YOU--BUT IT ISN'T THIS ROAD AT ALL.
YOU CROSS THE TEN-ACRE LOT, FOLLOW THE LANE TO THE HIGHWAY, GO NORTH TO THE FIVE BRANCHES, AND TAKE--LET ME SEE--
TO BE SURE, MISS--SEE AS FAR AS BUTTERFIELD, IF YOU LIKE.
YOU TAKE THE BRANCH NEXT TO THE WILLOW STUMP, I B'LIEVE--OR ELSE THE BRANCH BY THE GOPHER HOLES--OR ELSE--
WON'T ANY OF 'EM DO, MISS?
COURSE NOT, SHAGGY MAN--YOU MUST TAKE THE ***RIGHT*** ROAD TO GET TO BUTTERFIELD!
AND IS THAT THE ONE BY THE GOPHER STUMP, OR--?
I'LL HAVE TO SHOW YOU THE WAY, YOU HAVE NO SENSE. WAIT A MINUTE TILL I RUN IN THE HOUSE AND GET MY SUNBONNET.

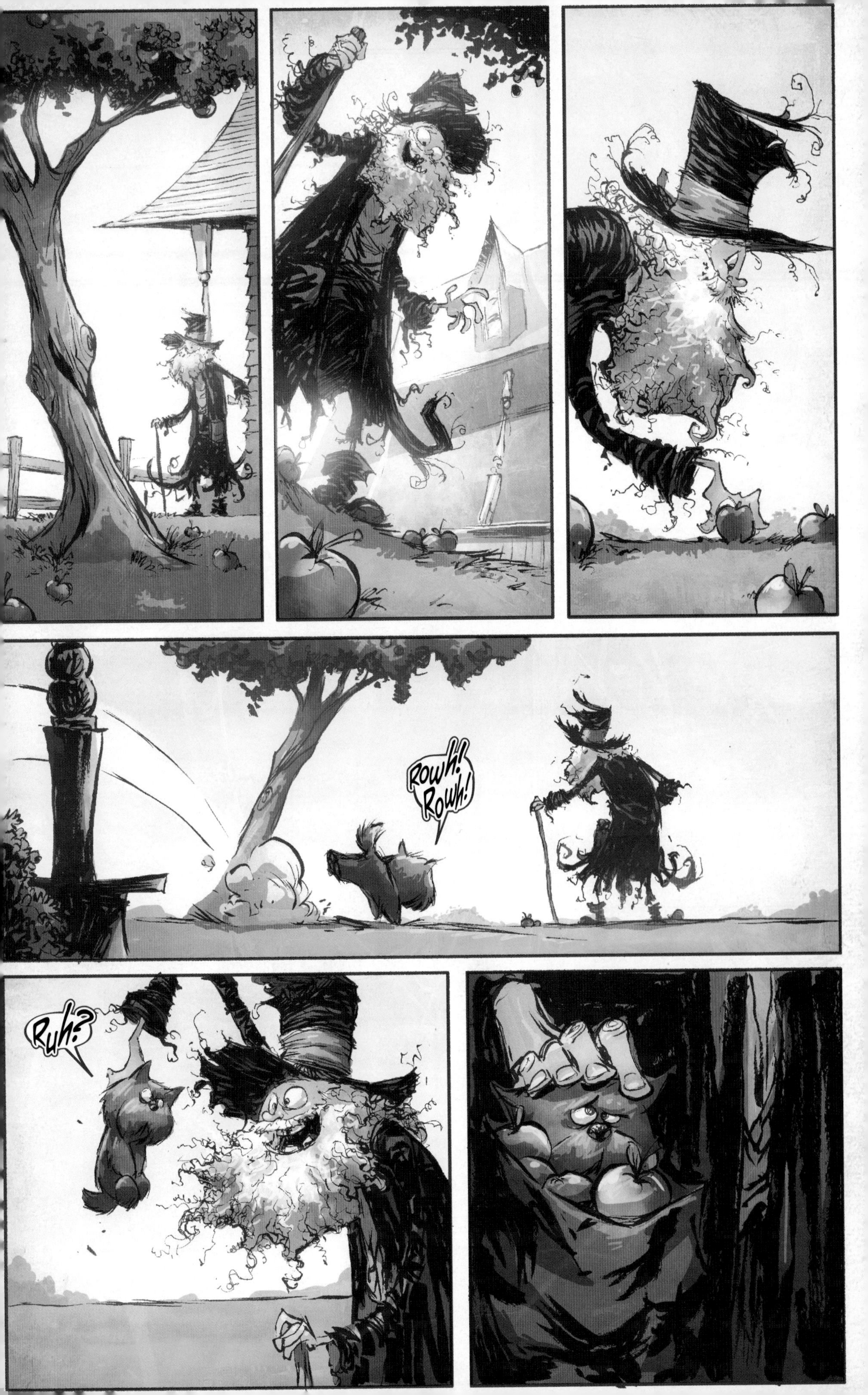
Rowh! Rowh!
Ruh?

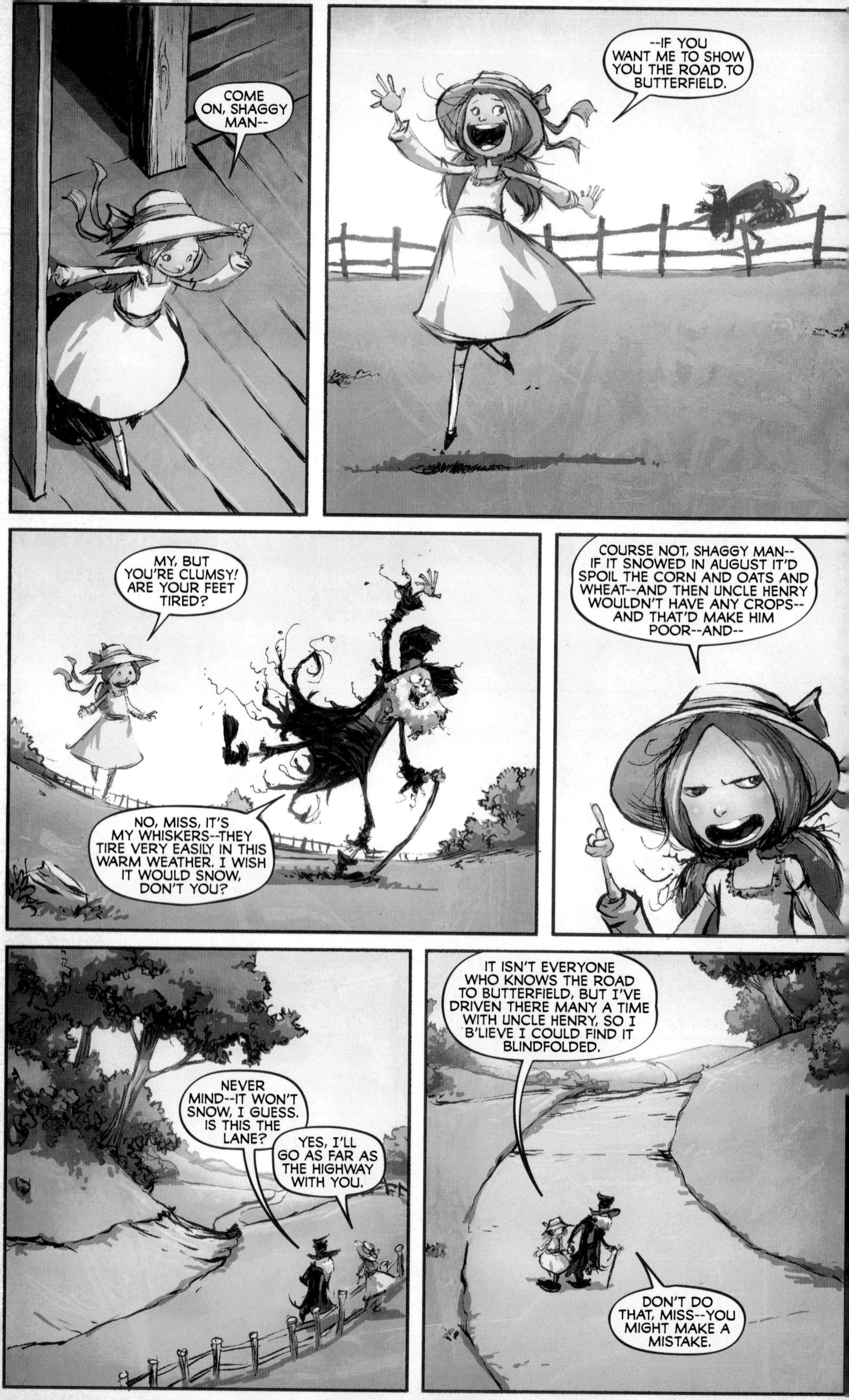
COME ON, SHAGGY MAN--
--IF YOU WANT ME TO SHOW YOU THE ROAD TO BUTTERFIELD.
MY, BUT YOU'RE CLUMSY! ARE YOUR FEET TIRED?
NO, MISS, IT'S MY WHISKERS--THEY TIRE VERY EASILY IN THIS WARM WEATHER. I WISH IT WOULD SNOW, DON'T YOU?
COURSE NOT, SHAGGY MAN--IF IT SNOWED IN AUGUST IT'D SPOIL THE CORN AND OATS AND WHEAT--AND THEN UNCLE HENRY WOULDN'T HAVE ANY CROPS--AND THAT'D MAKE HIM POOR--AND--
NEVER MIND--IT WON'T SNOW, I GUESS. IS THIS THE LANE?
YES, I'LL GO AS FAR AS THE HIGHWAY WITH YOU.
IT ISN'T EVERYONE WHO KNOWS THE ROAD TO BUTTERFIELD, BUT I'VE DRIVEN THERE MANY A TIME WITH UNCLE HENRY, SO I B'LIEVE I COULD FIND IT BLINDFOLDED.
DON'T DO THAT, MISS--YOU MIGHT MAKE A MISTAKE.

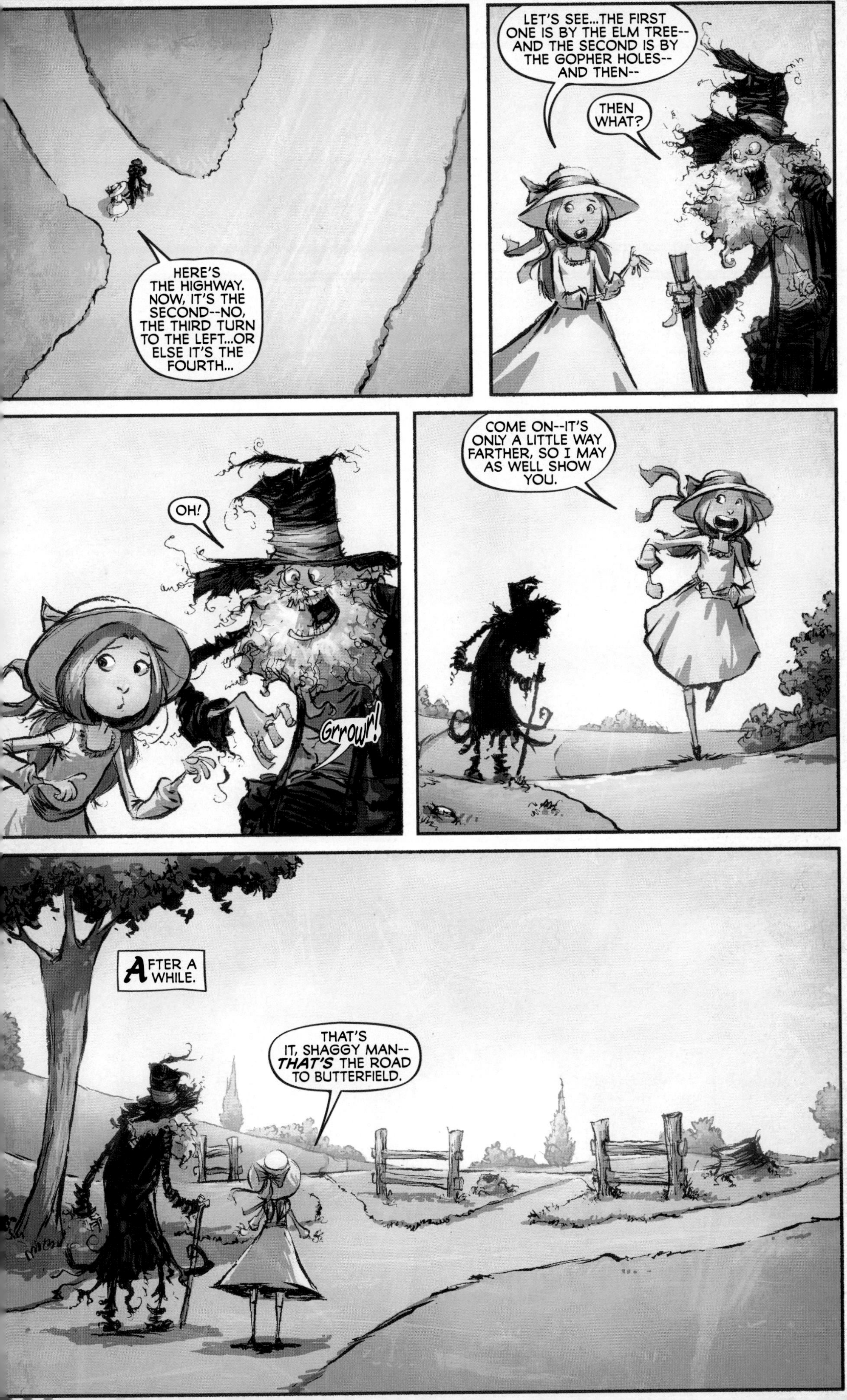
HERE'S THE HIGHWAY. NOW, IT'S THE SECOND--NO, THE THIRD TURN TO THE LEFT...OR ELSE IT'S THE FOURTH...
LET'S SEE...THE FIRST ONE IS BY THE ELM TREE-- AND THE SECOND IS BY THE GOPHER HOLES-- AND THEN--
THEN WHAT?
OH!
Grrowr!
COME ON--IT'S ONLY A LITTLE WAY FARTHER, SO I MAY AS WELL SHOW YOU.
AFTER A WHILE.
THAT'S IT, SHAGGY MAN-- *THAT'S* THE ROAD TO BUTTERFIELD.

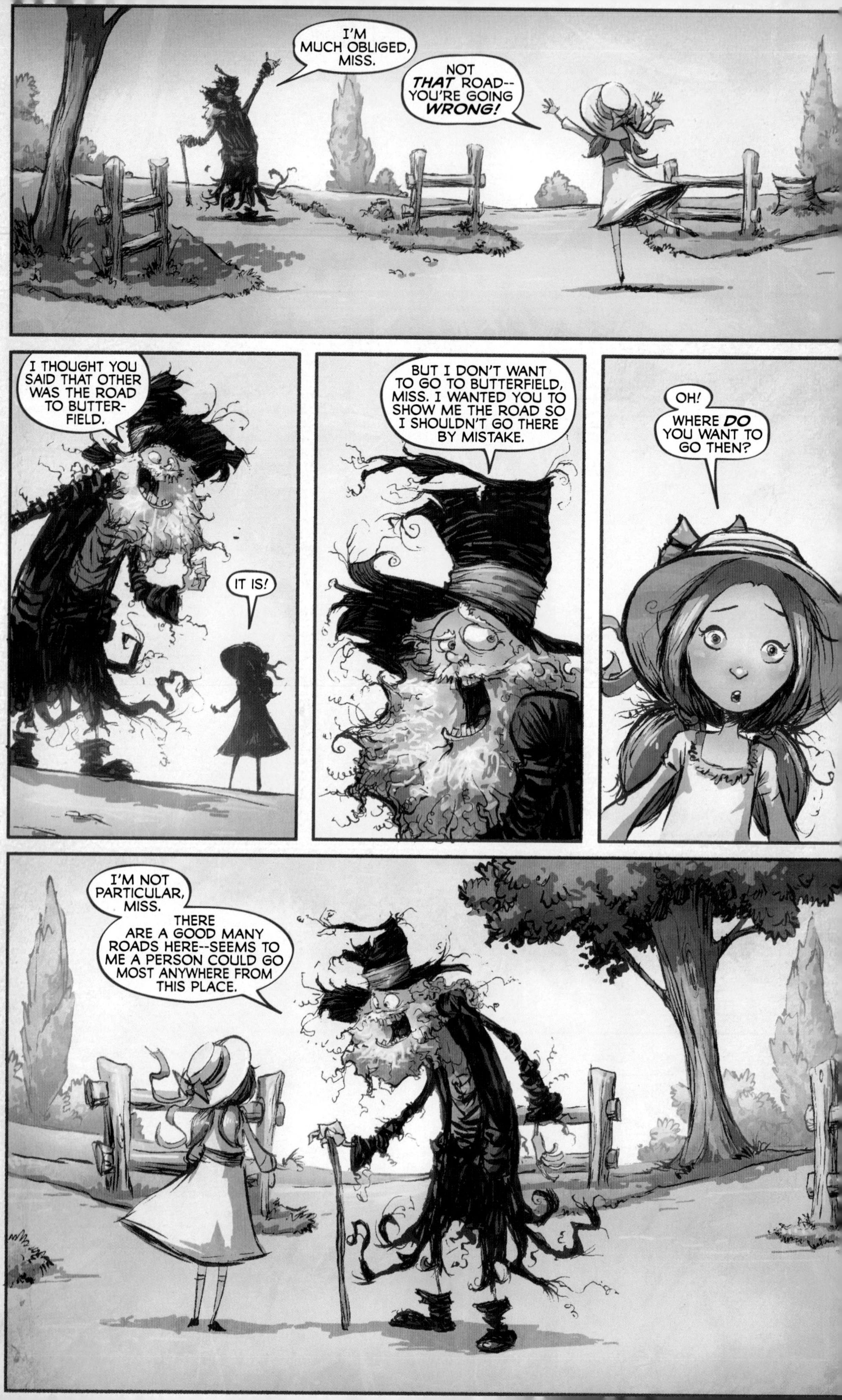
I'M MUCH OBLIGED, MISS.
NOT *THAT* ROAD-- YOU'RE GOING *WRONG!*
I THOUGHT YOU SAID THAT OTHER WAS THE ROAD TO BUTTER-FIELD.
IT IS!
BUT I DON'T WANT TO GO TO BUTTERFIELD, MISS. I WANTED YOU TO SHOW ME THE ROAD SO I SHOULDN'T GO THERE BY MISTAKE.
OH!
WHERE *DO* YOU WANT TO GO THEN?
I'M NOT PARTICULAR, MISS.
THERE ARE A GOOD MANY ROADS HERE--SEEMS TO ME A PERSON COULD GO MOST ANYWHERE FROM THIS PLACE.

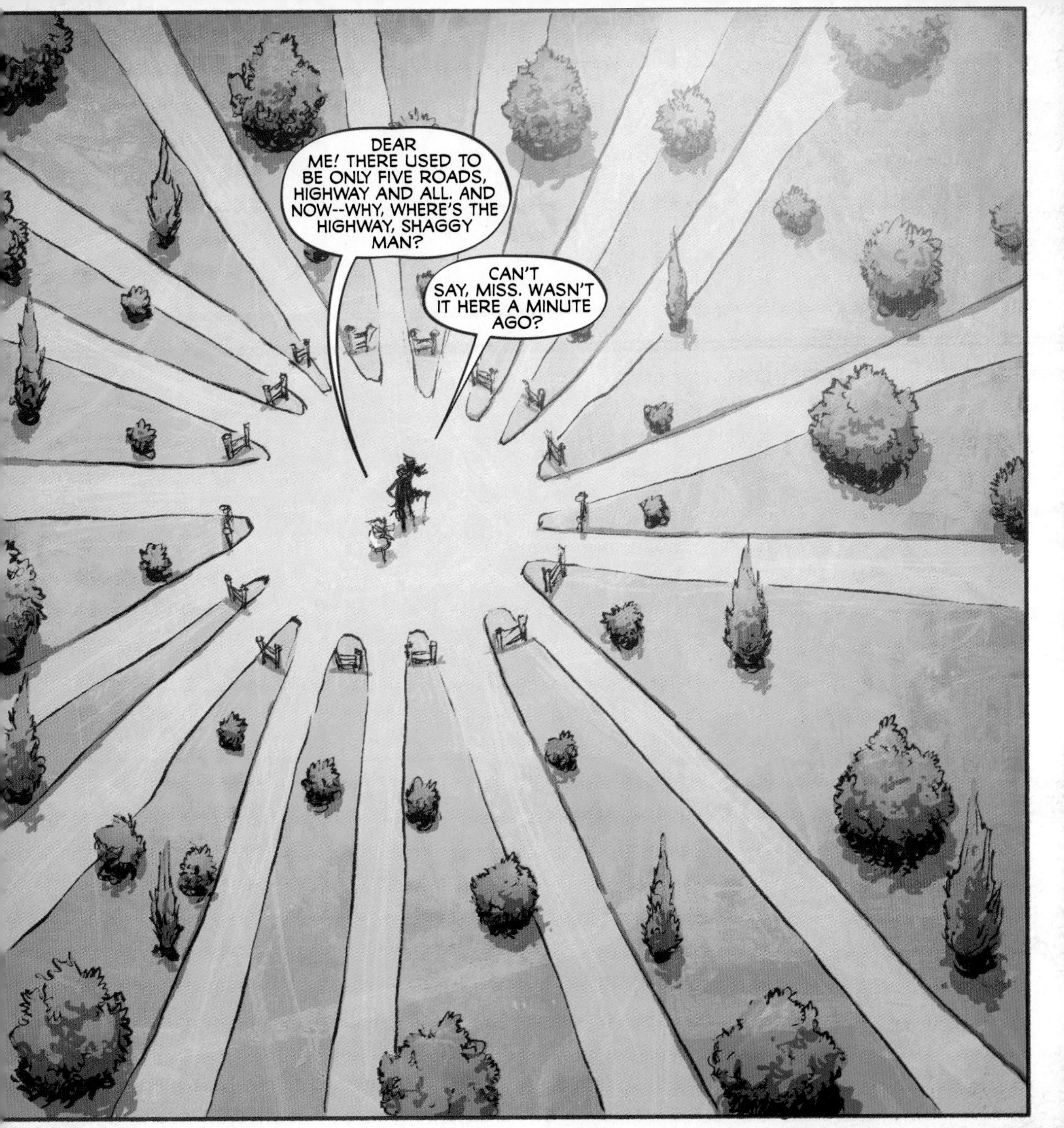
DEAR ME! THERE USED TO BE ONLY FIVE ROADS, HIGHWAY AND ALL. AND NOW--WHY, WHERE'S THE HIGHWAY, SHAGGY MAN?
CAN'T SAY, MISS. WASN'T IT HERE A MINUTE AGO?

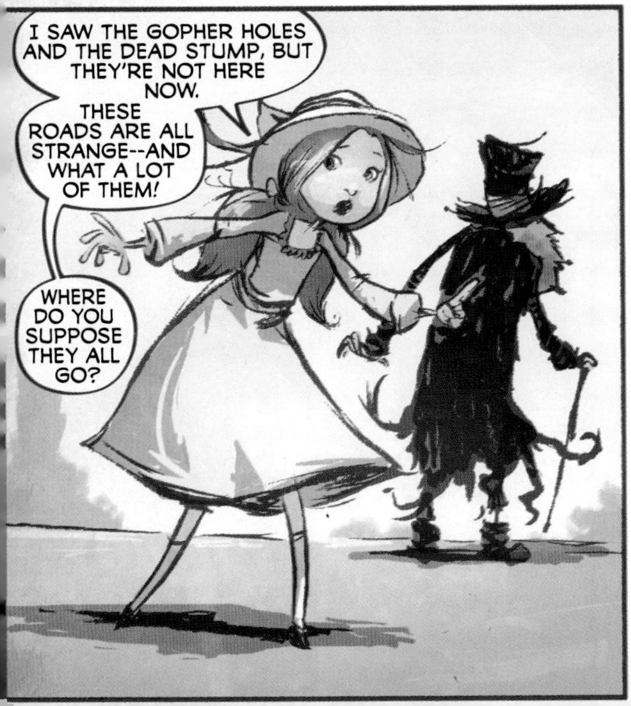
I SAW THE GOPHER HOLES AND THE DEAD STUMP, BUT THEY'RE NOT HERE NOW.
THESE ROADS ARE ALL STRANGE--AND WHAT A LOT OF THEM!
WHERE DO YOU SUPPOSE THEY ALL GO?

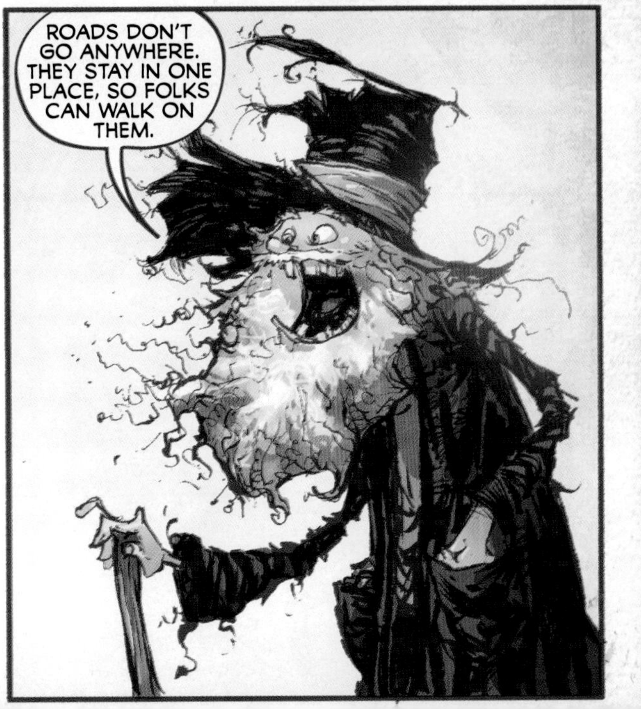
ROADS DON'T GO ANYWHERE. THEY STAY IN ONE PLACE, SO FOLKS CAN WALK ON THEM.

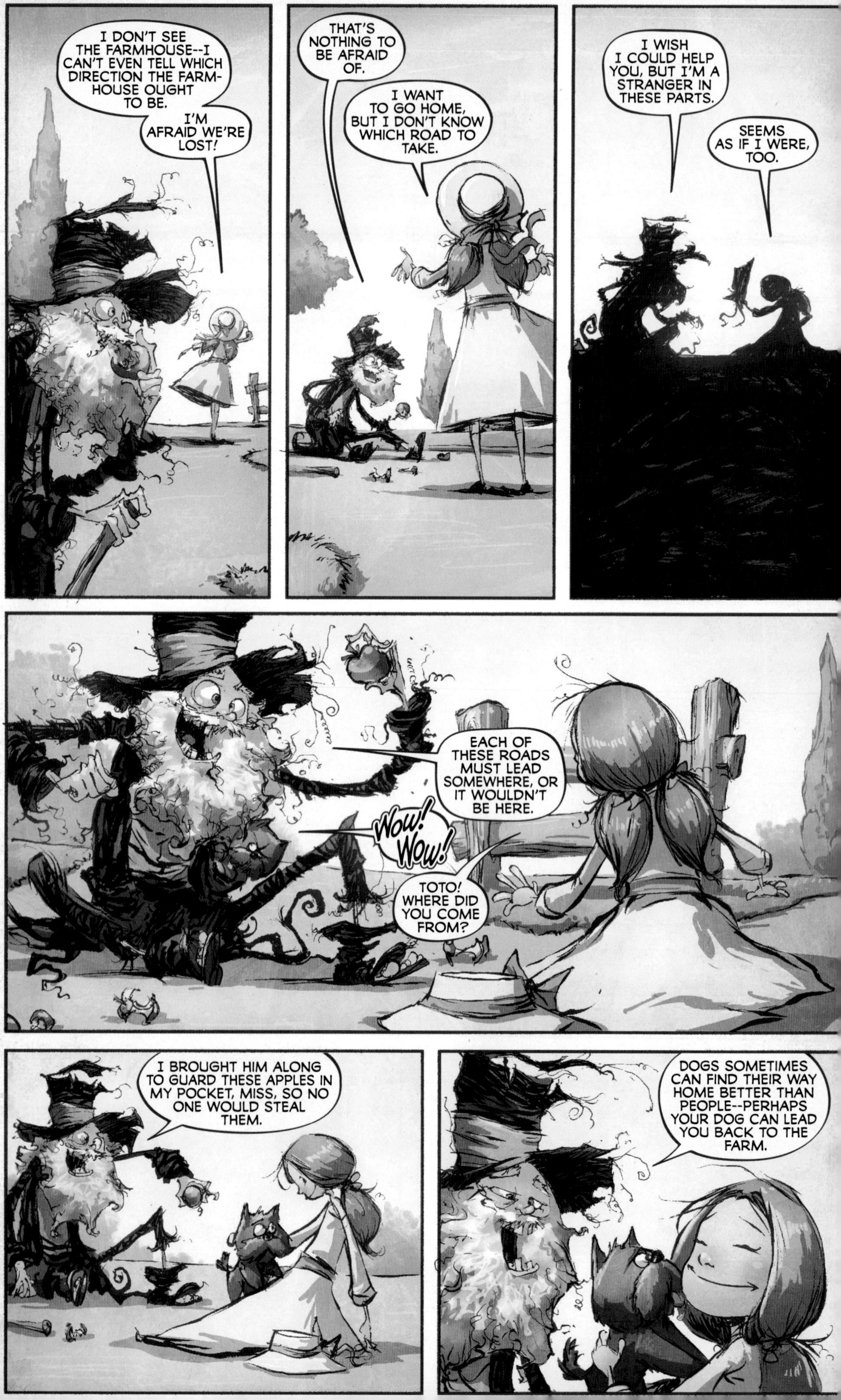
I DON'T SEE THE FARMHOUSE--I CAN'T EVEN TELL WHICH DIRECTION THE FARM-HOUSE OUGHT TO BE.
I'M AFRAID WE'RE LOST!
THAT'S NOTHING TO BE AFRAID OF.
I WANT TO GO HOME, BUT I DON'T KNOW WHICH ROAD TO TAKE.
I WISH I COULD HELP YOU, BUT I'M A STRANGER IN THESE PARTS.
SEEMS AS IF I WERE, TOO.
EACH OF THESE ROADS MUST LEAD SOMEWHERE, OR IT WOULDN'T BE HERE.
WOW! WOW!
TOTO! WHERE DID YOU COME FROM?
I BROUGHT HIM ALONG TO GUARD THESE APPLES IN MY POCKET, MISS, SO NO ONE WOULD STEAL THEM.
DOGS SOMETIMES CAN FIND THEIR WAY HOME BETTER THAN PEOPLE--PERHAPS YOUR DOG CAN LEAD YOU BACK TO THE FARM.

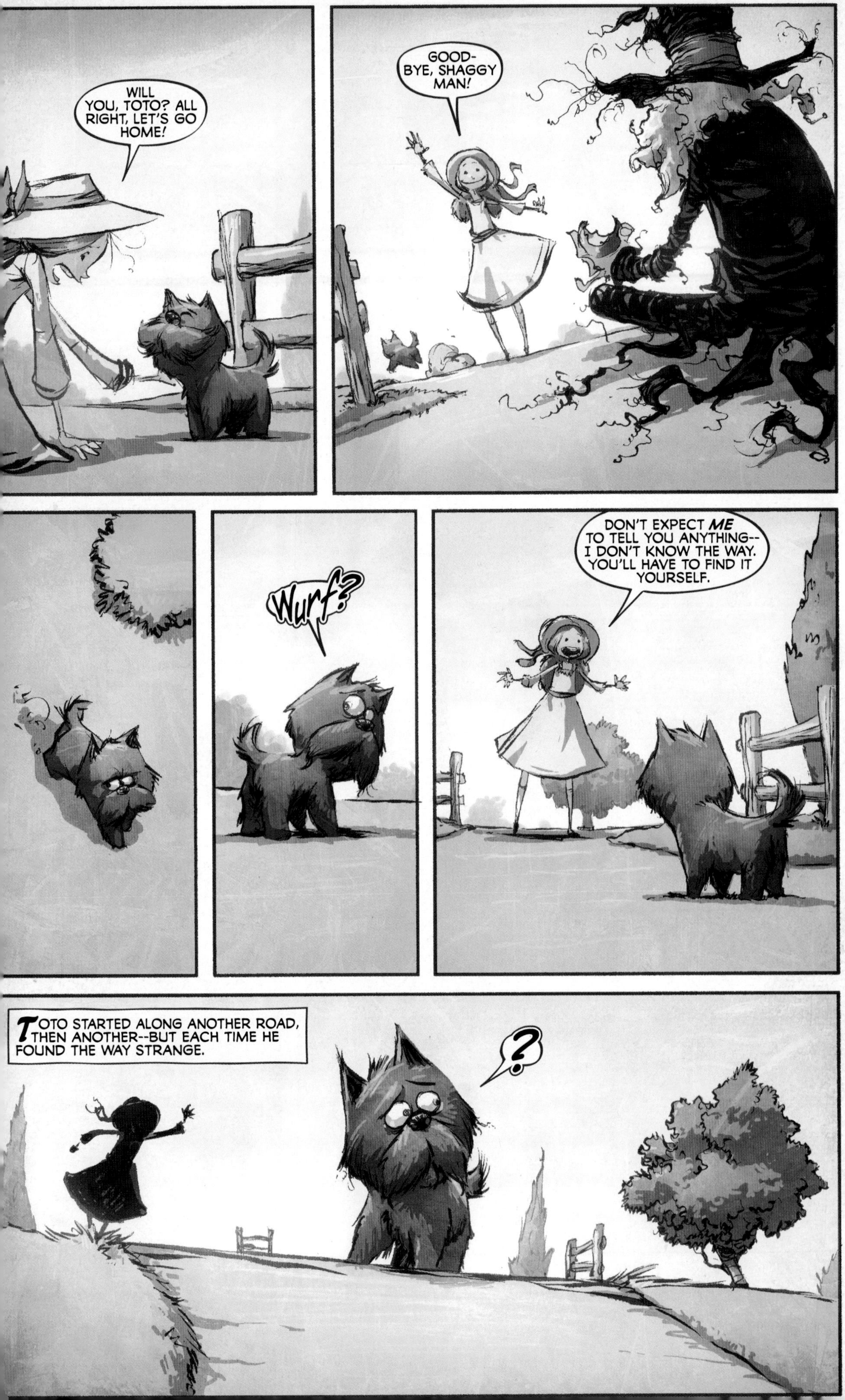
WILL YOU, TOTO? ALL RIGHT, LET'S GO HOME!
GOOD-BYE, SHAGGY MAN!
Wurf?
DON'T EXPECT ME TO TELL YOU ANYTHING--I DON'T KNOW THE WAY. YOU'LL HAVE TO FIND IT YOURSELF.
TOTO STARTED ALONG ANOTHER ROAD, THEN ANOTHER--BUT EACH TIME HE FOUND THE WAY STRANGE.
?

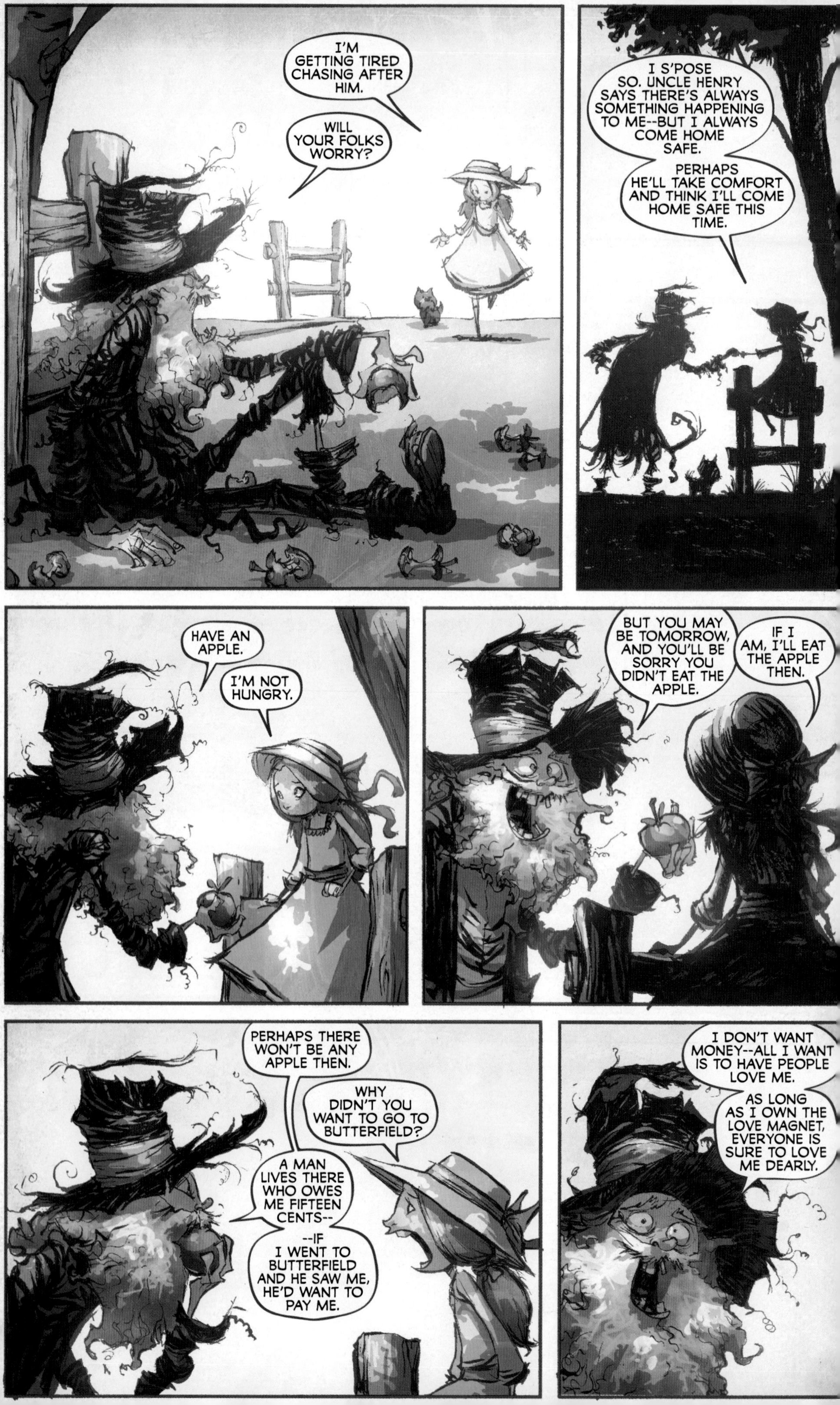
I'M GETTING TIRED CHASING AFTER HIM.
WILL YOUR FOLKS WORRY?
I S'POSE SO. UNCLE HENRY SAYS THERE'S ALWAYS SOMETHING HAPPENING TO ME--BUT I ALWAYS COME HOME SAFE.
PERHAPS HE'LL TAKE COMFORT AND THINK I'LL COME HOME SAFE THIS TIME.
HAVE AN APPLE.
I'M NOT HUNGRY.
BUT YOU MAY BE TOMORROW, AND YOU'LL BE SORRY YOU DIDN'T EAT THE APPLE.
IF I AM, I'LL EAT THE APPLE THEN.
PERHAPS THERE WON'T BE ANY APPLE THEN.
WHY DIDN'T YOU WANT TO GO TO BUTTERFIELD?
A MAN LIVES THERE WHO OWES ME FIFTEEN CENTS--
--IF I WENT TO BUTTERFIELD AND HE SAW ME, HE'D WANT TO PAY ME.
I DON'T WANT MONEY--ALL I WANT IS TO HAVE PEOPLE LOVE ME.
AS LONG AS I OWN THE LOVE MAGNET, EVERYONE IS SURE TO LOVE ME DEARLY.

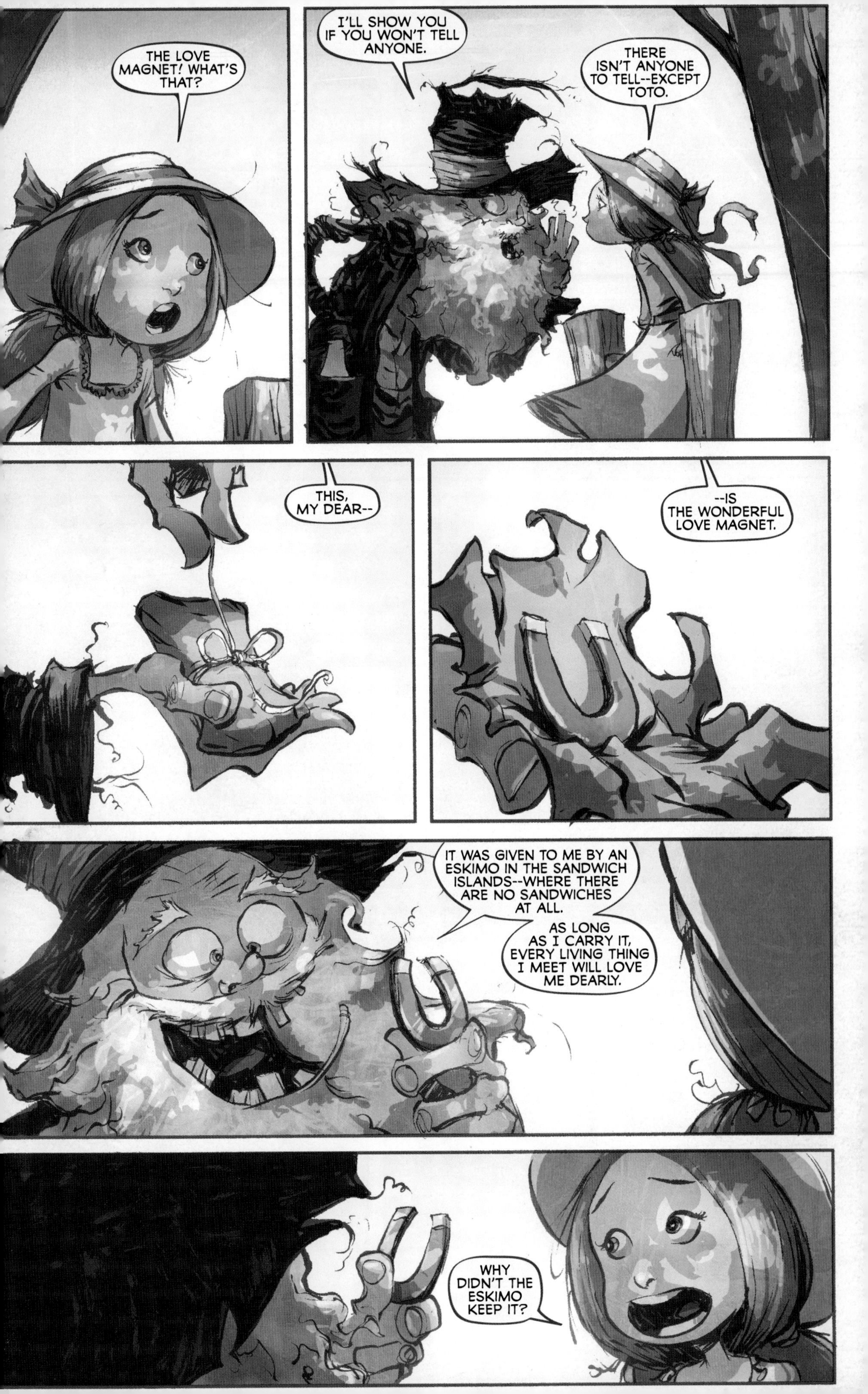
THE LOVE MAGNET! WHAT'S THAT?
I'LL SHOW YOU IF YOU WON'T TELL ANYONE.
THERE ISN'T ANYONE TO TELL--EXCEPT TOTO.
THIS, MY DEAR--
--IS THE WONDERFUL LOVE MAGNET.
IT WAS GIVEN TO ME BY AN ESKIMO IN THE SANDWICH ISLANDS--WHERE THERE ARE NO SANDWICHES AT ALL.
AS LONG AS I CARRY IT, EVERY LIVING THING I MEET WILL LOVE ME DEARLY.
WHY DIDN'T THE ESKIMO KEEP IT?

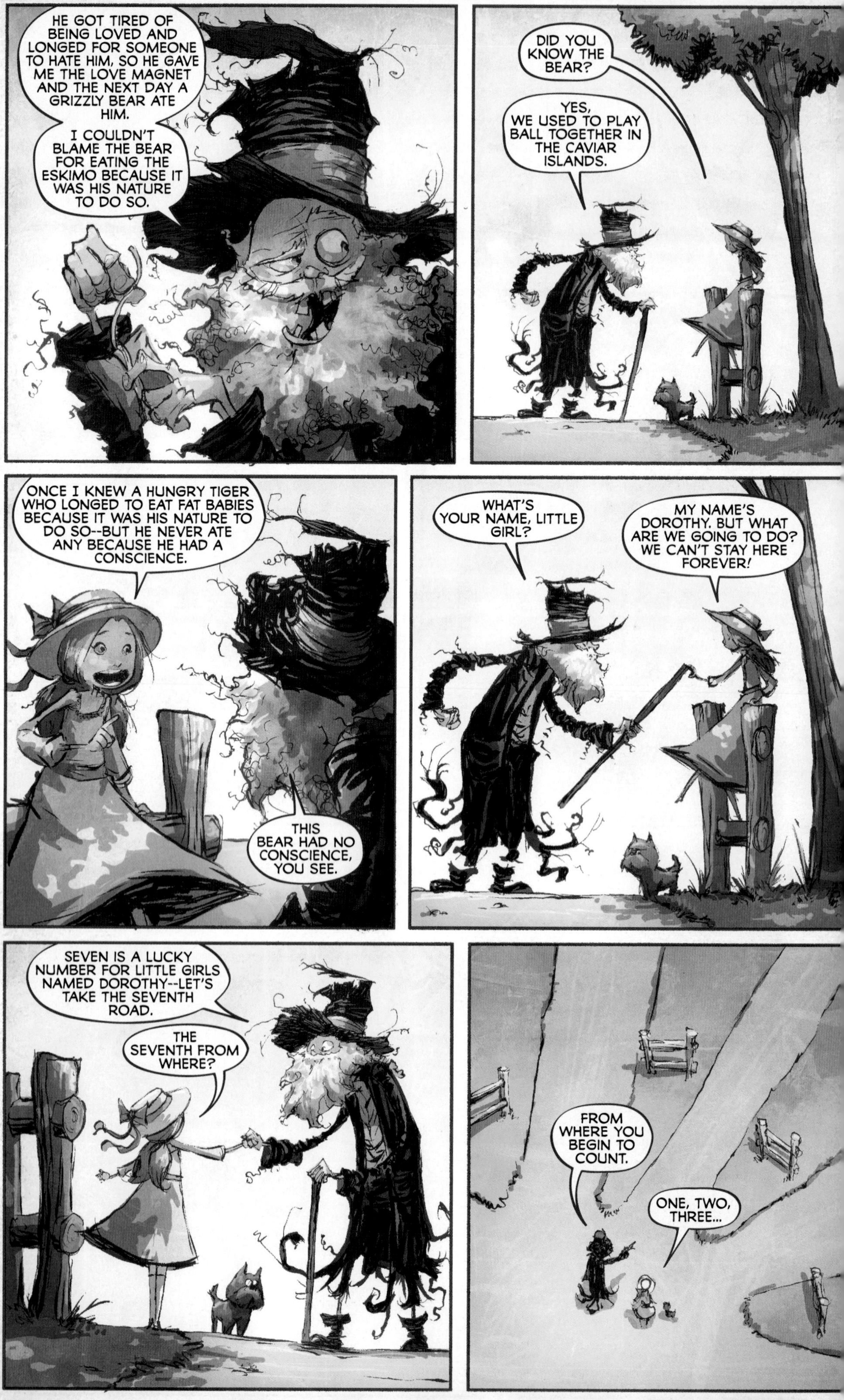
HE GOT TIRED OF BEING LOVED AND LONGED FOR SOMEONE TO HATE HIM, SO HE GAVE ME THE LOVE MAGNET AND THE NEXT DAY A GRIZZLY BEAR ATE HIM.
I COULDN'T BLAME THE BEAR FOR EATING THE ESKIMO BECAUSE IT WAS HIS NATURE TO DO SO.
DID YOU KNOW THE BEAR?
YES, WE USED TO PLAY BALL TOGETHER IN THE CAVIAR ISLANDS.
ONCE I KNEW A HUNGRY TIGER WHO LONGED TO EAT FAT BABIES BECAUSE IT WAS HIS NATURE TO DO SO--BUT HE NEVER ATE ANY BECAUSE HE HAD A CONSCIENCE.
THIS BEAR HAD NO CONSCIENCE, YOU SEE.
WHAT'S YOUR NAME, LITTLE GIRL?
MY NAME'S DOROTHY. BUT WHAT ARE WE GOING TO DO? WE CAN'T STAY HERE FOREVER!
SEVEN IS A LUCKY NUMBER FOR LITTLE GIRLS NAMED DOROTHY--LET'S TAKE THE SEVENTH ROAD.
THE SEVENTH FROM WHERE?
FROM WHERE YOU BEGIN TO COUNT.
ONE, TWO, THREE...

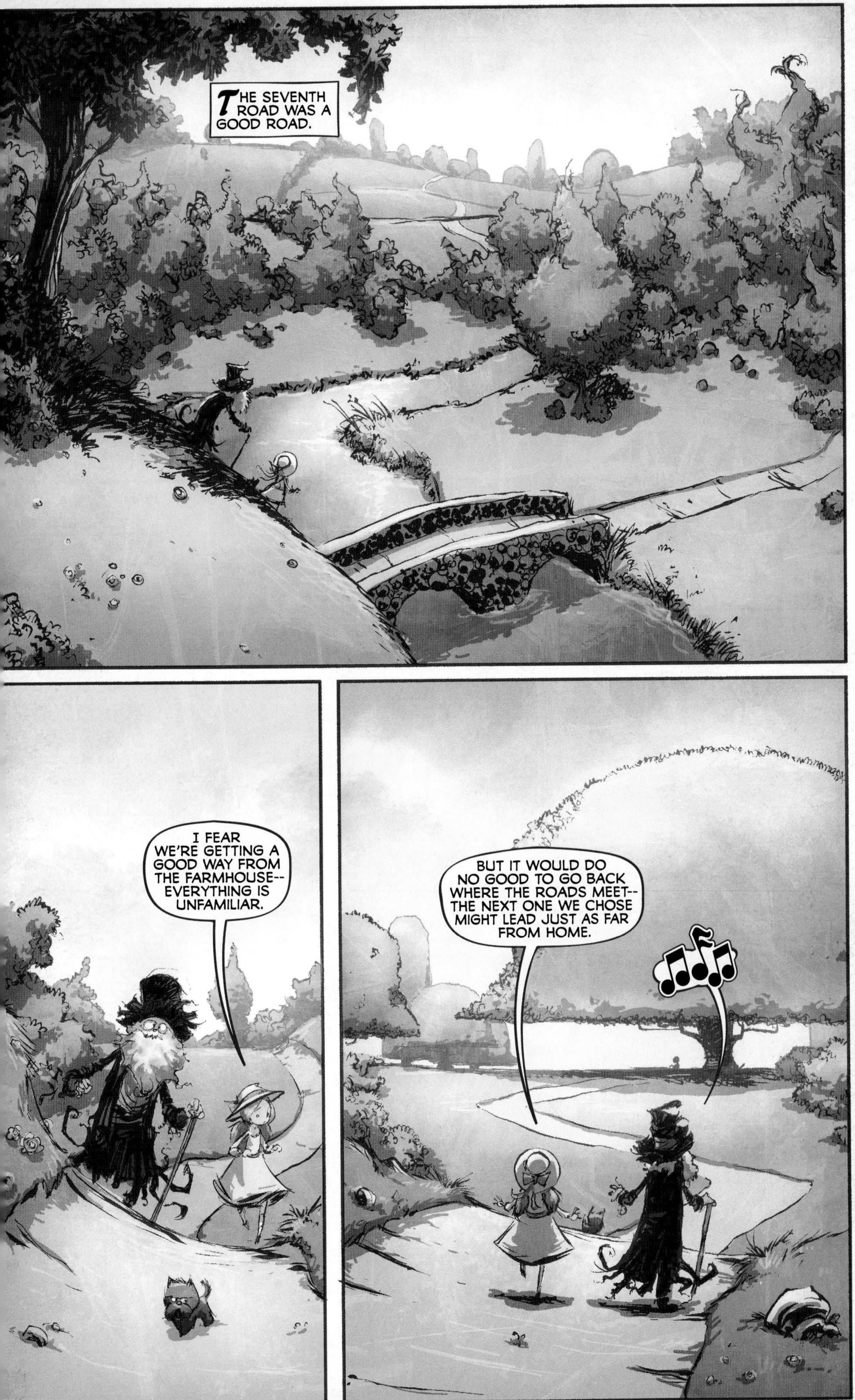
THE SEVENTH ROAD WAS A GOOD ROAD.
I FEAR WE'RE GETTING A GOOD WAY FROM THE FARMHOUSE-- EVERYTHING IS UNFAMILIAR.
BUT IT WOULD DO NO GOOD TO GO BACK WHERE THE ROADS MEET-- THE NEXT ONE WE CHOSE MIGHT LEAD JUST AS FAR FROM HOME.

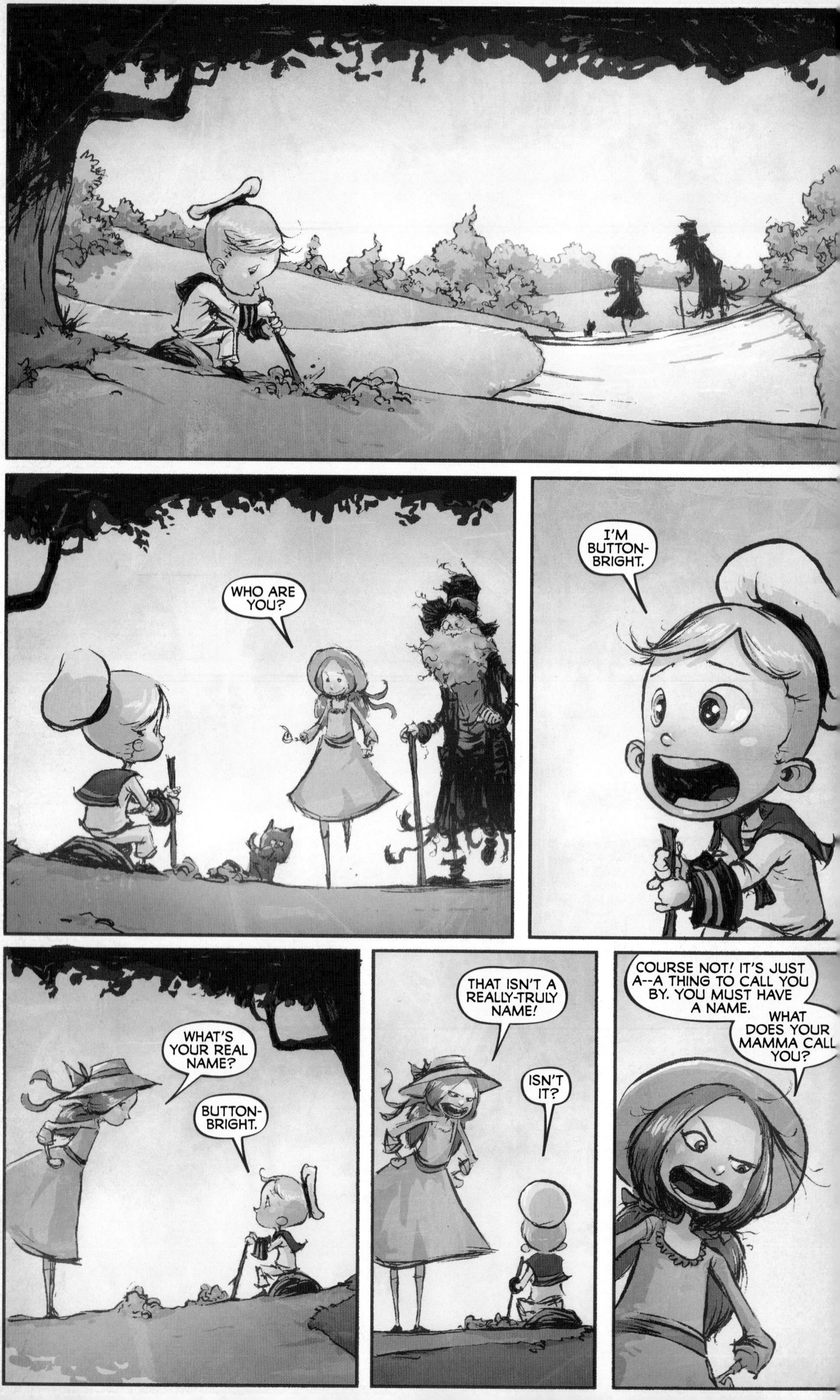
WHO ARE YOU?
I'M BUTTON-BRIGHT.
WHAT'S YOUR REAL NAME?
BUTTON-BRIGHT.
THAT ISN'T A REALLY-TRULY NAME!
ISN'T IT?
COURSE NOT! IT'S JUST A--A THING TO CALL YOU BY. YOU MUST HAVE A NAME.
WHAT DOES YOUR MAMMA CALL YOU?

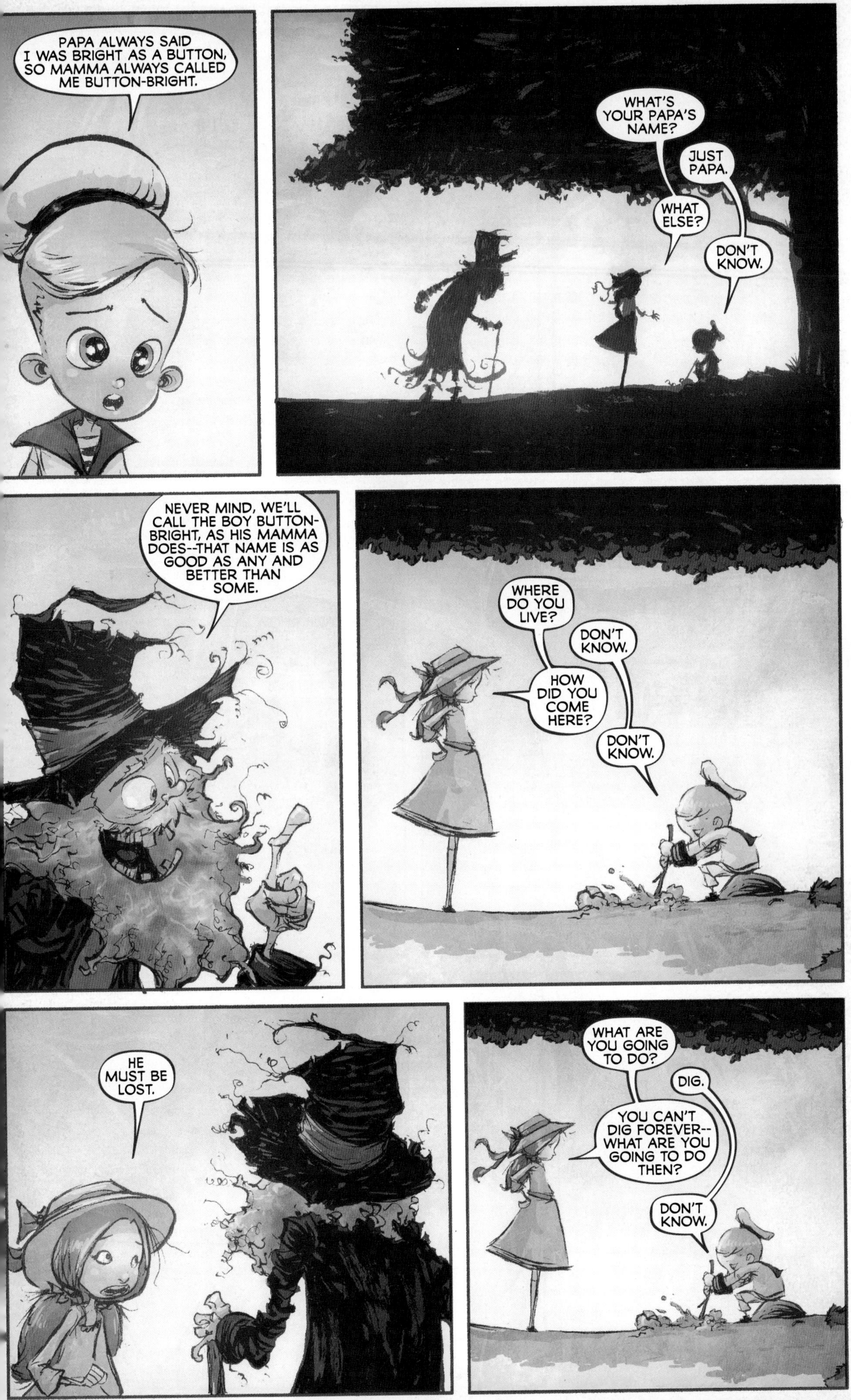
PAPA ALWAYS SAID I WAS BRIGHT AS A BUTTON, SO MAMMA ALWAYS CALLED ME BUTTON-BRIGHT.
WHAT'S YOUR PAPA'S NAME?
JUST PAPA.
WHAT ELSE?
DON'T KNOW.
NEVER MIND, WE'LL CALL THE BOY BUTTON-BRIGHT, AS HIS MAMMA DOES--THAT NAME IS AS GOOD AS ANY AND BETTER THAN SOME.
WHERE DO YOU LIVE?
DON'T KNOW.
HOW DID YOU COME HERE?
DON'T KNOW.
HE MUST BE LOST.
WHAT ARE YOU GOING TO DO?
DIG.
YOU CAN'T DIG FOREVER--WHAT ARE YOU GOING TO DO THEN?
DON'T KNOW.

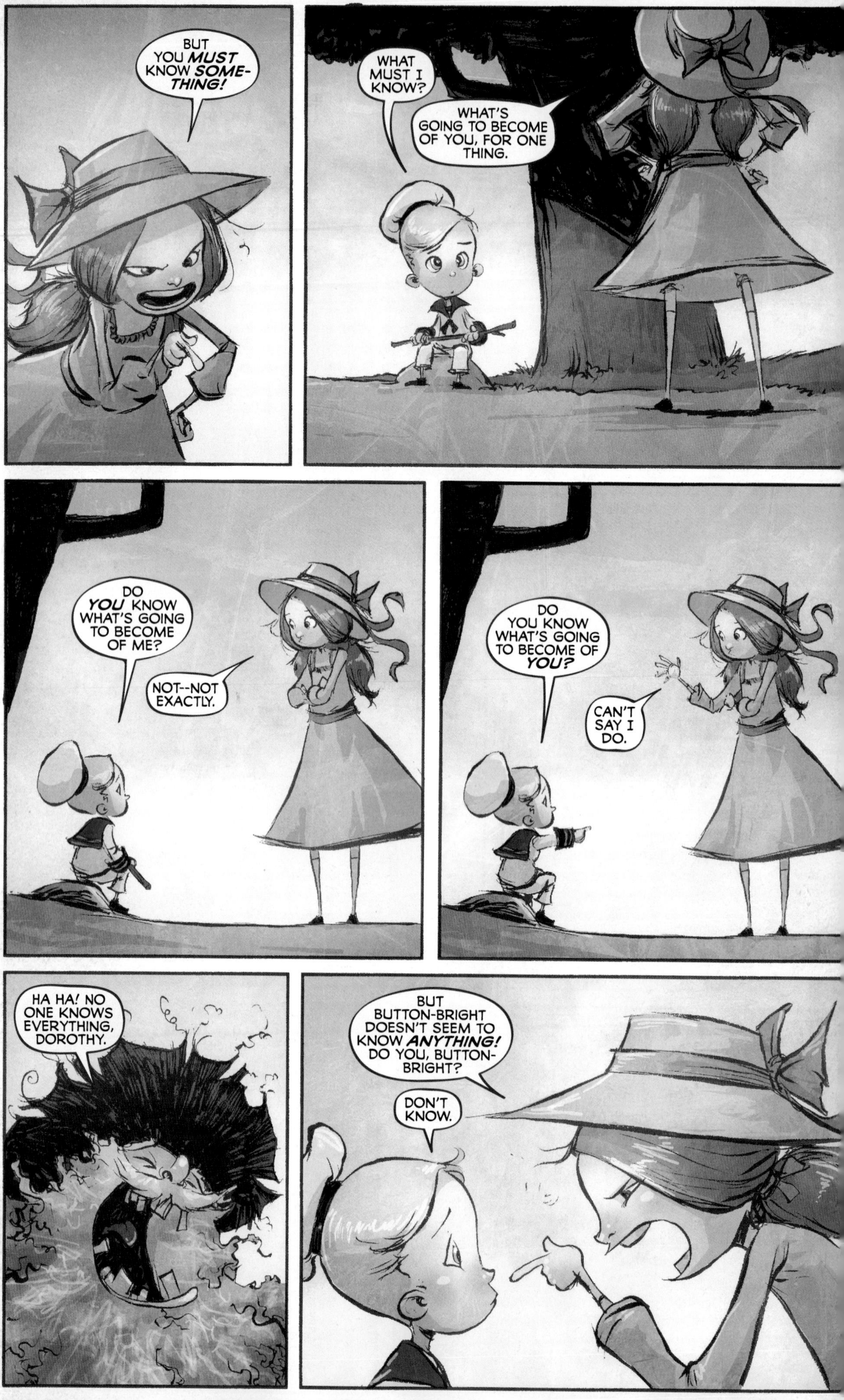
BUT YOU *MUST* KNOW *SOME-THING!*
WHAT MUST I KNOW?
WHAT'S GOING TO BECOME OF YOU, FOR ONE THING.
DO *YOU* KNOW WHAT'S GOING TO BECOME OF ME?
NOT--NOT EXACTLY.
DO YOU KNOW WHAT'S GOING TO BECOME OF *YOU?*
CAN'T SAY I DO.
HA HA! NO ONE KNOWS EVERYTHING, DOROTHY.
BUT BUTTON-BRIGHT DOESN'T SEEM TO KNOW *ANYTHING!* DO YOU, BUTTON-BRIGHT?
DON'T KNOW.

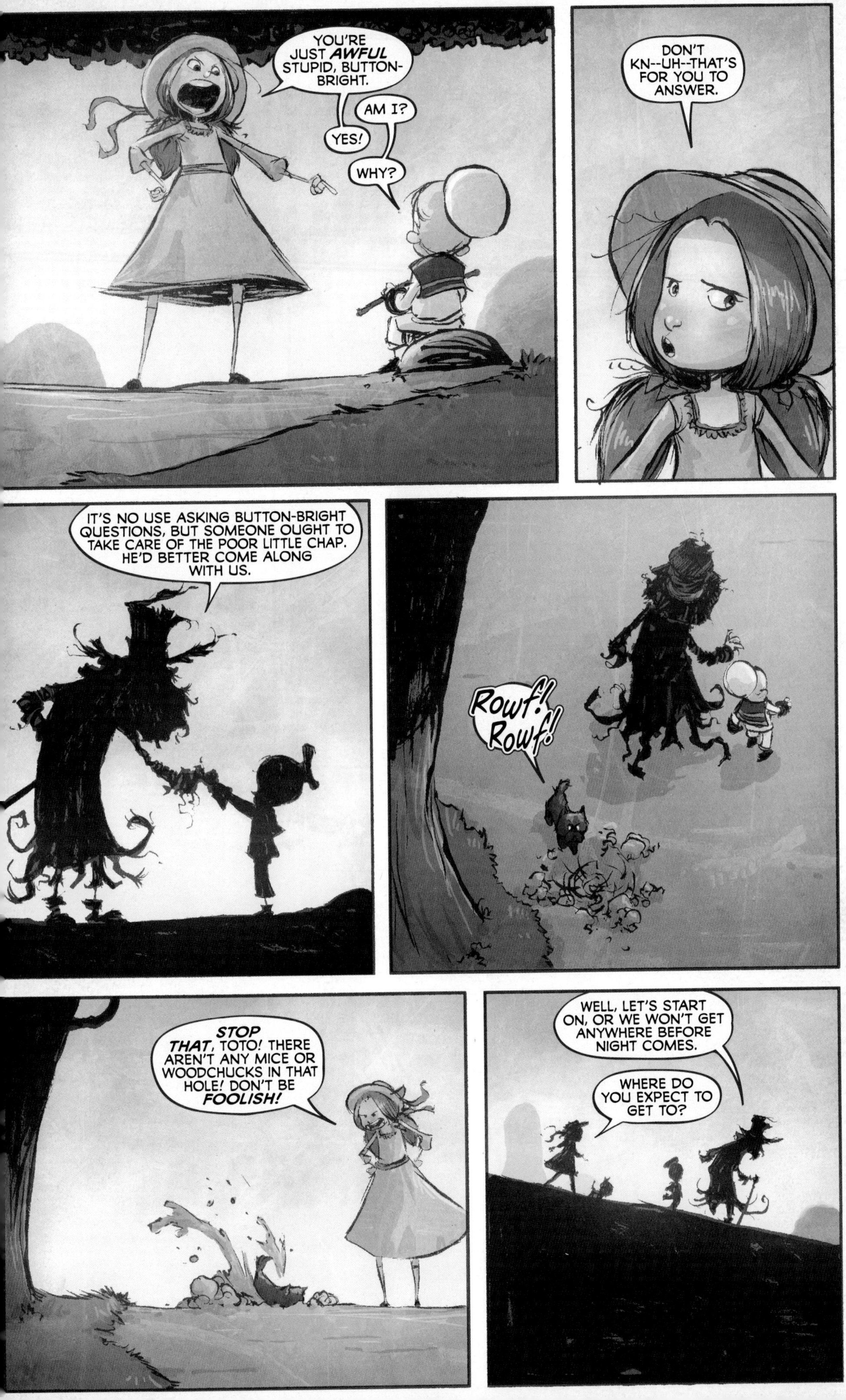
YOU'RE JUST AWFUL STUPID, BUTTON-BRIGHT.
AM I?
YES!
WHY?
DON'T KN--UH--THAT'S FOR YOU TO ANSWER.
IT'S NO USE ASKING BUTTON-BRIGHT QUESTIONS, BUT SOMEONE OUGHT TO TAKE CARE OF THE POOR LITTLE CHAP. HE'D BETTER COME ALONG WITH US.
Rowf! Rowf!
STOP THAT, TOTO! THERE AREN'T ANY MICE OR WOODCHUCKS IN THAT HOLE! DON'T BE FOOLISH!
WELL, LET'S START ON, OR WE WON'T GET ANYWHERE BEFORE NIGHT COMES.
WHERE DO YOU EXPECT TO GET TO?

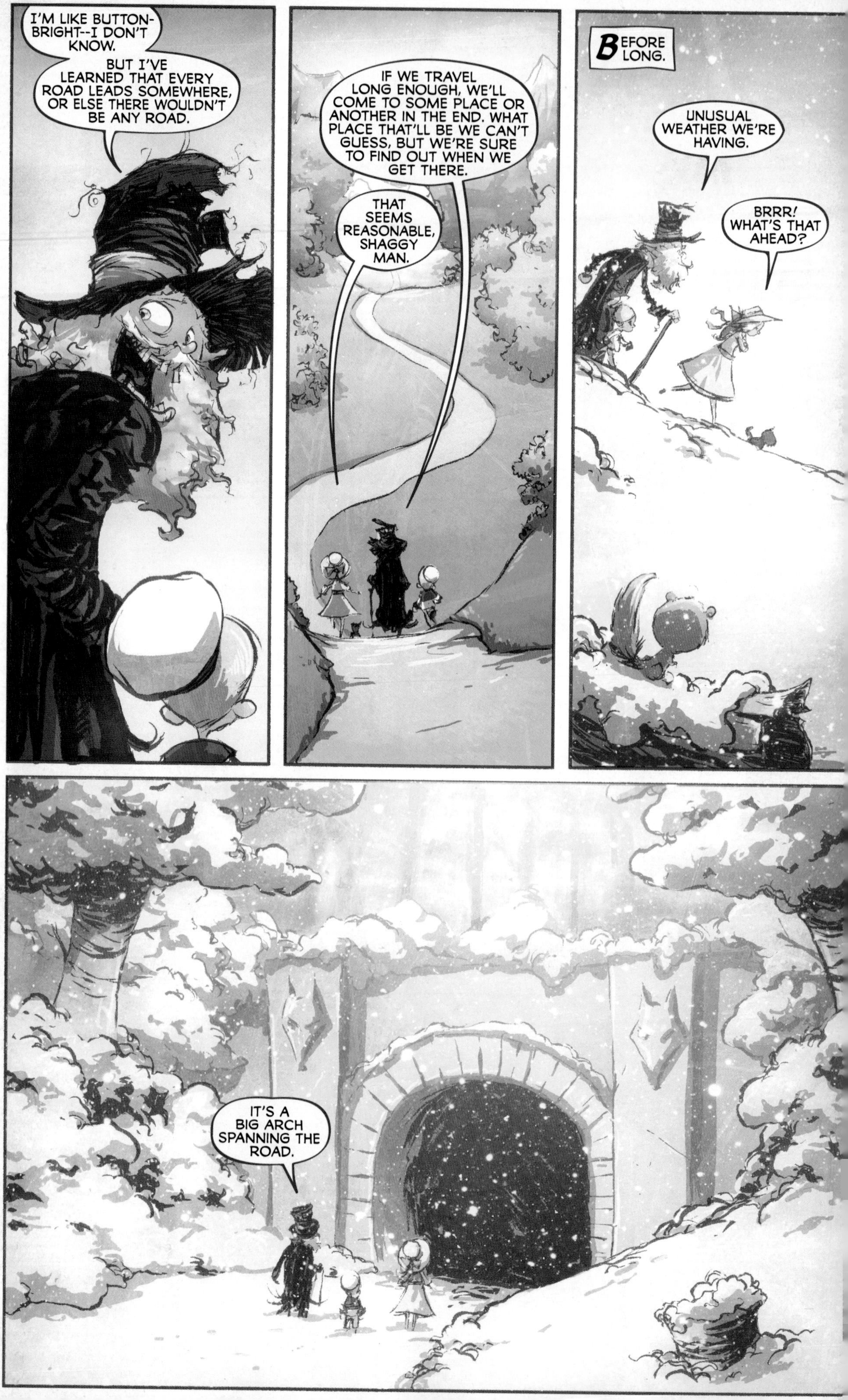
I'M LIKE BUTTON-BRIGHT--I DON'T KNOW.
BUT I'VE LEARNED THAT EVERY ROAD LEADS SOMEWHERE, OR ELSE THERE WOULDN'T BE ANY ROAD.
IF WE TRAVEL LONG ENOUGH, WE'LL COME TO SOME PLACE OR ANOTHER IN THE END. WHAT PLACE THAT'LL BE WE CAN'T GUESS, BUT WE'RE SURE TO FIND OUT WHEN WE GET THERE.
THAT SEEMS REASONABLE, SHAGGY MAN.
BEFORE LONG.
UNUSUAL WEATHER WE'RE HAVING.
BRRR! WHAT'S THAT AHEAD?
IT'S A BIG ARCH SPANNING THE ROAD.

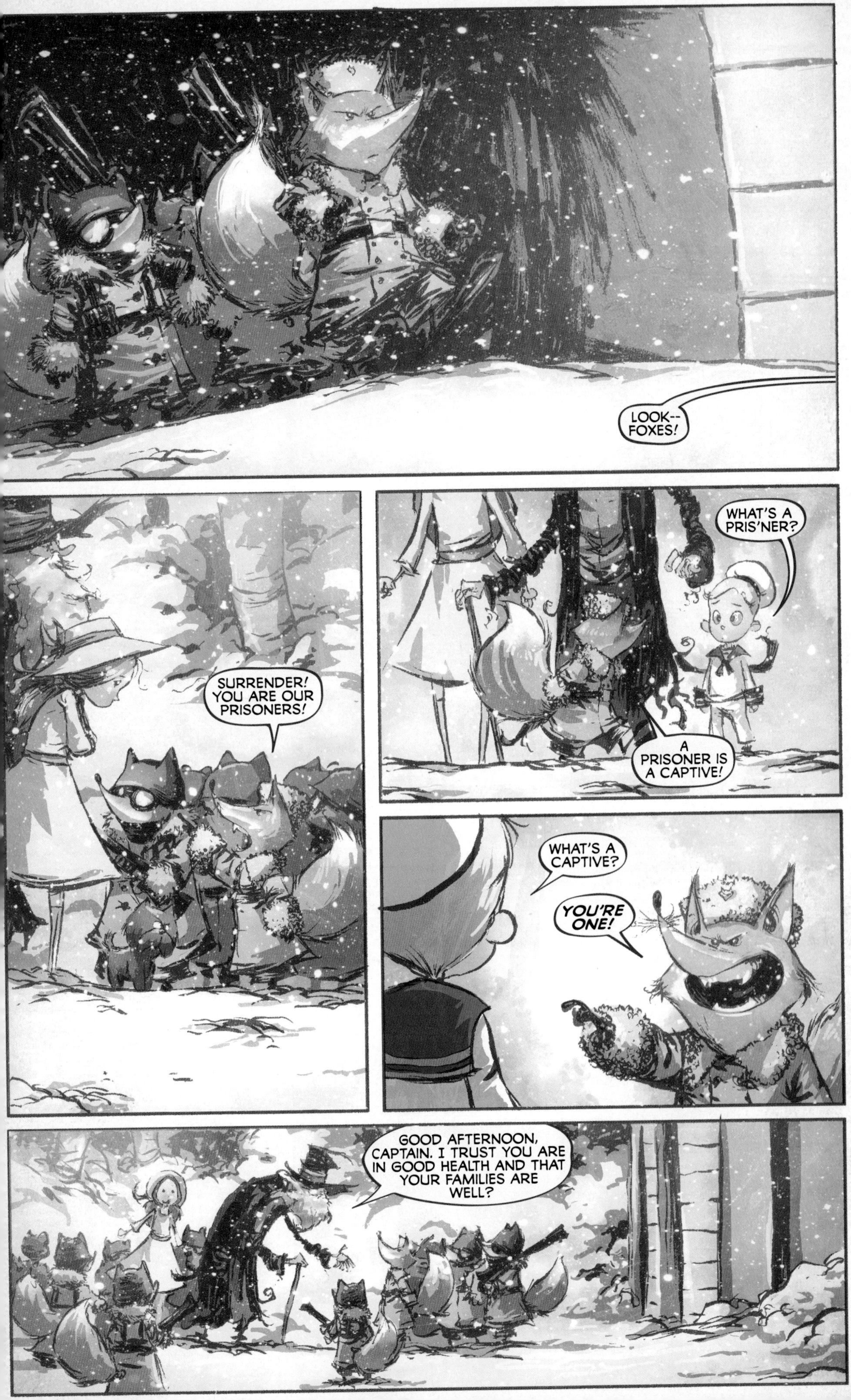
LOOK--
FOXES!
SURRENDER! YOU ARE OUR PRISONERS!
WHAT'S A PRIS'NER?
A PRISONER IS A CAPTIVE!
WHAT'S A CAPTIVE?
YOU'RE ONE!
GOOD AFTERNOON, CAPTAIN. I TRUST YOU ARE IN GOOD HEALTH AND THAT YOUR FAMILIES ARE WELL?

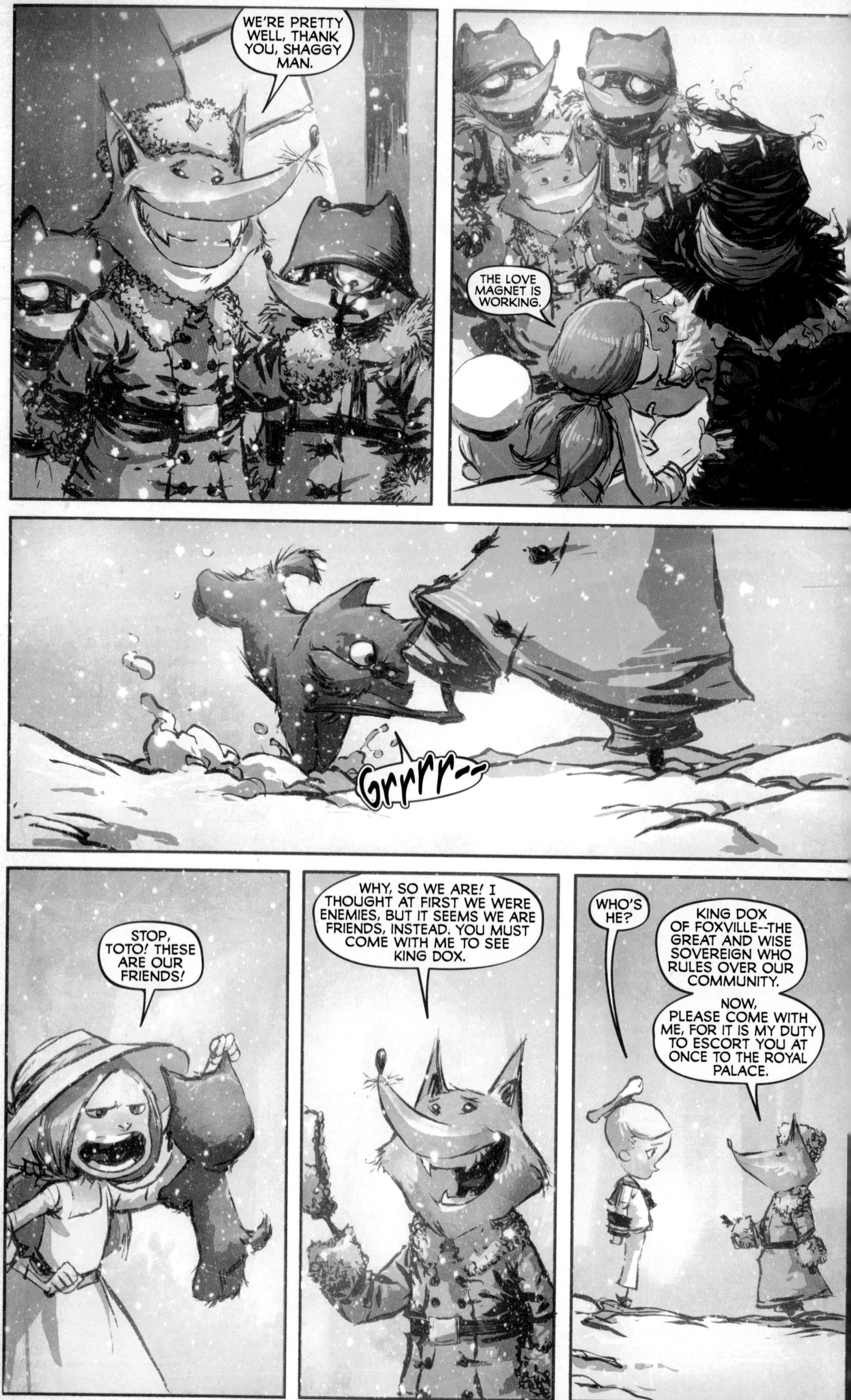
WE'RE PRETTY WELL, THANK YOU, SHAGGY MAN.
THE LOVE MAGNET IS WORKING.
GRRRR--
STOP, TOTO! THESE ARE OUR FRIENDS!
WHY, SO WE ARE! I THOUGHT AT FIRST WE WERE ENEMIES, BUT IT SEEMS WE ARE FRIENDS, INSTEAD. YOU MUST COME WITH ME TO SEE KING DOX.
WHO'S HE?
KING DOX OF FOXVILLE--THE GREAT AND WISE SOVEREIGN WHO RULES OVER OUR COMMUNITY.
NOW, PLEASE COME WITH ME, FOR IT IS MY DUTY TO ESCORT YOU AT ONCE TO THE ROYAL PALACE.

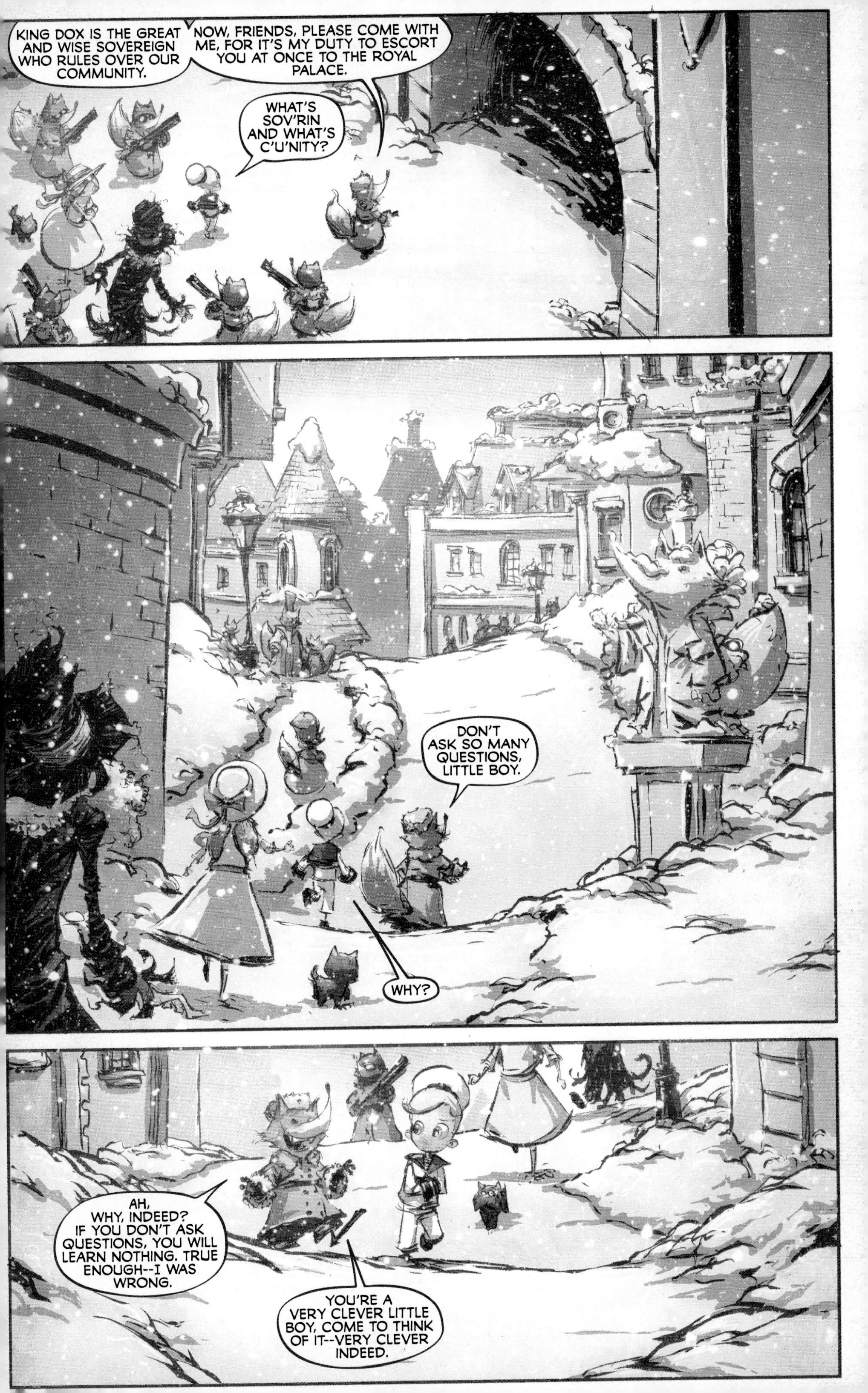
KING DOX IS THE GREAT AND WISE SOVEREIGN WHO RULES OVER OUR COMMUNITY.
NOW, FRIENDS, PLEASE COME WITH ME, FOR IT'S MY DUTY TO ESCORT YOU AT ONCE TO THE ROYAL PALACE.
WHAT'S SOV'RIN AND WHAT'S C'U'NITY?
DON'T ASK SO MANY QUESTIONS, LITTLE BOY.
WHY?
AH, WHY, INDEED? IF YOU DON'T ASK QUESTIONS, YOU WILL LEARN NOTHING. TRUE ENOUGH--I WAS WRONG.
YOU'RE A VERY CLEVER LITTLE BOY, COME TO THINK OF IT--VERY CLEVER INDEED.

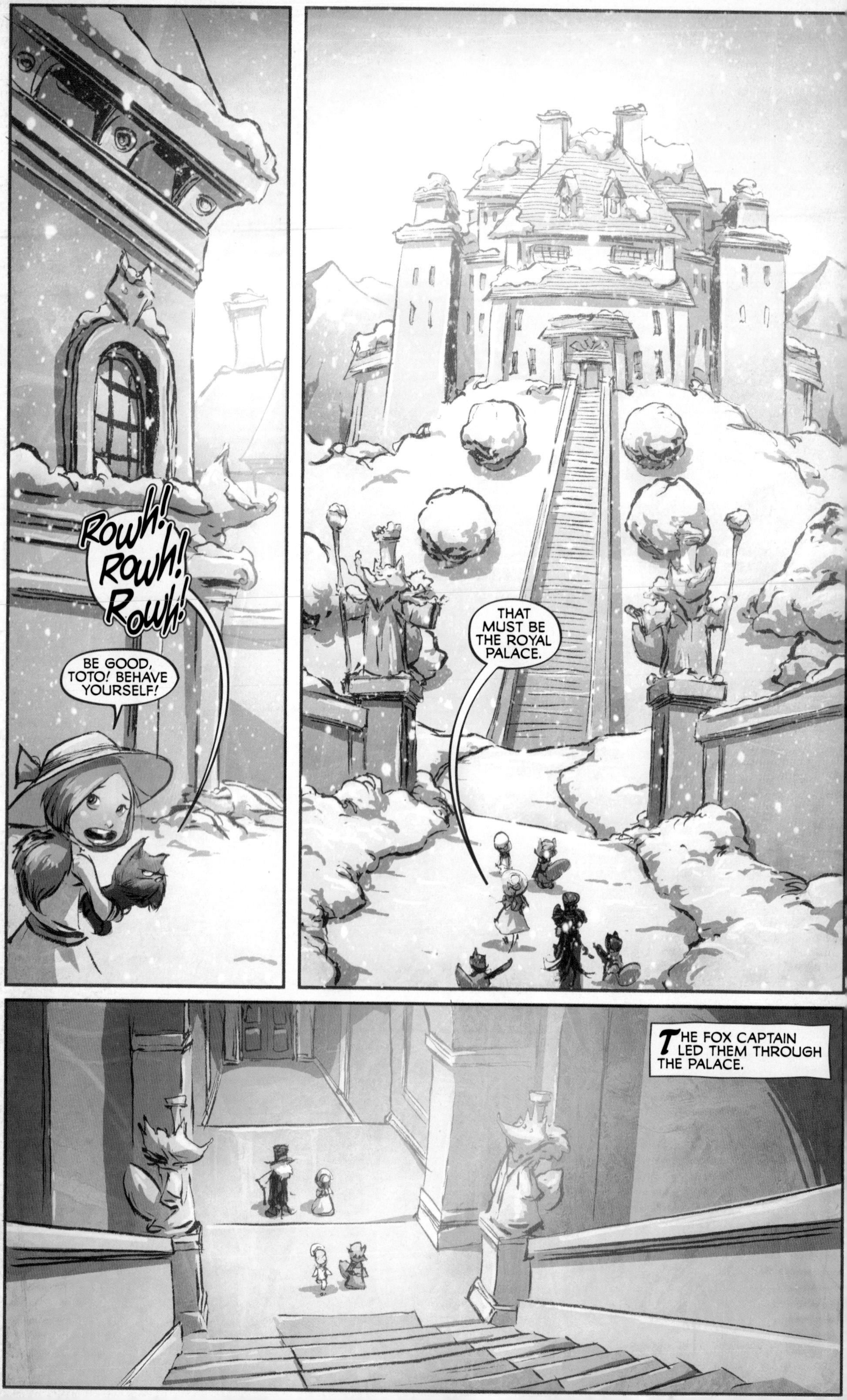

ROWH! ROWH! ROWH!
BE GOOD, TOTO! BEHAVE YOURSELF!
THAT MUST BE THE ROYAL PALACE.
THE FOX CAPTAIN LED THEM THROUGH THE PALACE.

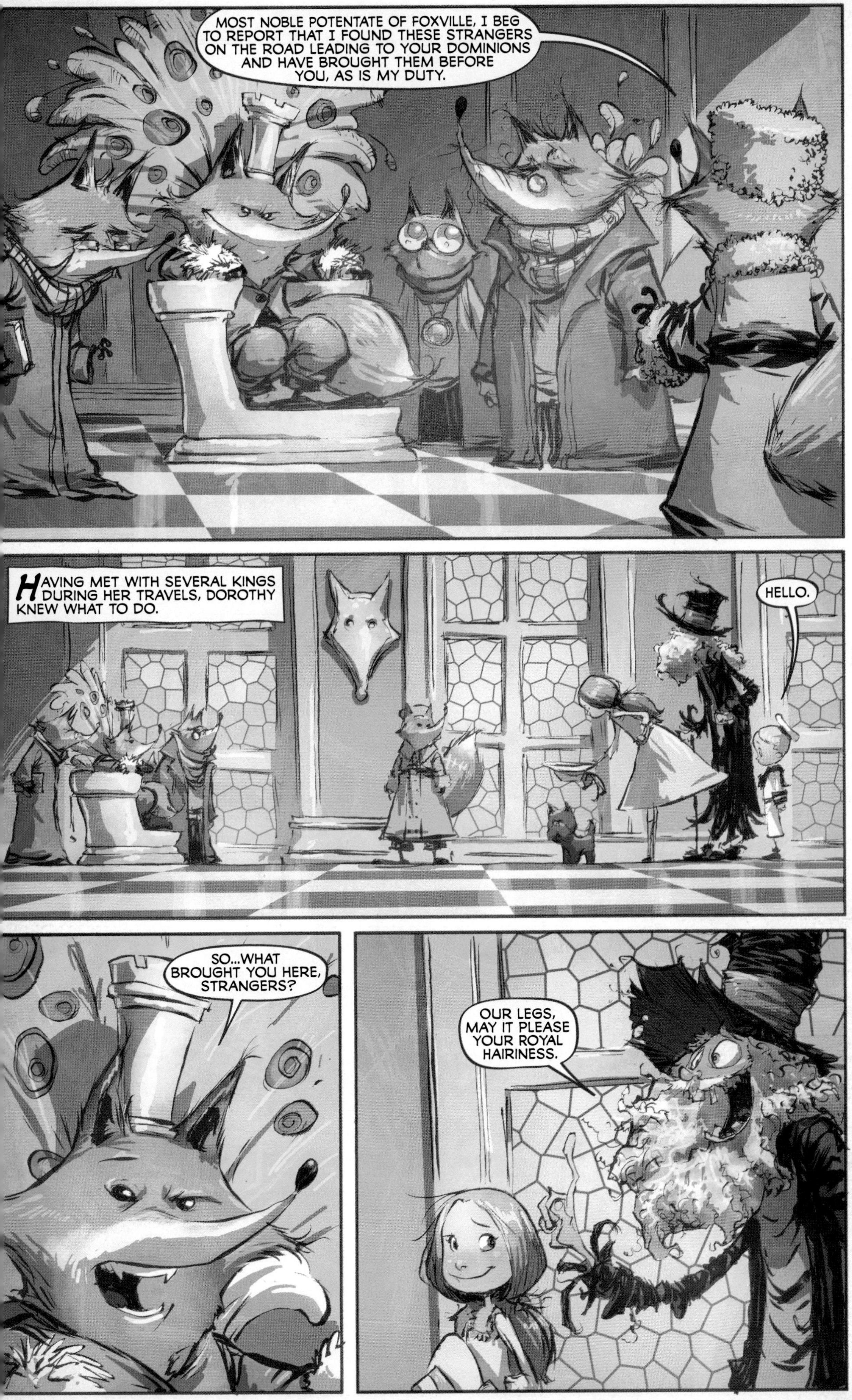
MOST NOBLE POTENTATE OF FOXVILLE, I BEG TO REPORT THAT I FOUND THESE STRANGERS ON THE ROAD LEADING TO YOUR DOMINIONS AND HAVE BROUGHT THEM BEFORE YOU, AS IS MY DUTY.
HAVING MET WITH SEVERAL KINGS DURING HER TRAVELS, DOROTHY KNEW WHAT TO DO.
HELLO.
SO...WHAT BROUGHT YOU HERE, STRANGERS?
OUR LEGS, MAY IT PLEASE YOUR ROYAL HAIRINESS.

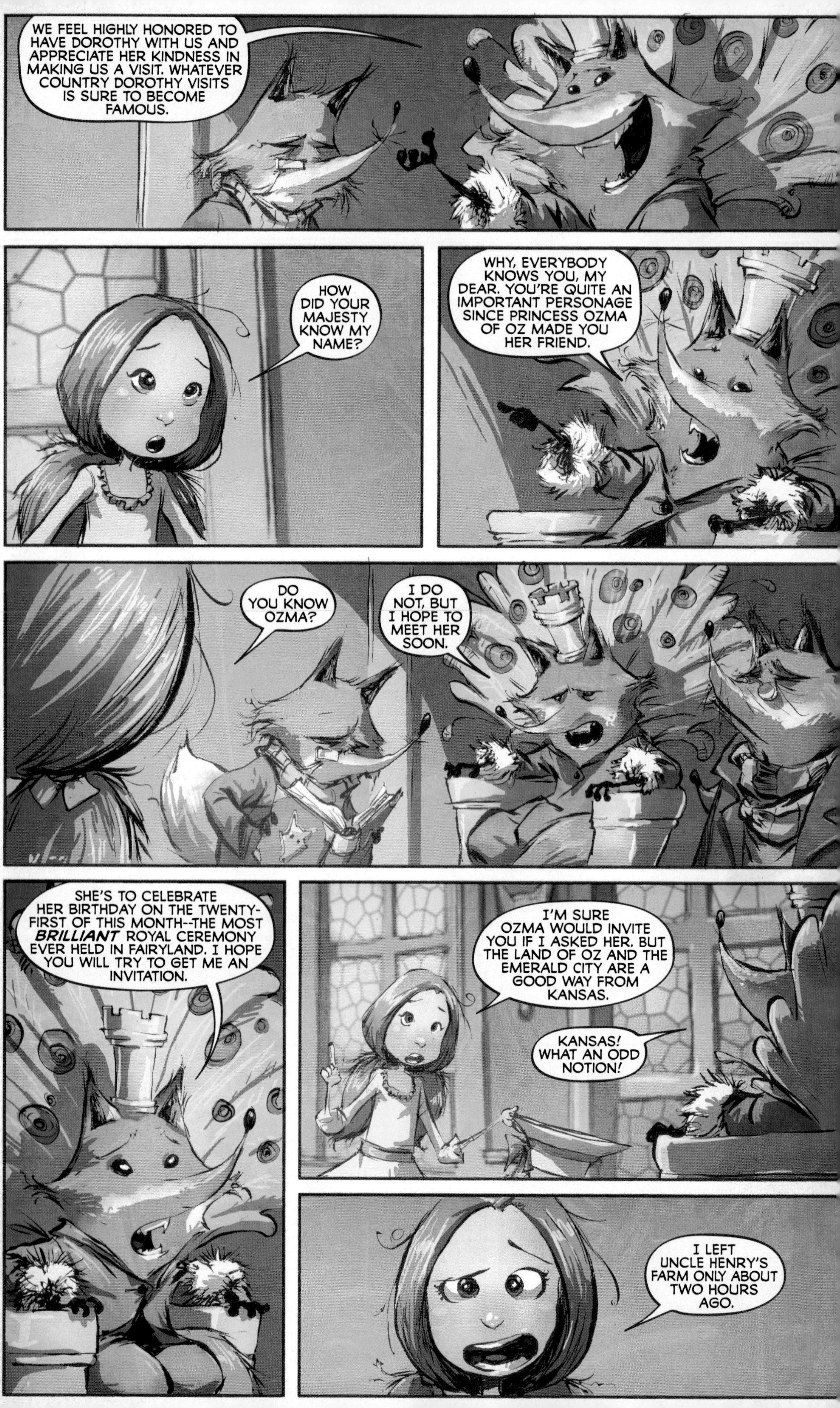
WE FEEL HIGHLY HONORED TO HAVE DOROTHY WITH US AND APPRECIATE HER KINDNESS IN MAKING US A VISIT. WHATEVER COUNTRY DOROTHY VISITS IS SURE TO BECOME FAMOUS.
HOW DID YOUR MAJESTY KNOW MY NAME?
WHY, EVERYBODY KNOWS YOU, MY DEAR. YOU'RE QUITE AN IMPORTANT PERSONAGE SINCE PRINCESS OZMA OF OZ MADE YOU HER FRIEND.
DO YOU KNOW OZMA?
I DO NOT, BUT I HOPE TO MEET HER SOON.
SHE'S TO CELEBRATE HER BIRTHDAY ON THE TWENTY-FIRST OF THIS MONTH--THE MOST *BRILLIANT* ROYAL CEREMONY EVER HELD IN FAIRYLAND. I HOPE YOU WILL TRY TO GET ME AN INVITATION.
I'M SURE OZMA WOULD INVITE YOU IF I ASKED HER. BUT THE LAND OF OZ AND THE EMERALD CITY ARE A GOOD WAY FROM KANSAS.
KANSAS! WHAT AN ODD NOTION!
I LEFT UNCLE HENRY'S FARM ONLY ABOUT TWO HOURS AGO.

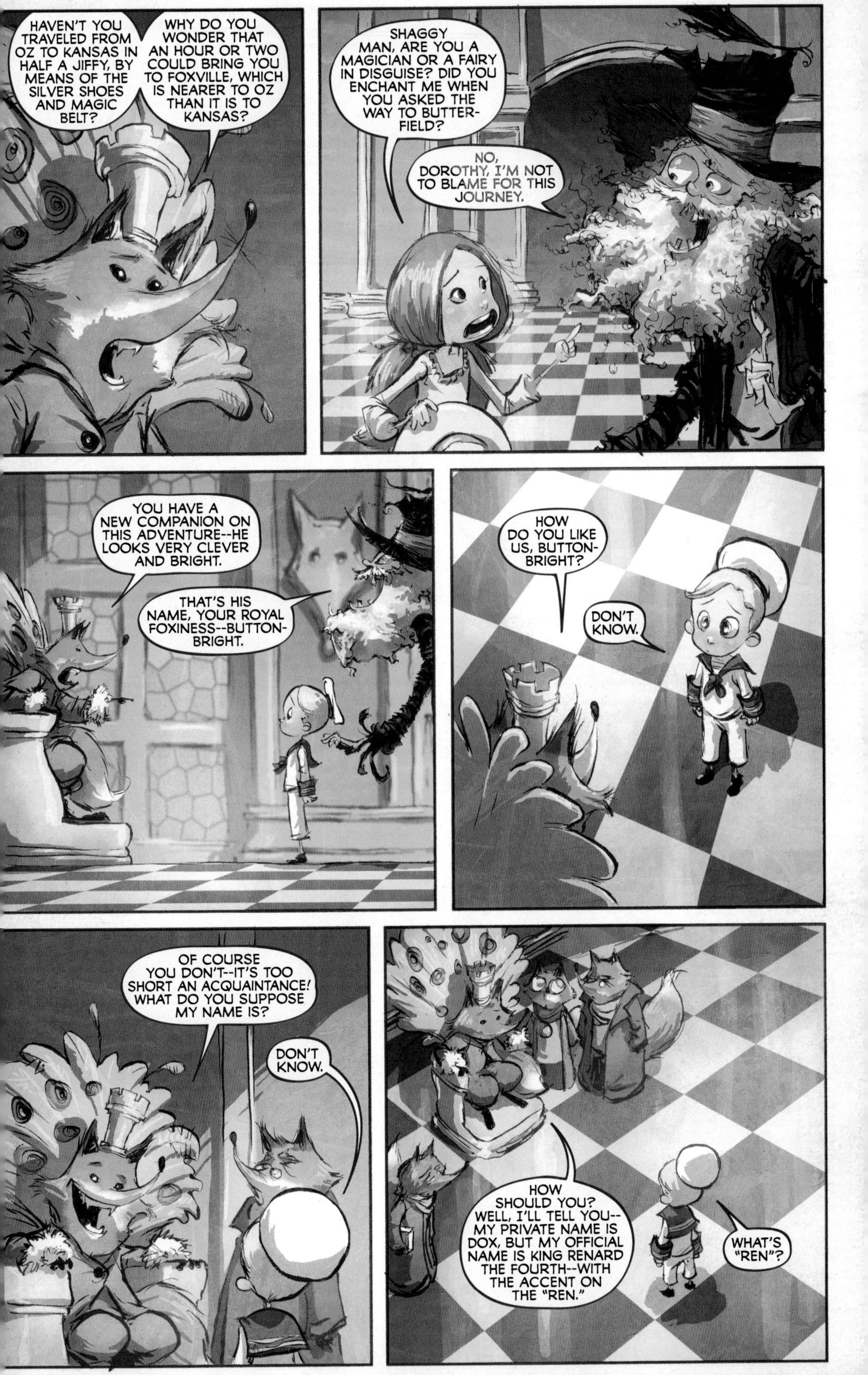
HAVEN'T YOU TRAVELED FROM OZ TO KANSAS IN HALF A JIFFY, BY MEANS OF THE SILVER SHOES AND MAGIC BELT?
WHY DO YOU WONDER THAT AN HOUR OR TWO COULD BRING YOU TO FOXVILLE, WHICH IS NEARER TO OZ THAN IT IS TO KANSAS?
SHAGGY MAN, ARE YOU A MAGICIAN OR A FAIRY IN DISGUISE? DID YOU ENCHANT ME WHEN YOU ASKED THE WAY TO BUTTER-FIELD?
NO, DOROTHY, I'M NOT TO BLAME FOR THIS JOURNEY.
YOU HAVE A NEW COMPANION ON THIS ADVENTURE--HE LOOKS VERY CLEVER AND BRIGHT.
THAT'S HIS NAME, YOUR ROYAL FOXINESS--BUTTON-BRIGHT.
HOW DO YOU LIKE US, BUTTON-BRIGHT?
DON'T KNOW.
OF COURSE YOU DON'T--IT'S TOO SHORT AN ACQUAINTANCE! WHAT DO YOU SUPPOSE MY NAME IS?
DON'T KNOW.
HOW SHOULD YOU? WELL, I'LL TELL YOU--MY PRIVATE NAME IS DOX, BUT MY OFFICIAL NAME IS KING RENARD THE FOURTH--WITH THE ACCENT ON THE "REN."
WHAT'S "REN"?

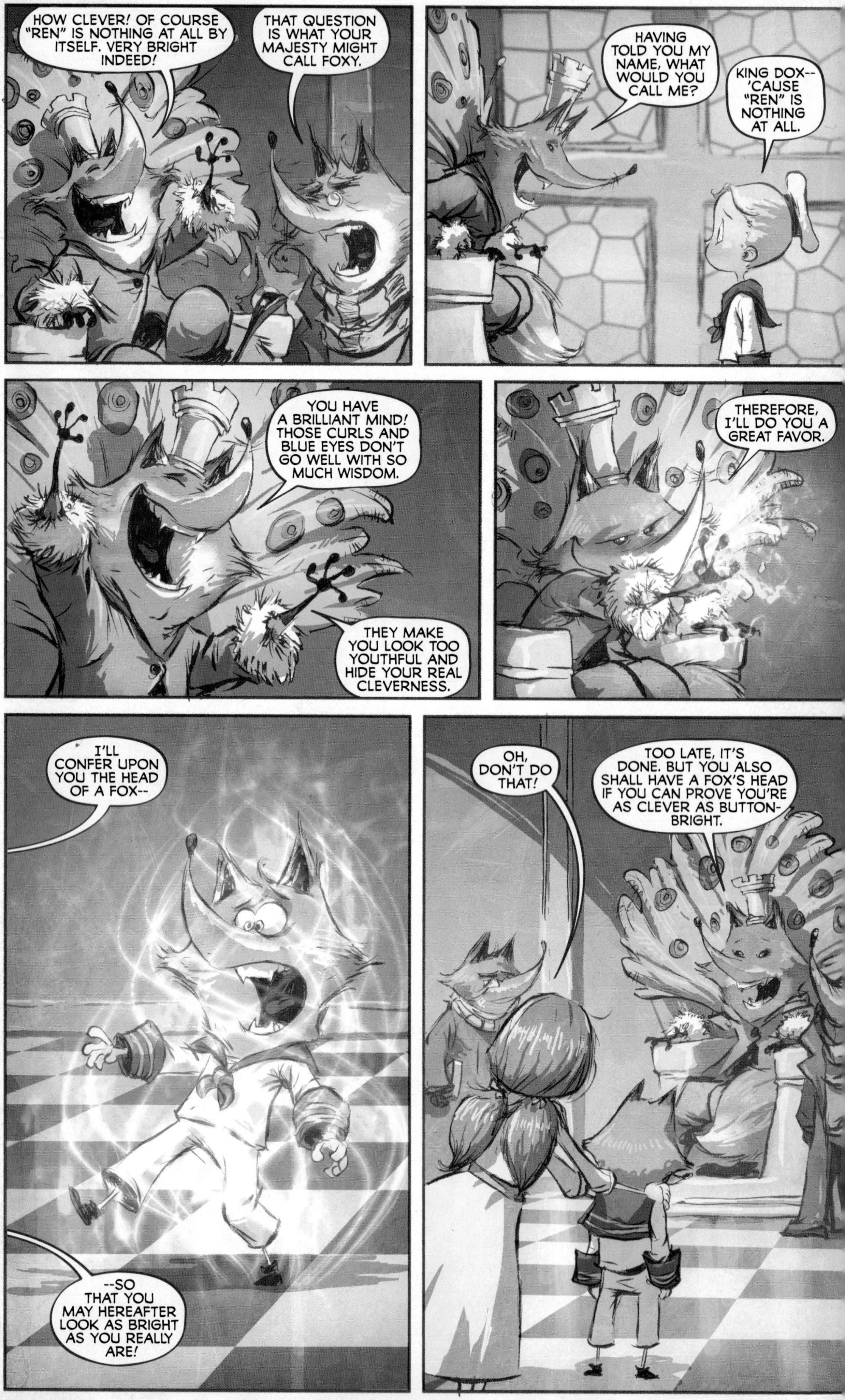
HOW CLEVER! OF COURSE "REN" IS NOTHING AT ALL BY ITSELF. VERY BRIGHT INDEED!
THAT QUESTION IS WHAT YOUR MAJESTY MIGHT CALL FOXY.
HAVING TOLD YOU MY NAME, WHAT WOULD YOU CALL ME?
KING DOX--'CAUSE "REN" IS NOTHING AT ALL.
YOU HAVE A BRILLIANT MIND! THOSE CURLS AND BLUE EYES DON'T GO WELL WITH SO MUCH WISDOM.
THEY MAKE YOU LOOK TOO YOUTHFUL AND HIDE YOUR REAL CLEVERNESS.
THEREFORE, I'LL DO YOU A GREAT FAVOR.
I'LL CONFER UPON YOU THE HEAD OF A FOX--
--SO THAT YOU MAY HEREAFTER LOOK AS BRIGHT AS YOU REALLY ARE!
OH, DON'T DO THAT!
TOO LATE, IT'S DONE. BUT YOU ALSO SHALL HAVE A FOX'S HEAD IF YOU CAN PROVE YOU'RE AS CLEVER AS BUTTON-BRIGHT.

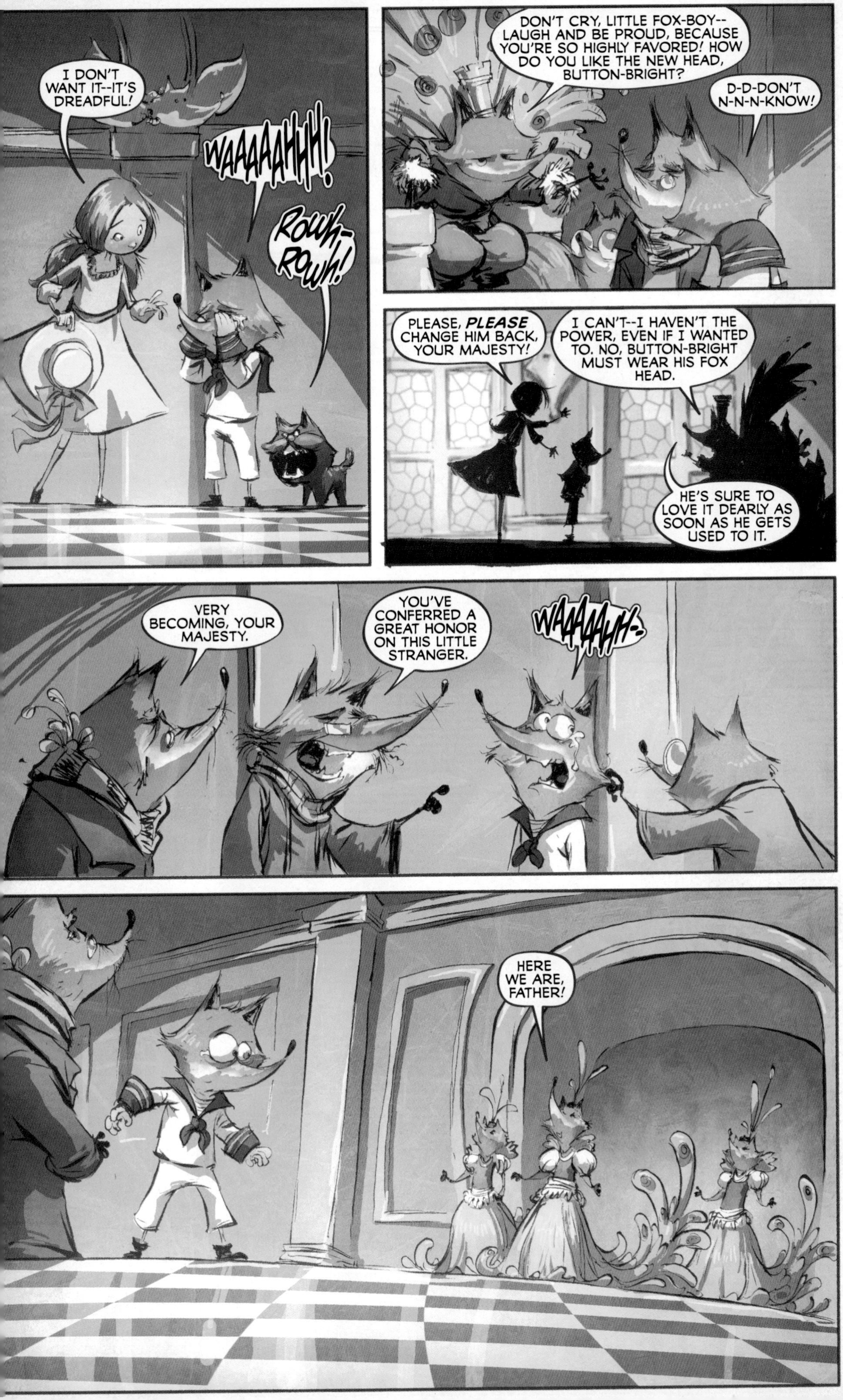
I DON'T WANT IT--IT'S DREADFUL!
WAAAAAHHH!
ROWH-ROWH!
DON'T CRY, LITTLE FOX-BOY-- LAUGH AND BE PROUD, BECAUSE YOU'RE SO HIGHLY FAVORED! HOW DO YOU LIKE THE NEW HEAD, BUTTON-BRIGHT?
D-D-DON'T N-N-N-KNOW!
PLEASE, *PLEASE* CHANGE HIM BACK, YOUR MAJESTY!
I CAN'T--I HAVEN'T THE POWER, EVEN IF I WANTED TO. NO, BUTTON-BRIGHT MUST WEAR HIS FOX HEAD.
HE'S SURE TO LOVE IT DEARLY AS SOON AS HE GETS USED TO IT.
VERY BECOMING, YOUR MAJESTY.
YOU'VE CONFERRED A GREAT HONOR ON THIS LITTLE STRANGER.
WAAAAAHH-
HERE WE ARE, FATHER!

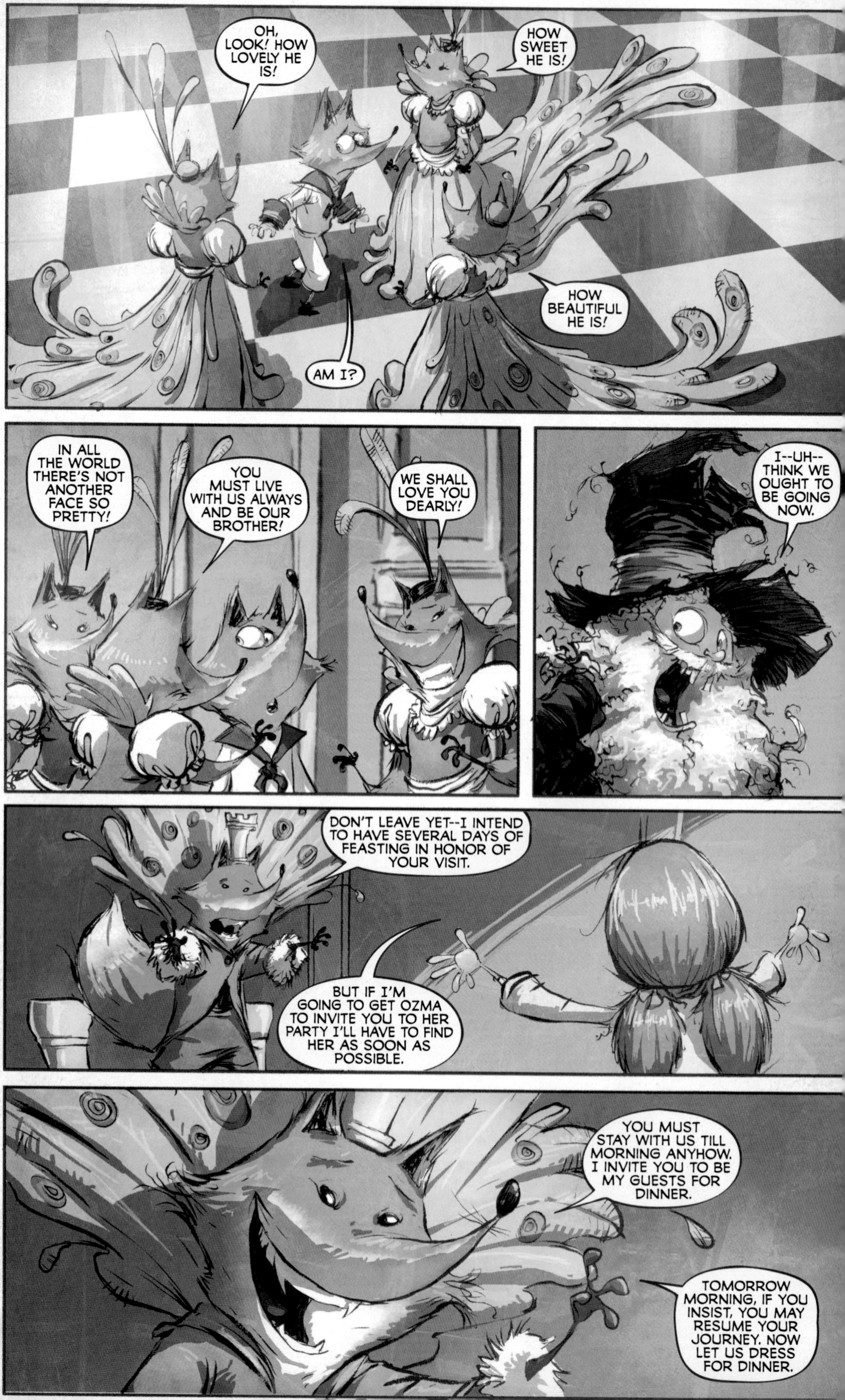
OH, LOOK! HOW LOVELY HE IS!
HOW SWEET HE IS!
HOW BEAUTIFUL HE IS!
AM I?
IN ALL THE WORLD THERE'S NOT ANOTHER FACE SO PRETTY!
YOU MUST LIVE WITH US ALWAYS AND BE OUR BROTHER!
WE SHALL LOVE YOU DEARLY!
I--UH-- THINK WE OUGHT TO BE GOING NOW.
DON'T LEAVE YET--I INTEND TO HAVE SEVERAL DAYS OF FEASTING IN HONOR OF YOUR VISIT.
BUT IF I'M GOING TO GET OZMA TO INVITE YOU TO HER PARTY I'LL HAVE TO FIND HER AS SOON AS POSSIBLE.
YOU MUST STAY WITH US TILL MORNING ANYHOW. I INVITE YOU TO BE MY GUESTS FOR DINNER.
TOMORROW MORNING, IF YOU INSIST, YOU MAY RESUME YOUR JOURNEY. NOW LET US DRESS FOR DINNER.

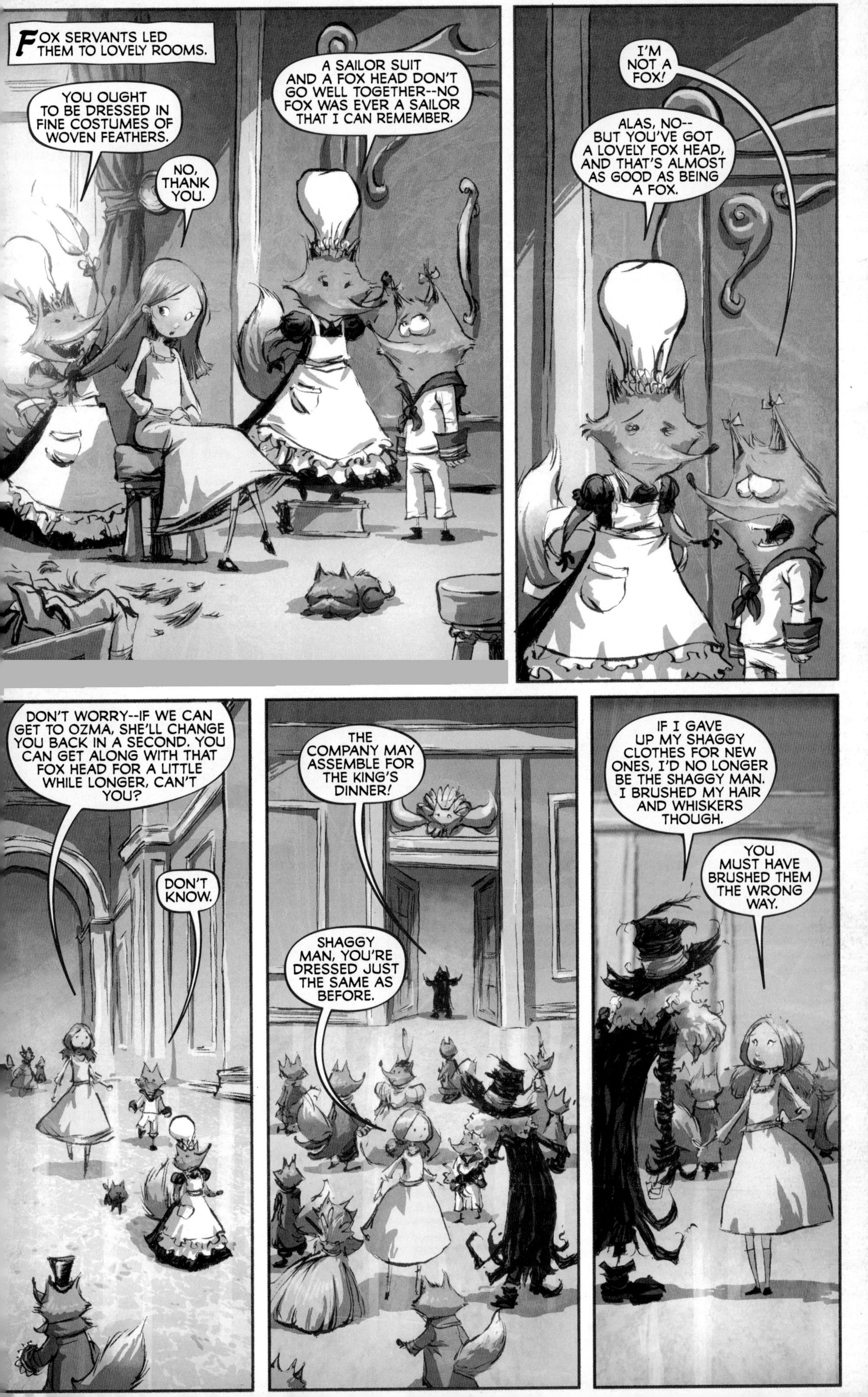
FOX SERVANTS LED THEM TO LOVELY ROOMS.
YOU OUGHT TO BE DRESSED IN FINE COSTUMES OF WOVEN FEATHERS.
NO, THANK YOU.
A SAILOR SUIT AND A FOX HEAD DON'T GO WELL TOGETHER--NO FOX WAS EVER A SAILOR THAT I CAN REMEMBER.
I'M NOT A FOX!
ALAS, NO-- BUT YOU'VE GOT A LOVELY FOX HEAD, AND THAT'S ALMOST AS GOOD AS BEING A FOX.
DON'T WORRY--IF WE CAN GET TO OZMA, SHE'LL CHANGE YOU BACK IN A SECOND. YOU CAN GET ALONG WITH THAT FOX HEAD FOR A LITTLE WHILE LONGER, CAN'T YOU?
DON'T KNOW.
THE COMPANY MAY ASSEMBLE FOR THE KING'S DINNER!
SHAGGY MAN, YOU'RE DRESSED JUST THE SAME AS BEFORE.
IF I GAVE UP MY SHAGGY CLOTHES FOR NEW ONES, I'D NO LONGER BE THE SHAGGY MAN. I BRUSHED MY HAIR AND WHISKERS THOUGH.
YOU MUST HAVE BRUSHED THEM THE WRONG WAY.

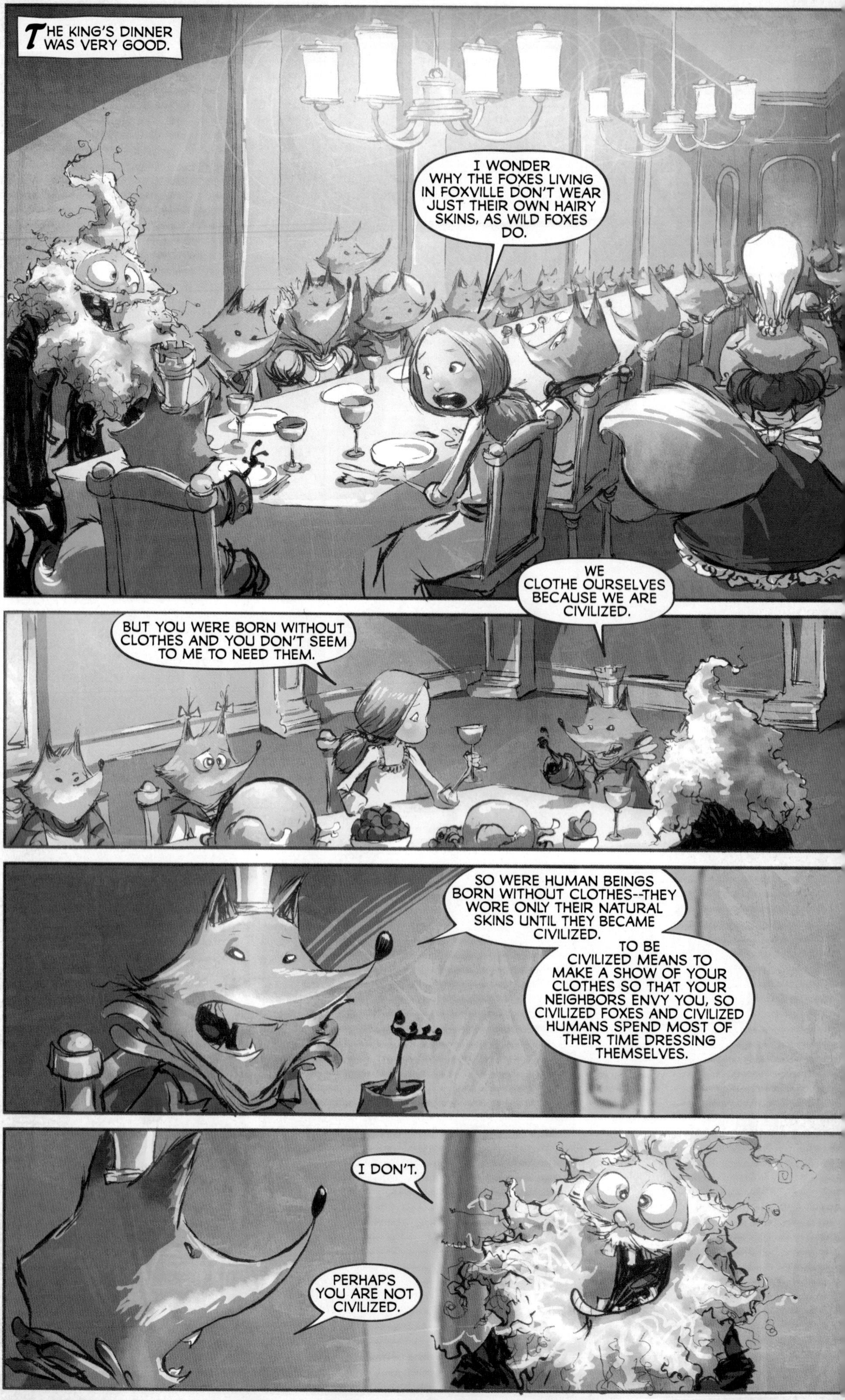
THE KING'S DINNER WAS VERY GOOD.
I WONDER WHY THE FOXES LIVING IN FOXVILLE DON'T WEAR JUST THEIR OWN HAIRY SKINS, AS WILD FOXES DO.
WE CLOTHE OURSELVES BECAUSE WE ARE CIVILIZED.
BUT YOU WERE BORN WITHOUT CLOTHES AND YOU DON'T SEEM TO ME TO NEED THEM.
SO WERE HUMAN BEINGS BORN WITHOUT CLOTHES--THEY WORE ONLY THEIR NATURAL SKINS UNTIL THEY BECAME CIVILIZED.
TO BE CIVILIZED MEANS TO MAKE A SHOW OF YOUR CLOTHES SO THAT YOUR NEIGHBORS ENVY YOU, SO CIVILIZED FOXES AND CIVILIZED HUMANS SPEND MOST OF THEIR TIME DRESSING THEMSELVES.
I DON'T.
PERHAPS YOU ARE NOT CIVILIZED.

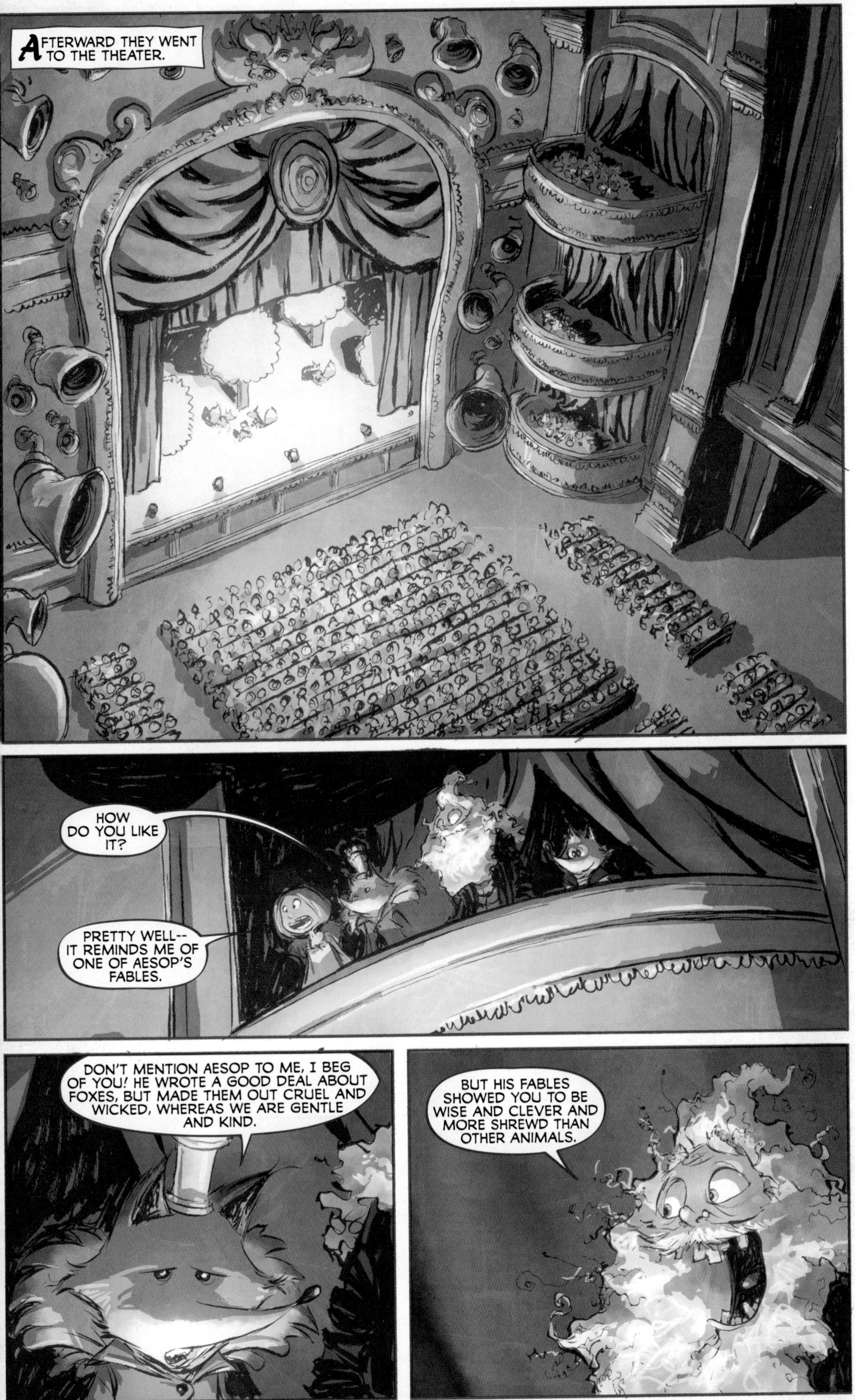
AFTERWARD THEY WENT TO THE THEATER.
HOW DO YOU LIKE IT?
PRETTY WELL-- IT REMINDS ME OF ONE OF AESOP'S FABLES.
DON'T MENTION AESOP TO ME, I BEG OF YOU! HE WROTE A GOOD DEAL ABOUT FOXES, BUT MADE THEM OUT CRUEL AND WICKED, WHEREAS WE ARE GENTLE AND KIND.
BUT HIS FABLES SHOWED YOU TO BE WISE AND CLEVER AND MORE SHREWD THAN OTHER ANIMALS.

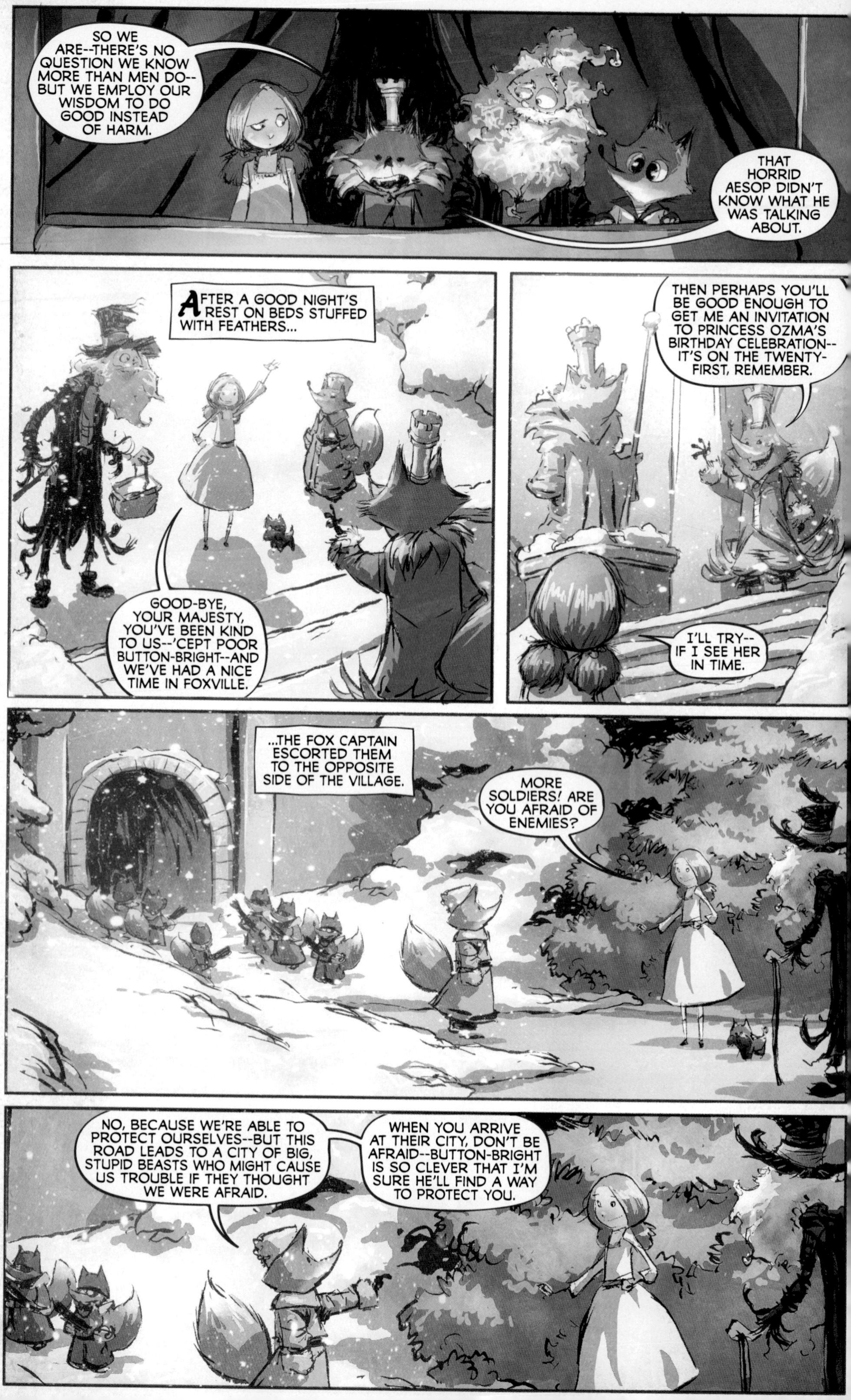
SO WE ARE--THERE'S NO QUESTION WE KNOW MORE THAN MEN DO--BUT WE EMPLOY OUR WISDOM TO DO GOOD INSTEAD OF HARM.
THAT HORRID AESOP DIDN'T KNOW WHAT HE WAS TALKING ABOUT.
AFTER A GOOD NIGHT'S REST ON BEDS STUFFED WITH FEATHERS...
GOOD-BYE, YOUR MAJESTY, YOU'VE BEEN KIND TO US--'CEPT POOR BUTTON-BRIGHT--AND WE'VE HAD A NICE TIME IN FOXVILLE.
THEN PERHAPS YOU'LL BE GOOD ENOUGH TO GET ME AN INVITATION TO PRINCESS OZMA'S BIRTHDAY CELEBRATION--IT'S ON THE TWENTY-FIRST, REMEMBER.
I'LL TRY--IF I SEE HER IN TIME.
...THE FOX CAPTAIN ESCORTED THEM TO THE OPPOSITE SIDE OF THE VILLAGE.
MORE SOLDIERS! ARE YOU AFRAID OF ENEMIES?
NO, BECAUSE WE'RE ABLE TO PROTECT OURSELVES--BUT THIS ROAD LEADS TO A CITY OF BIG, STUPID BEASTS WHO MIGHT CAUSE US TROUBLE IF THEY THOUGHT WE WERE AFRAID.
WHEN YOU ARRIVE AT THEIR CITY, DON'T BE AFRAID--BUTTON-BRIGHT IS SO CLEVER THAT I'M SURE HE'LL FIND A WAY TO PROTECT YOU.

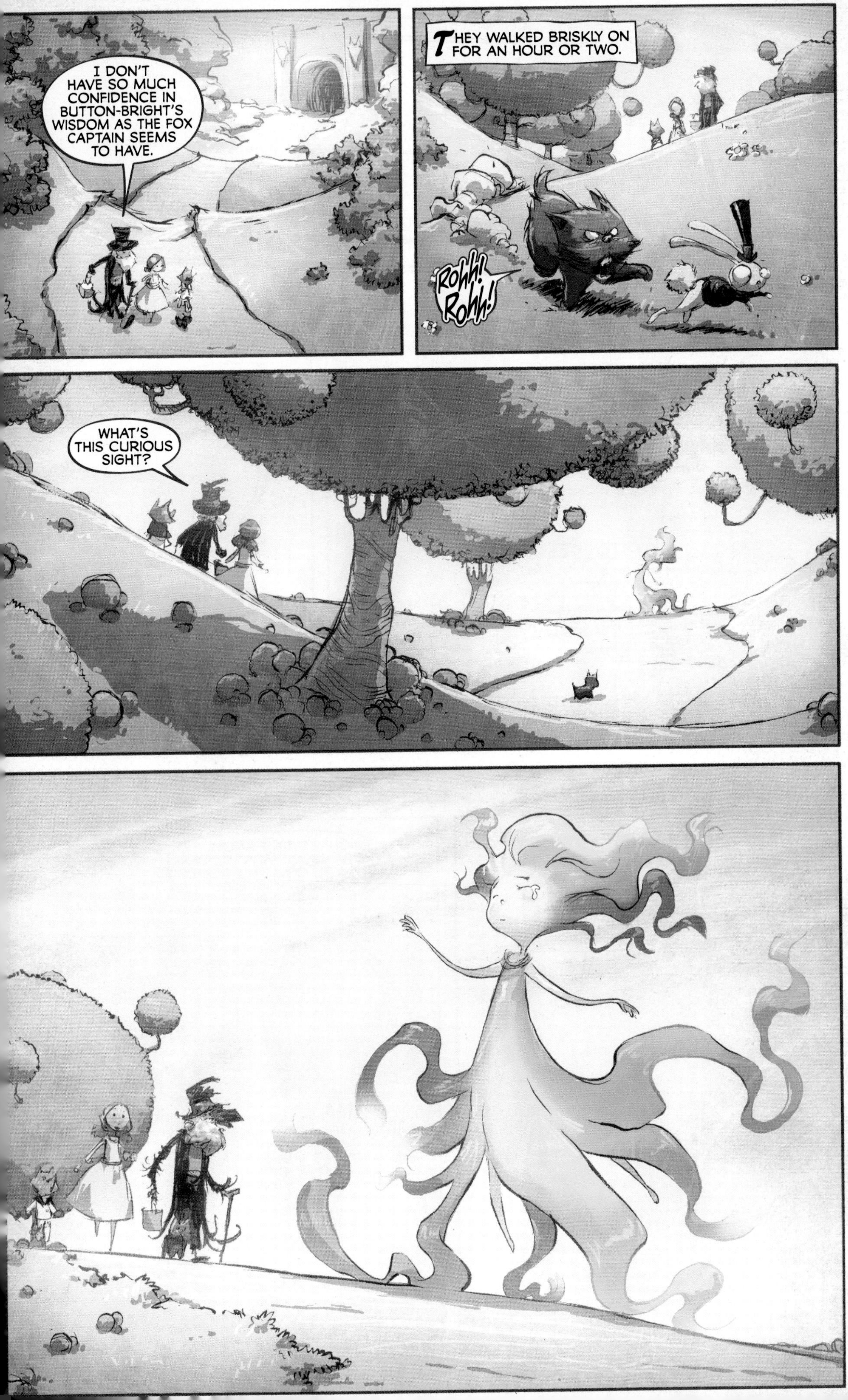
I DON'T HAVE SO MUCH CONFIDENCE IN BUTTON-BRIGHT'S WISDOM AS THE FOX CAPTAIN SEEMS TO HAVE.
THEY WALKED BRISKLY ON FOR AN HOUR OR TWO.
ROHH! ROHH!
WHAT'S THIS CURIOUS SIGHT?

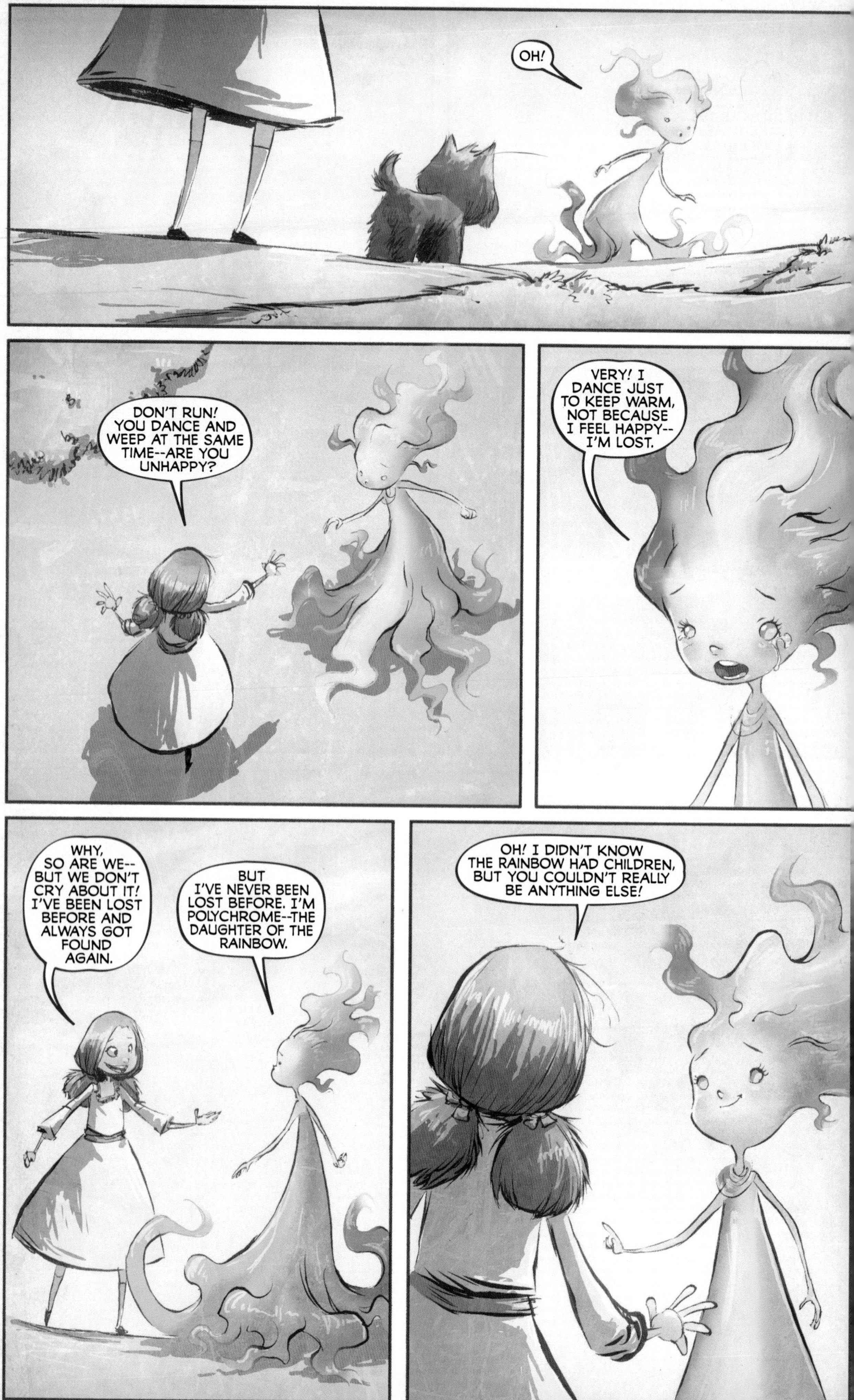
OH!
DON'T RUN! YOU DANCE AND WEEP AT THE SAME TIME--ARE YOU UNHAPPY?
VERY! I DANCE JUST TO KEEP WARM, NOT BECAUSE I FEEL HAPPY-- I'M LOST.
WHY, SO ARE WE-- BUT WE DON'T CRY ABOUT IT! I'VE BEEN LOST BEFORE AND ALWAYS GOT FOUND AGAIN.
BUT I'VE NEVER BEEN LOST BEFORE. I'M POLYCHROME--THE DAUGHTER OF THE RAINBOW.
OH! I DIDN'T KNOW THE RAINBOW HAD CHILDREN, BUT YOU COULDN'T REALLY BE ANYTHING ELSE!

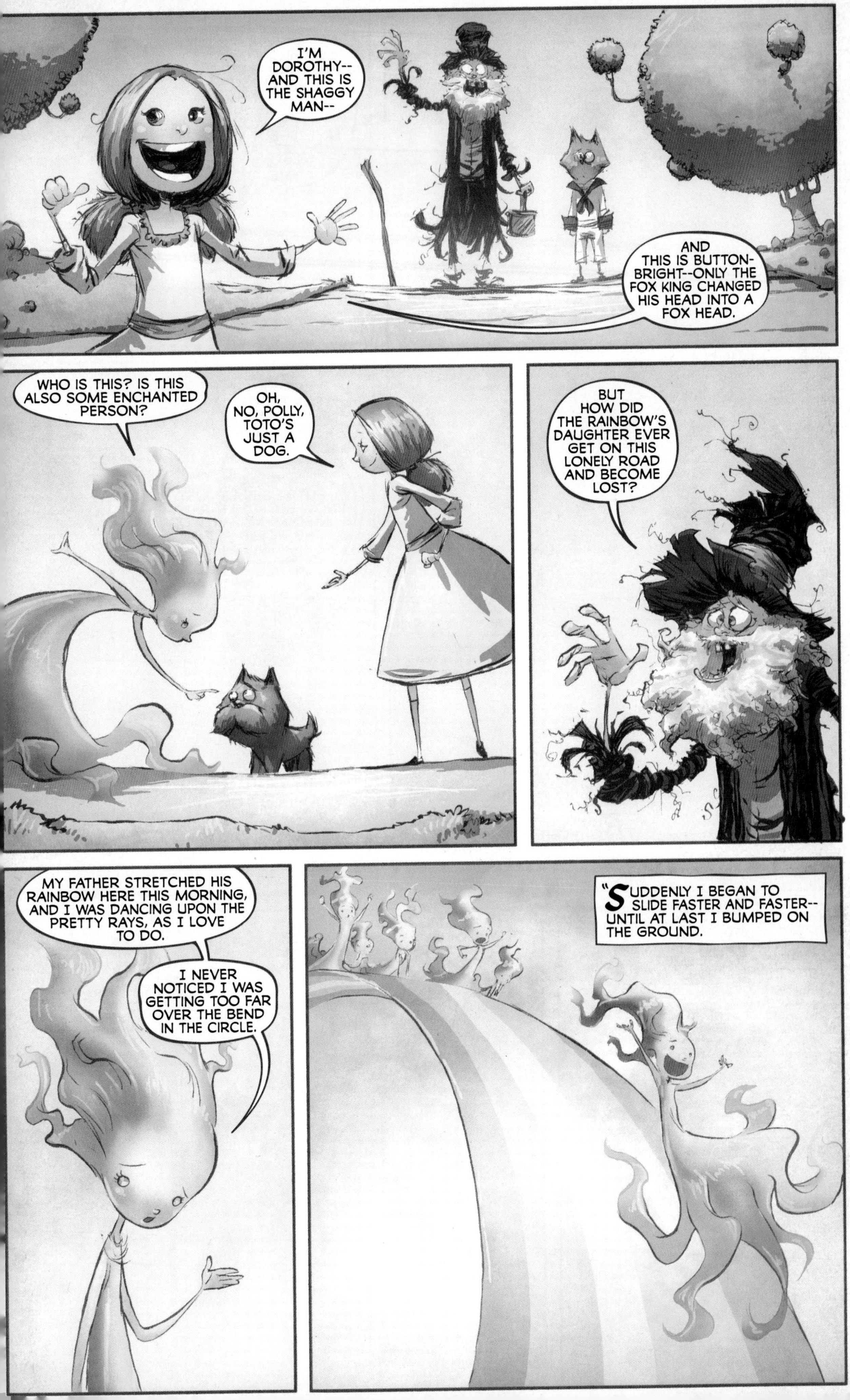
I'M DOROTHY-- AND THIS IS THE SHAGGY MAN--
AND THIS IS BUTTON-BRIGHT--ONLY THE FOX KING CHANGED HIS HEAD INTO A FOX HEAD.
WHO IS THIS? IS THIS ALSO SOME ENCHANTED PERSON?
OH, NO, POLLY, TOTO'S JUST A DOG.
BUT HOW DID THE RAINBOW'S DAUGHTER EVER GET ON THIS LONELY ROAD AND BECOME LOST?
MY FATHER STRETCHED HIS RAINBOW HERE THIS MORNING, AND I WAS DANCING UPON THE PRETTY RAYS, AS I LOVE TO DO.
I NEVER NOTICED I WAS GETTING TOO FAR OVER THE BEND IN THE CIRCLE.
"SUDDENLY I BEGAN TO SLIDE FASTER AND FASTER--UNTIL AT LAST I BUMPED ON THE GROUND.

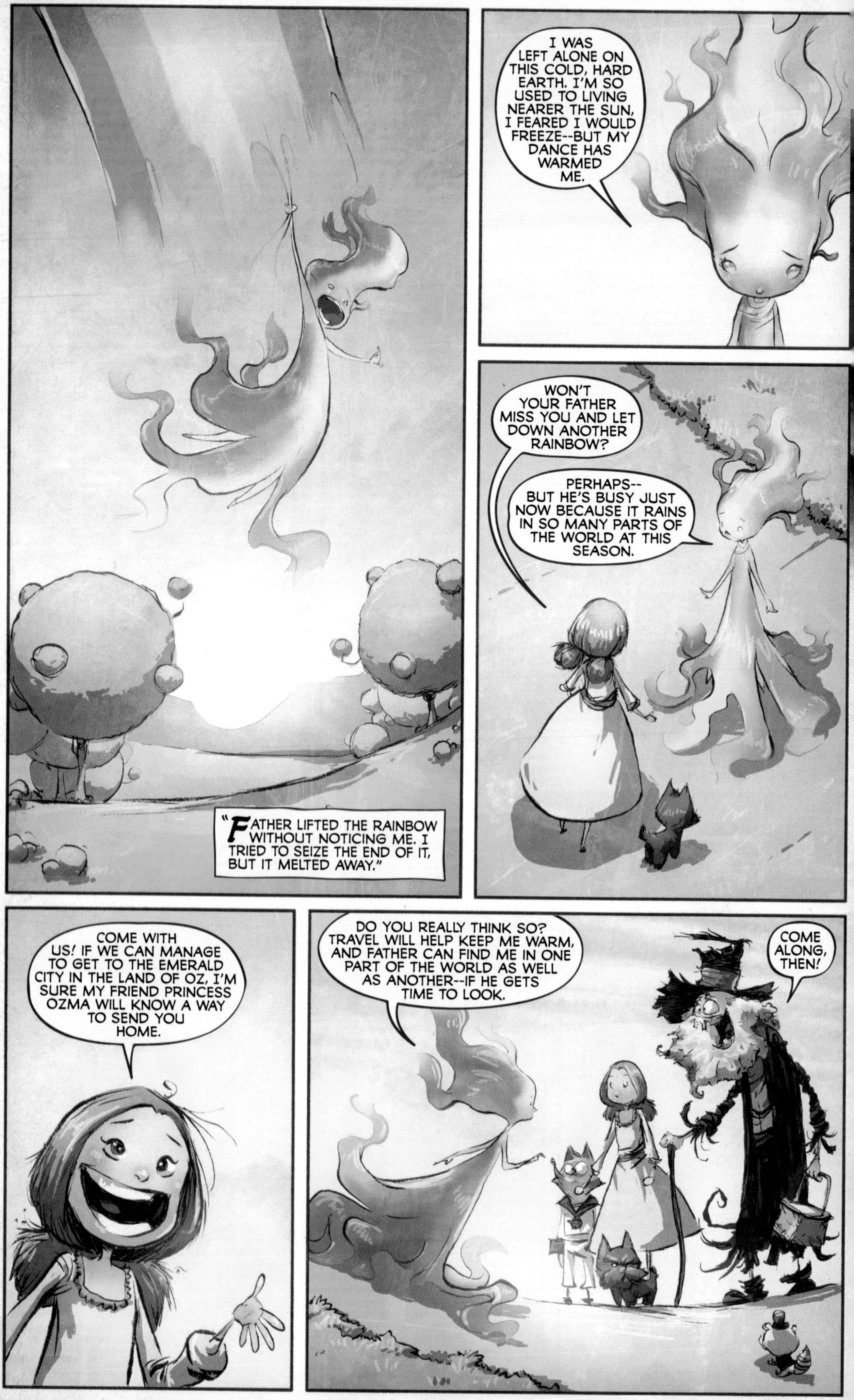
"FATHER LIFTED THE RAINBOW WITHOUT NOTICING ME. I TRIED TO SEIZE THE END OF IT, BUT IT MELTED AWAY."
I WAS LEFT ALONE ON THIS COLD, HARD EARTH. I'M SO USED TO LIVING NEARER THE SUN, I FEARED I WOULD FREEZE--BUT MY DANCE HAS WARMED ME.
WON'T YOUR FATHER MISS YOU AND LET DOWN ANOTHER RAINBOW?
PERHAPS-- BUT HE'S BUSY JUST NOW BECAUSE IT RAINS IN SO MANY PARTS OF THE WORLD AT THIS SEASON.
COME WITH US! IF WE CAN MANAGE TO GET TO THE EMERALD CITY IN THE LAND OF OZ, I'M SURE MY FRIEND PRINCESS OZMA WILL KNOW A WAY TO SEND YOU HOME.
DO YOU REALLY THINK SO? TRAVEL WILL HELP KEEP ME WARM, AND FATHER CAN FIND ME IN ONE PART OF THE WORLD AS WELL AS ANOTHER--IF HE GETS TIME TO LOOK.
COME ALONG, THEN!

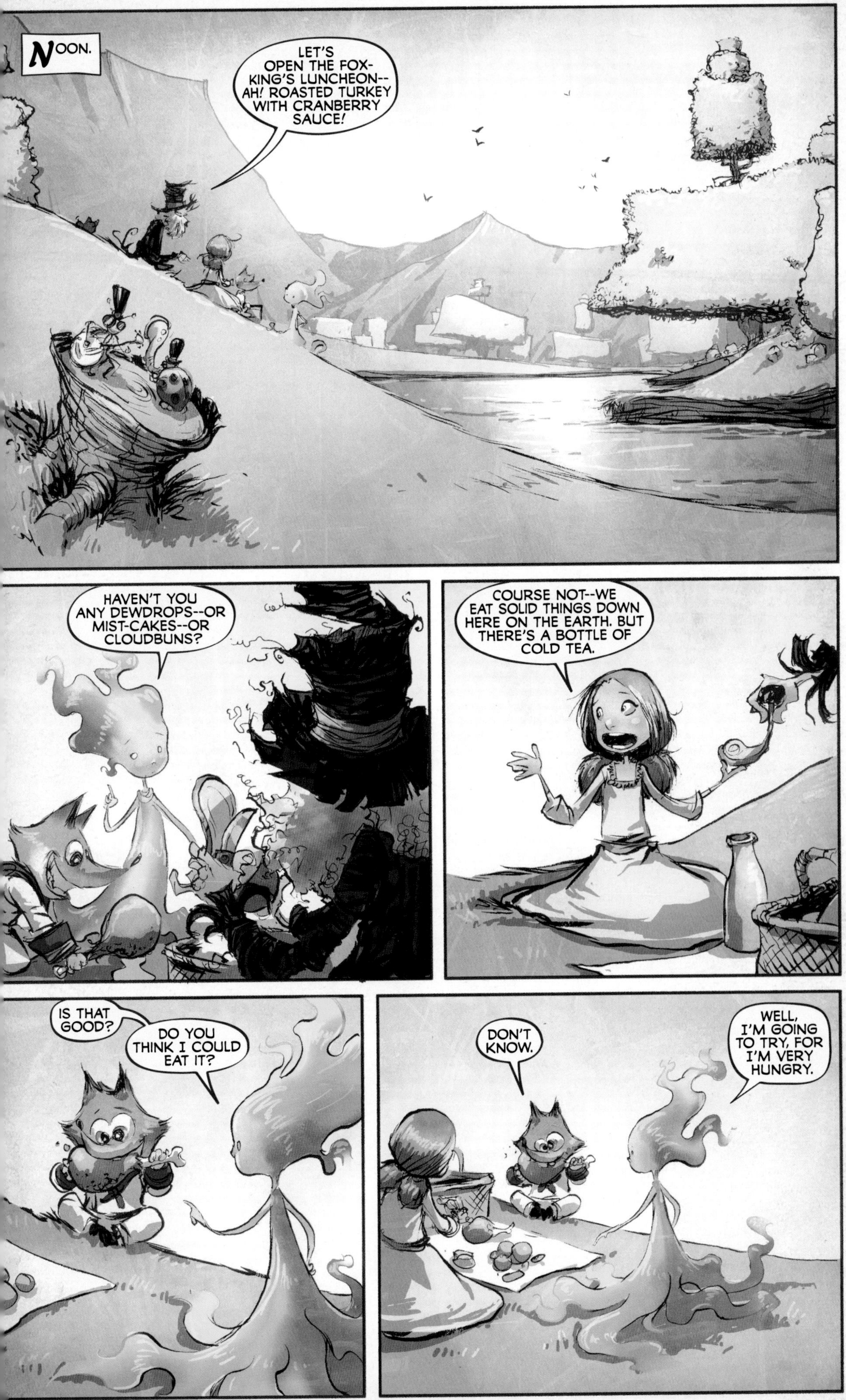
NOON.
LET'S OPEN THE FOX-KING'S LUNCHEON--AH! ROASTED TURKEY WITH CRANBERRY SAUCE!
HAVEN'T YOU ANY DEWDROPS--OR MIST-CAKES--OR CLOUDBUNS?
COURSE NOT--WE EAT SOLID THINGS DOWN HERE ON THE EARTH. BUT THERE'S A BOTTLE OF COLD TEA.
IS THAT GOOD?
DO YOU THINK I COULD EAT IT?
DON'T KNOW.
WELL, I'M GOING TO TRY, FOR I'M VERY HUNGRY.

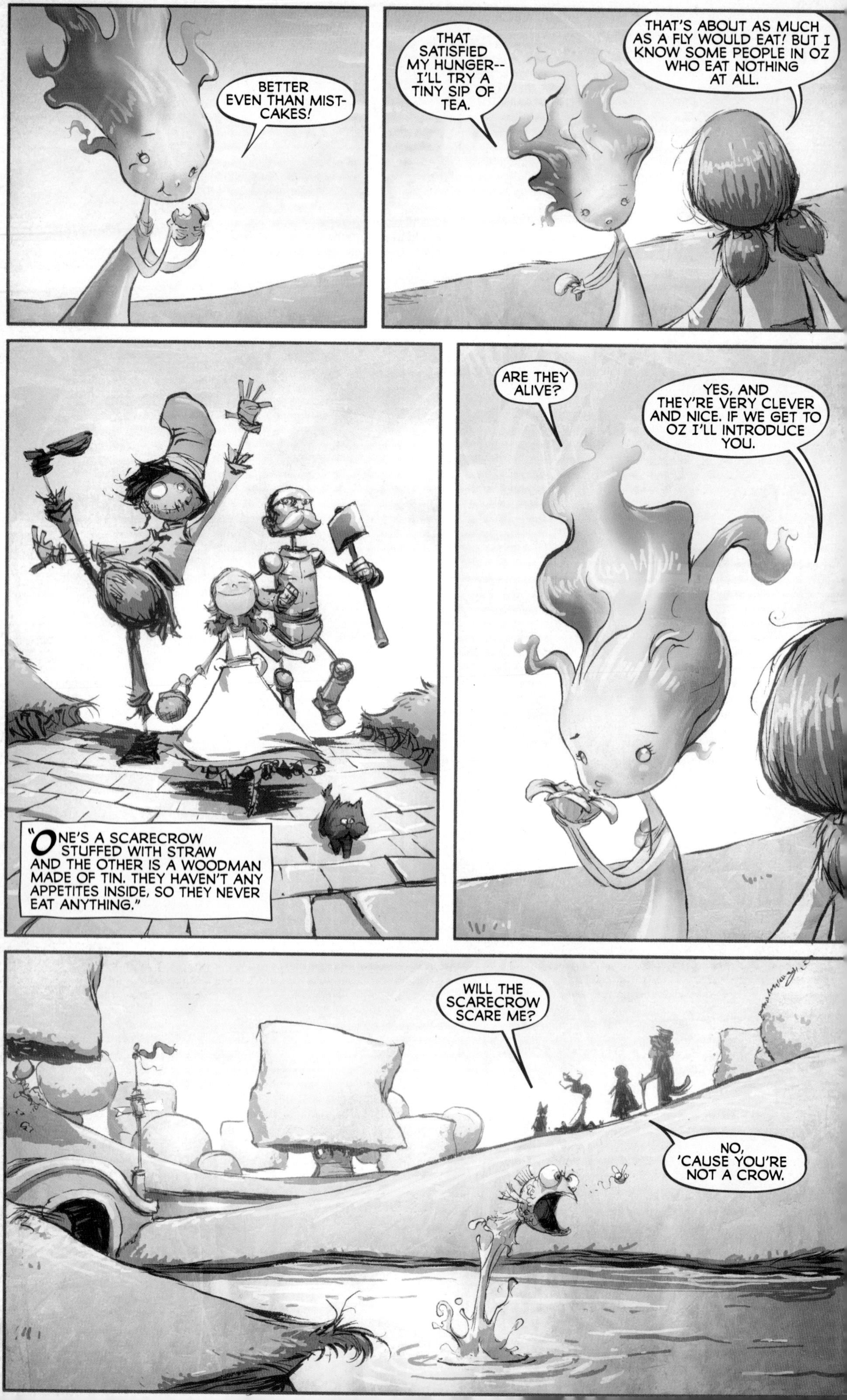
BETTER EVEN THAN MIST-CAKES!
THAT SATISFIED MY HUNGER-- I'LL TRY A TINY SIP OF TEA.
THAT'S ABOUT AS MUCH AS A FLY WOULD EAT! BUT I KNOW SOME PEOPLE IN OZ WHO EAT NOTHING AT ALL.
"ONE'S A SCARECROW STUFFED WITH STRAW AND THE OTHER IS A WOODMAN MADE OF TIN. THEY HAVEN'T ANY APPETITES INSIDE, SO THEY NEVER EAT ANYTHING."
ARE THEY ALIVE?
YES, AND THEY'RE VERY CLEVER AND NICE. IF WE GET TO OZ I'LL INTRODUCE YOU.
WILL THE SCARECROW SCARE ME?
NO, 'CAUSE YOU'RE NOT A CROW.

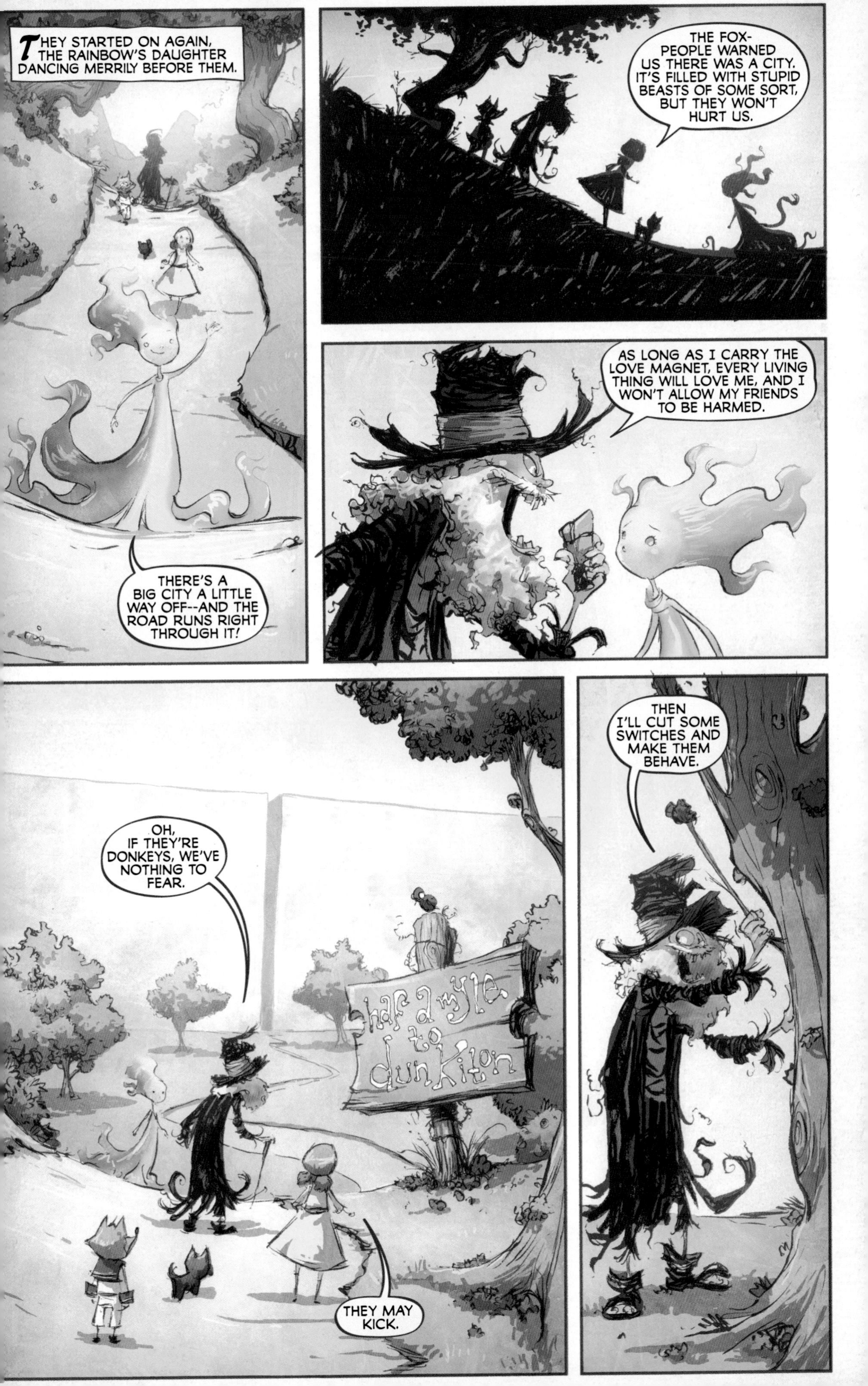
THEY STARTED ON AGAIN, THE RAINBOW'S DAUGHTER DANCING MERRILY BEFORE THEM.
THERE'S A BIG CITY A LITTLE WAY OFF--AND THE ROAD RUNS RIGHT THROUGH IT!
THE FOX-PEOPLE WARNED US THERE WAS A CITY. IT'S FILLED WITH STUPID BEASTS OF SOME SORT, BUT THEY WON'T HURT US.
AS LONG AS I CARRY THE LOVE MAGNET, EVERY LIVING THING WILL LOVE ME, AND I WON'T ALLOW MY FRIENDS TO BE HARMED.
haf a myle to dunkiton
OH, IF THEY'RE DONKEYS, WE'VE NOTHING TO FEAR.
THEY MAY KICK.
THEN I'LL CUT SOME SWITCHES AND MAKE THEM BEHAVE.

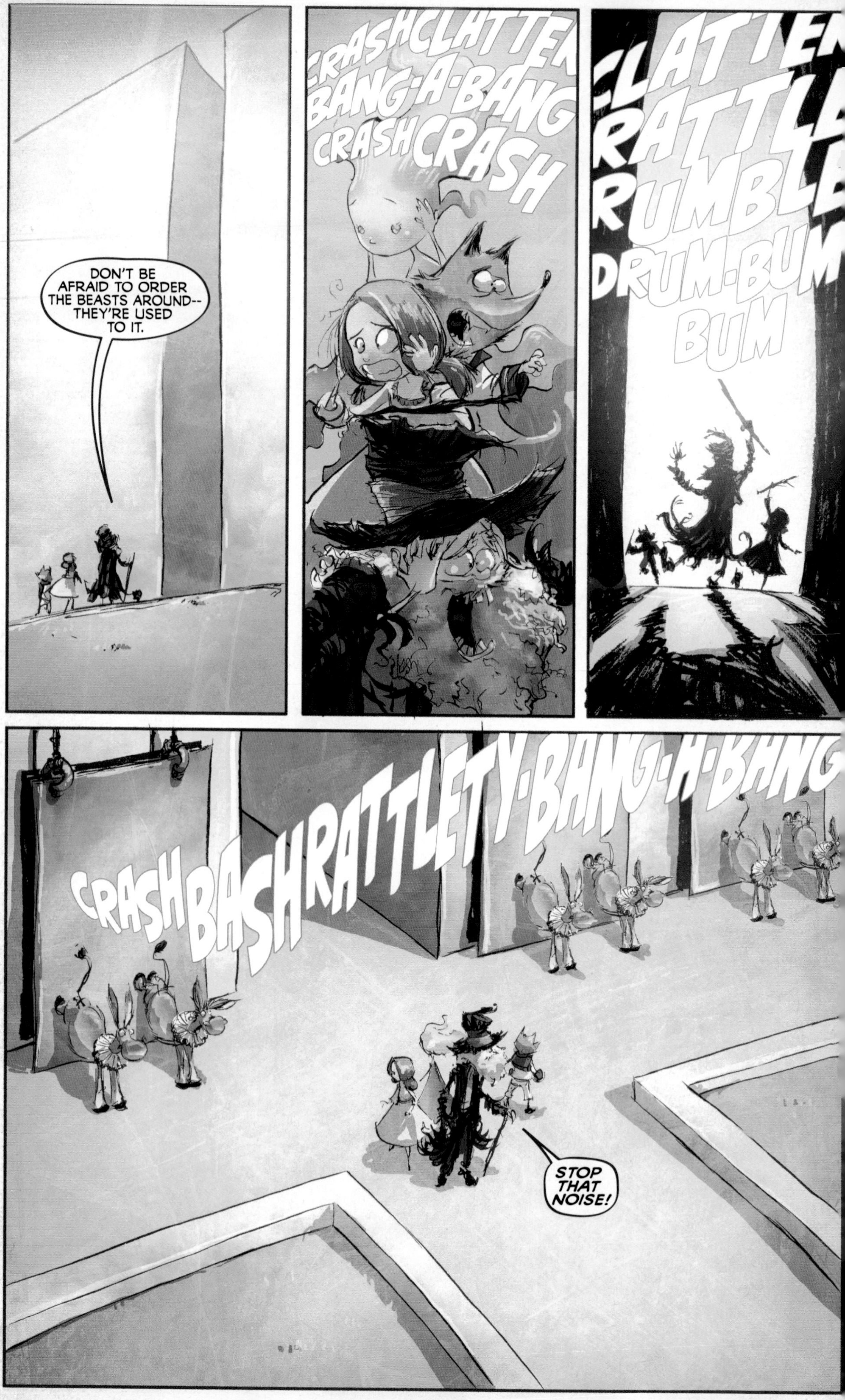
DON'T BE AFRAID TO ORDER THE BEASTS AROUND-- THEY'RE USED TO IT.
CRASHCLATTER BANG-A-BANG CRASHCRASH
CLATTER RATTLE RUMBLE DRUM-BUM BUM
CRASHBASHRATTLETY-BANG-A-BANG
STOP THAT NOISE!

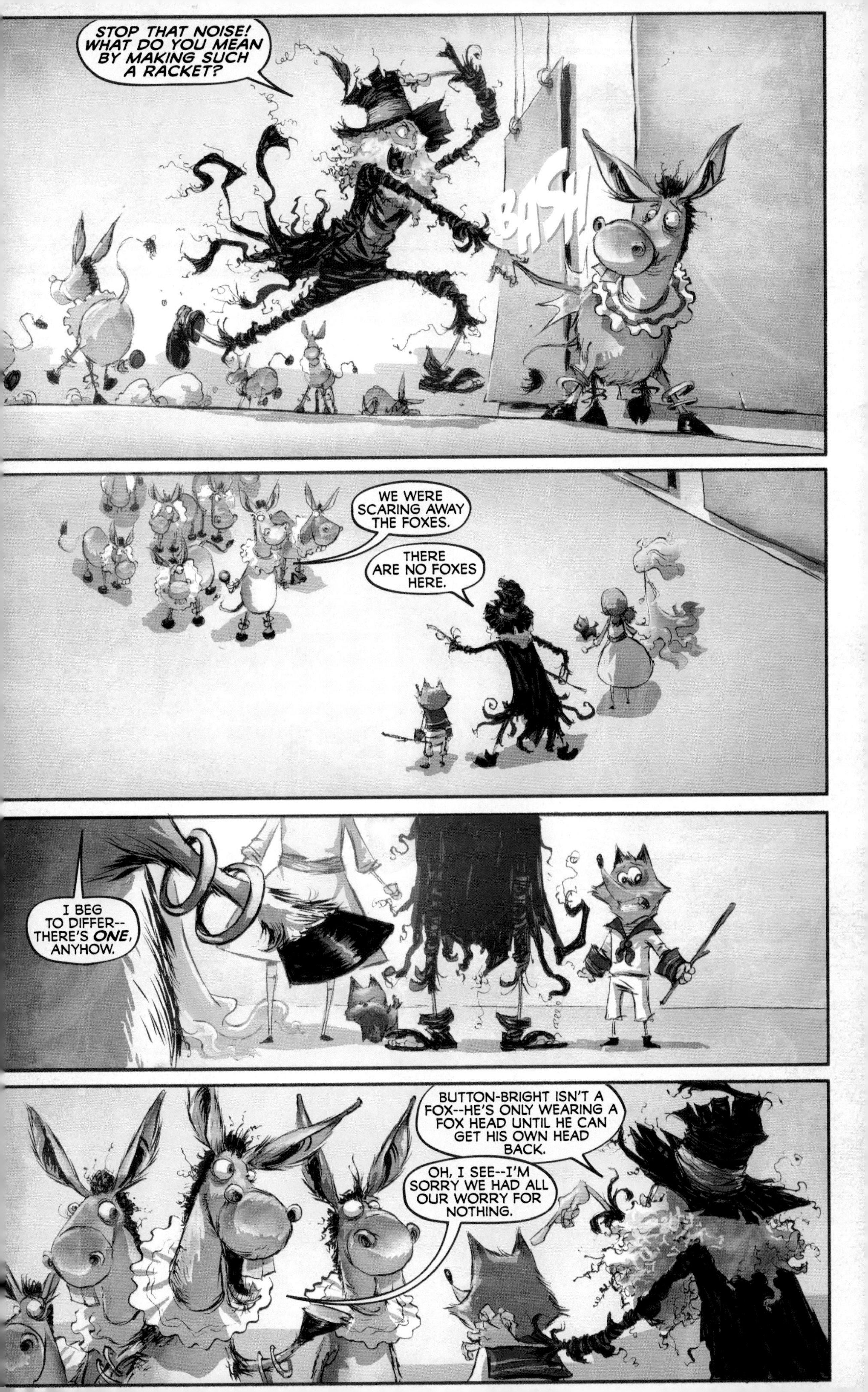
STOP THAT NOISE! WHAT DO YOU MEAN BY MAKING SUCH A RACKET?
BASH!
WE WERE SCARING AWAY THE FOXES.
THERE ARE NO FOXES HERE.
I BEG TO DIFFER--THERE'S ONE, ANYHOW.
BUTTON-BRIGHT ISN'T A FOX--HE'S ONLY WEARING A FOX HEAD UNTIL HE CAN GET HIS OWN HEAD BACK.
OH, I SEE--I'M SORRY WE HAD ALL OUR WORRY FOR NOTHING.

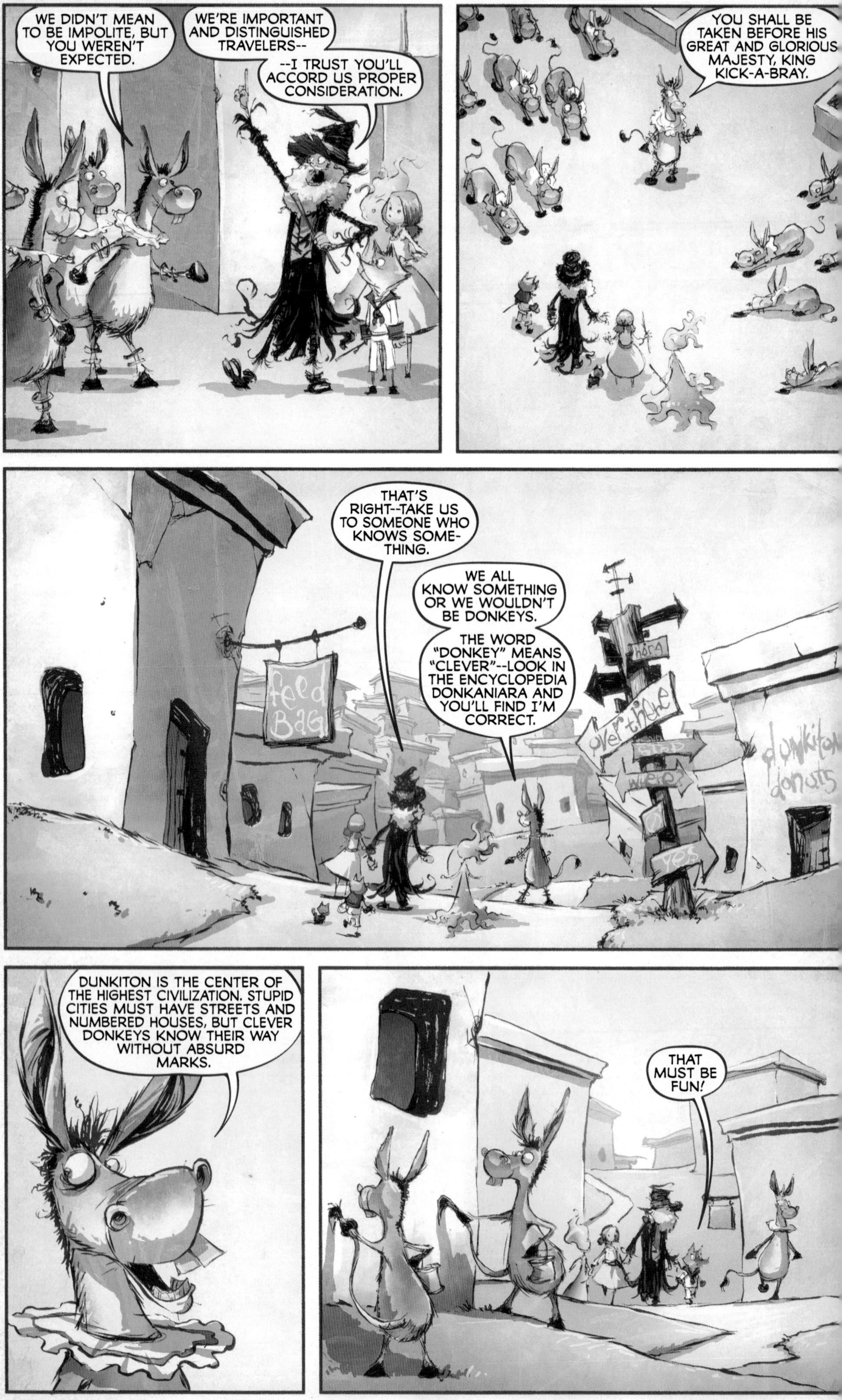
WE DIDN'T MEAN TO BE IMPOLITE, BUT YOU WEREN'T EXPECTED.
WE'RE IMPORTANT AND DISTINGUISHED TRAVELERS--
--I TRUST YOU'LL ACCORD US PROPER CONSIDERATION.
YOU SHALL BE TAKEN BEFORE HIS GREAT AND GLORIOUS MAJESTY, KING KICK-A-BRAY.
THAT'S RIGHT--TAKE US TO SOMEONE WHO KNOWS SOME-THING.
WE ALL KNOW SOMETHING OR WE WOULDN'T BE DONKEYS.
THE WORD "DONKEY" MEANS "CLEVER"--LOOK IN THE ENCYCLOPEDIA DONKANIARA AND YOU'LL FIND I'M CORRECT.
feed BaG
over there
where?
yes
donkiton donats
DUNKITON IS THE CENTER OF THE HIGHEST CIVILIZATION. STUPID CITIES MUST HAVE STREETS AND NUMBERED HOUSES, BUT CLEVER DONKEYS KNOW THEIR WAY WITHOUT ABSURD MARKS.
THAT MUST BE FUN!

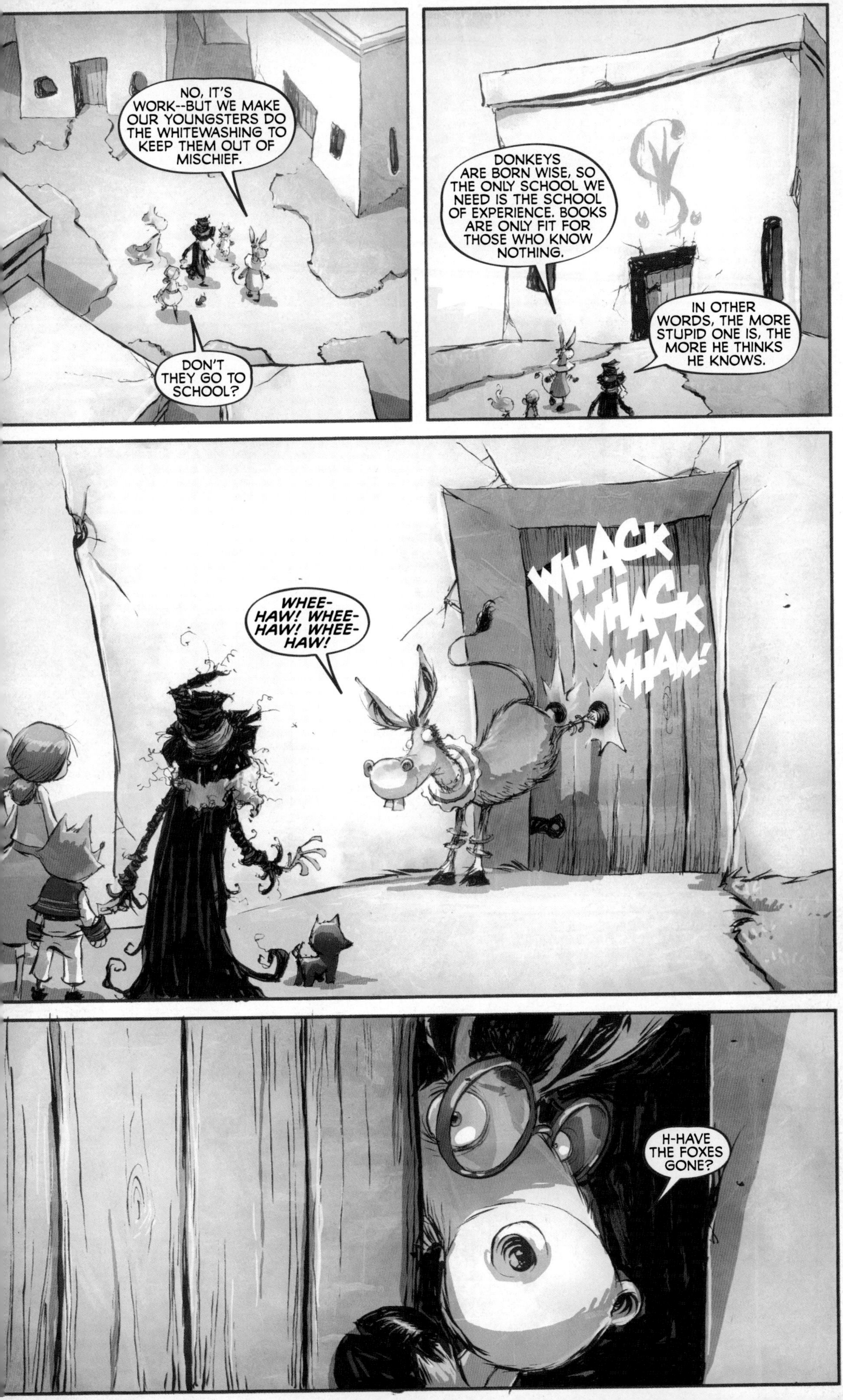
NO, IT'S WORK--BUT WE MAKE OUR YOUNGSTERS DO THE WHITEWASHING TO KEEP THEM OUT OF MISCHIEF.
DON'T THEY GO TO SCHOOL?
DONKEYS ARE BORN WISE, SO THE ONLY SCHOOL WE NEED IS THE SCHOOL OF EXPERIENCE. BOOKS ARE ONLY FIT FOR THOSE WHO KNOW NOTHING.
IN OTHER WORDS, THE MORE STUPID ONE IS, THE MORE HE THINKS HE KNOWS.
WHEE-HAW! WHEE-HAW! WHEE-HAW!
WHACK
WHACK
WHAM!
H-HAVE THE FOXES GONE?

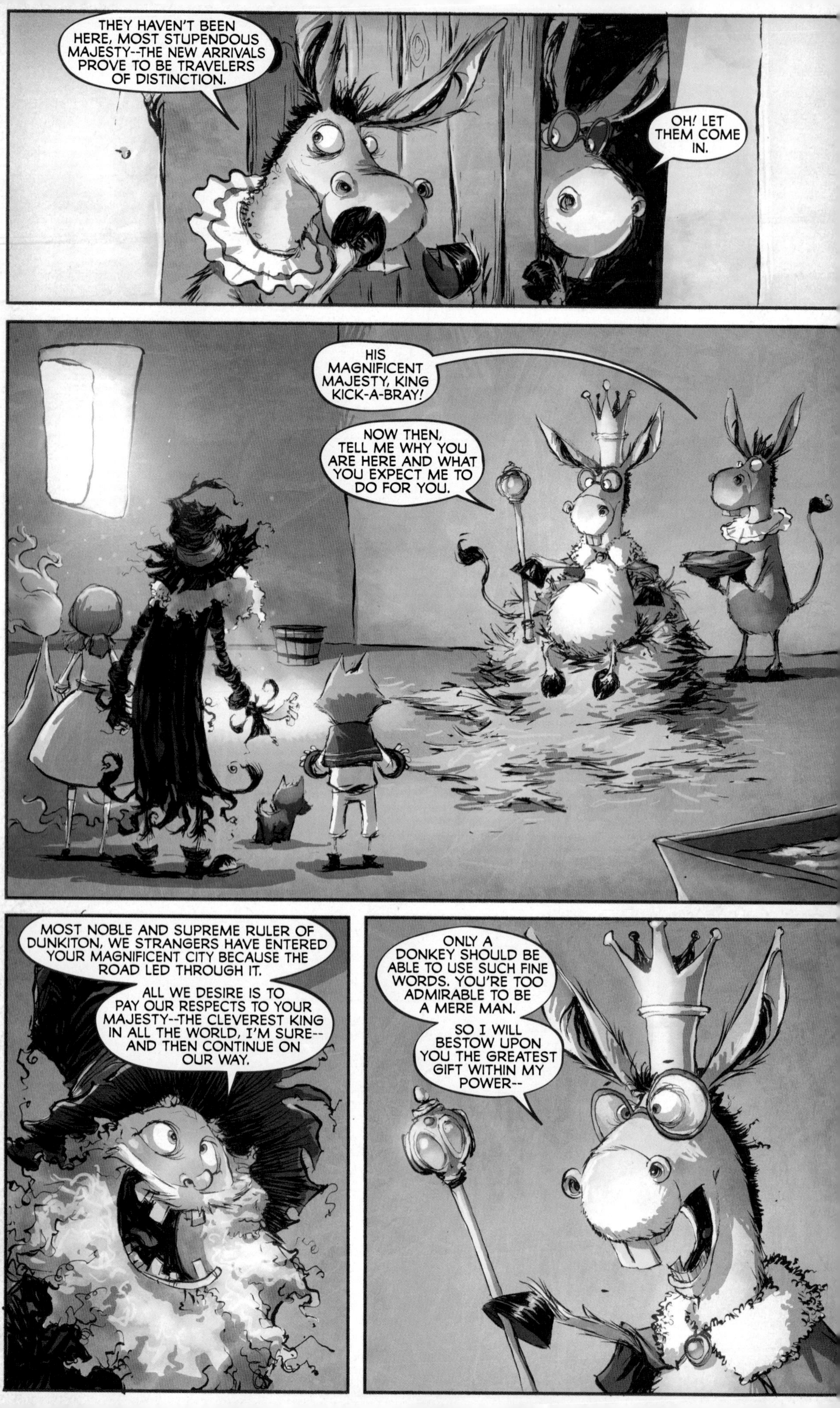
THEY HAVEN'T BEEN HERE, MOST STUPENDOUS MAJESTY--THE NEW ARRIVALS PROVE TO BE TRAVELERS OF DISTINCTION.
OH! LET THEM COME IN.
HIS MAGNIFICENT MAJESTY, KING KICK-A-BRAY!
NOW THEN, TELL ME WHY YOU ARE HERE AND WHAT YOU EXPECT ME TO DO FOR YOU.
MOST NOBLE AND SUPREME RULER OF DUNKITON, WE STRANGERS HAVE ENTERED YOUR MAGNIFICENT CITY BECAUSE THE ROAD LED THROUGH IT.
ALL WE DESIRE IS TO PAY OUR RESPECTS TO YOUR MAJESTY--THE CLEVEREST KING IN ALL THE WORLD, I'M SURE--AND THEN CONTINUE ON OUR WAY.
ONLY A DONKEY SHOULD BE ABLE TO USE SUCH FINE WORDS. YOU'RE TOO ADMIRABLE TO BE A MERE MAN.
SO I WILL BESTOW UPON YOU THE GREATEST GIFT WITHIN MY POWER--

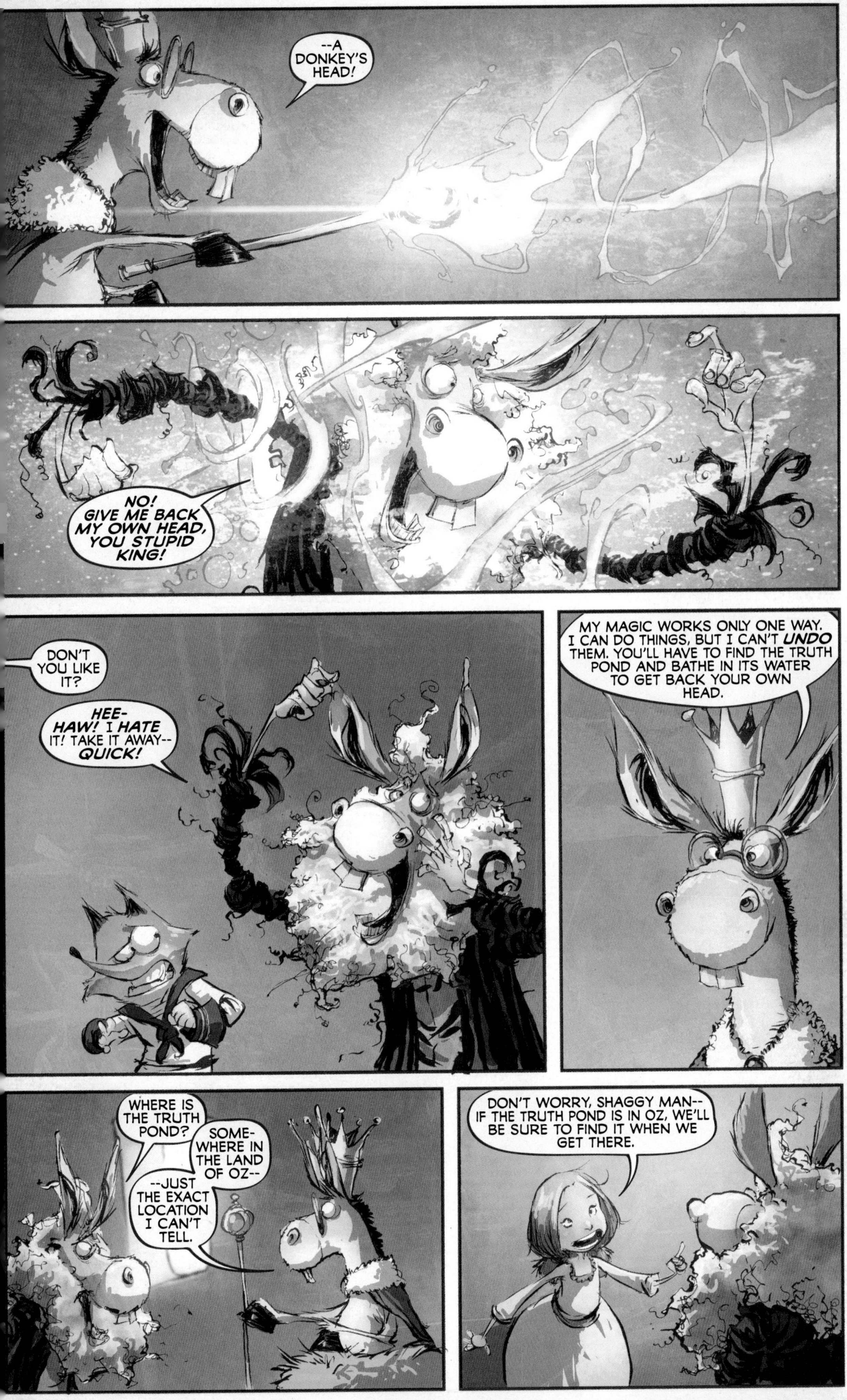
--A DONKEY'S HEAD!
NO! GIVE ME BACK MY OWN HEAD, YOU STUPID KING!
DON'T YOU LIKE IT?
HEE-HAW! I HATE IT! TAKE IT AWAY--QUICK!
MY MAGIC WORKS ONLY ONE WAY. I CAN DO THINGS, BUT I CAN'T UNDO THEM. YOU'LL HAVE TO FIND THE TRUTH POND AND BATHE IN ITS WATER TO GET BACK YOUR OWN HEAD.
WHERE IS THE TRUTH POND?
SOME-WHERE IN THE LAND OF OZ--
--JUST THE EXACT LOCATION I CAN'T TELL.
DON'T WORRY, SHAGGY MAN--IF THE TRUTH POND IS IN OZ, WE'LL BE SURE TO FIND IT WHEN WE GET THERE.

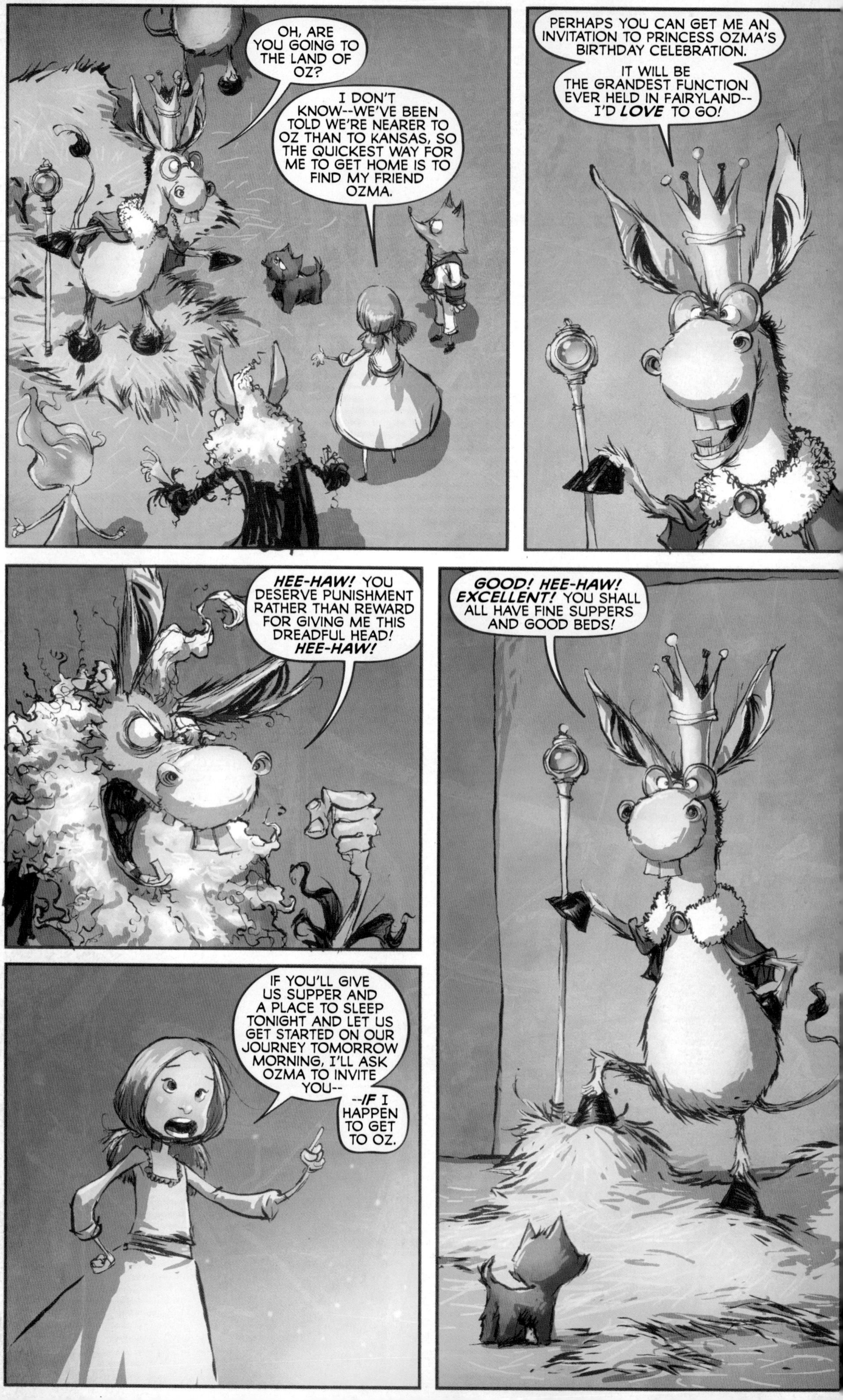
OH, ARE YOU GOING TO THE LAND OF OZ?
I DON'T KNOW--WE'VE BEEN TOLD WE'RE NEARER TO OZ THAN TO KANSAS, SO THE QUICKEST WAY FOR ME TO GET HOME IS TO FIND MY FRIEND OZMA.
PERHAPS YOU CAN GET ME AN INVITATION TO PRINCESS OZMA'S BIRTHDAY CELEBRATION.
IT WILL BE THE GRANDEST FUNCTION EVER HELD IN FAIRYLAND-- I'D LOVE TO GO!
HEE-HAW! YOU DESERVE PUNISHMENT RATHER THAN REWARD FOR GIVING ME THIS DREADFUL HEAD! HEE-HAW!
IF YOU'LL GIVE US SUPPER AND A PLACE TO SLEEP TONIGHT AND LET US GET STARTED ON OUR JOURNEY TOMORROW MORNING, I'LL ASK OZMA TO INVITE YOU--
--IF I HAPPEN TO GET TO OZ.
GOOD! HEE-HAW! EXCELLENT! YOU SHALL ALL HAVE FINE SUPPERS AND GOOD BEDS!

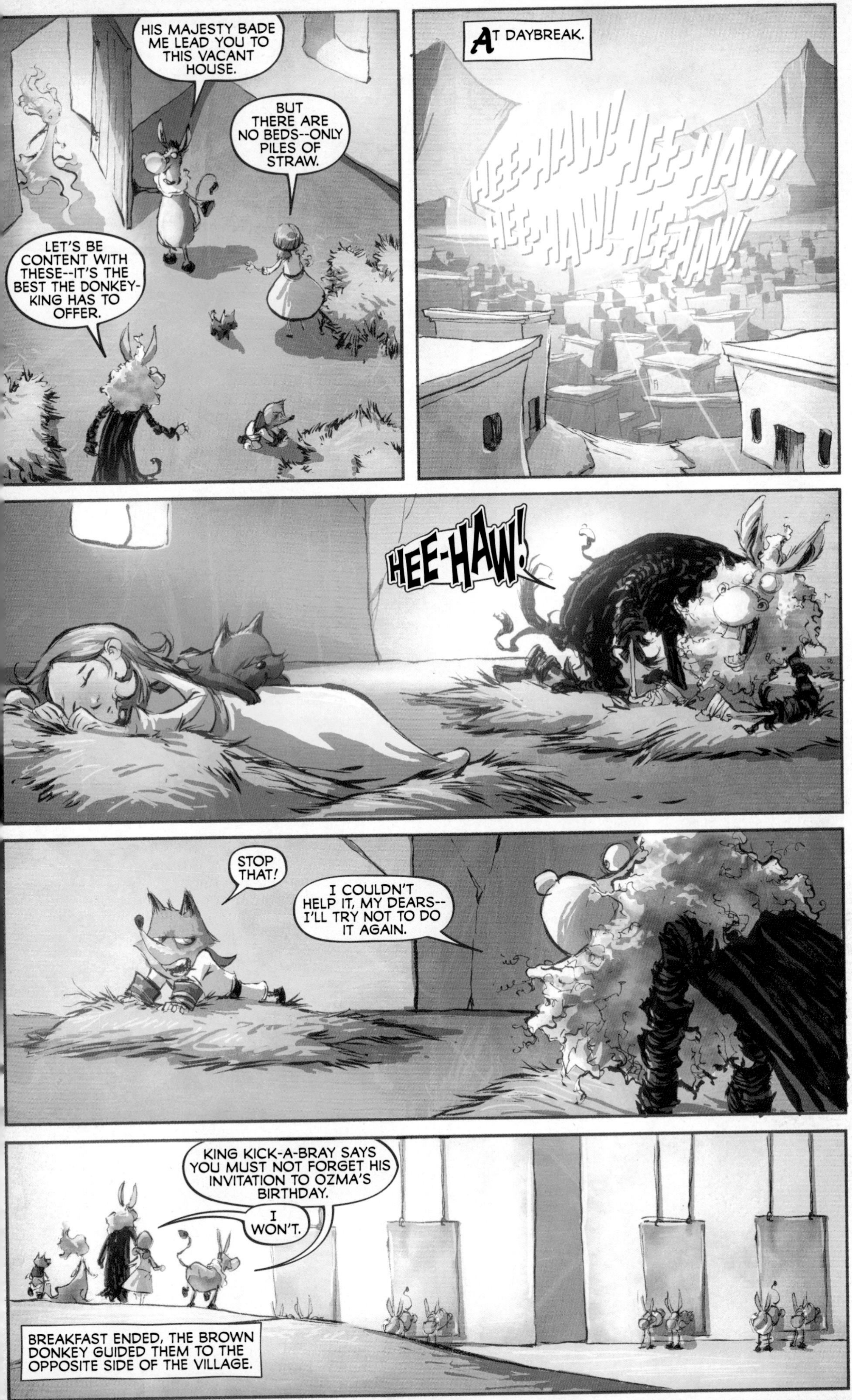
HIS MAJESTY BADE ME LEAD YOU TO THIS VACANT HOUSE.
BUT THERE ARE NO BEDS--ONLY PILES OF STRAW.
LET'S BE CONTENT WITH THESE--IT'S THE BEST THE DONKEY-KING HAS TO OFFER.
AT DAYBREAK.
HEE-HAW! HEE-HAW! HEE-HAW! HEE-HAW!
HEE-HAW!
STOP THAT!
I COULDN'T HELP IT, MY DEARS--I'LL TRY NOT TO DO IT AGAIN.
KING KICK-A-BRAY SAYS YOU MUST NOT FORGET HIS INVITATION TO OZMA'S BIRTHDAY.
I WON'T.
BREAKFAST ENDED, THE BROWN DONKEY GUIDED THEM TO THE OPPOSITE SIDE OF THE VILLAGE.

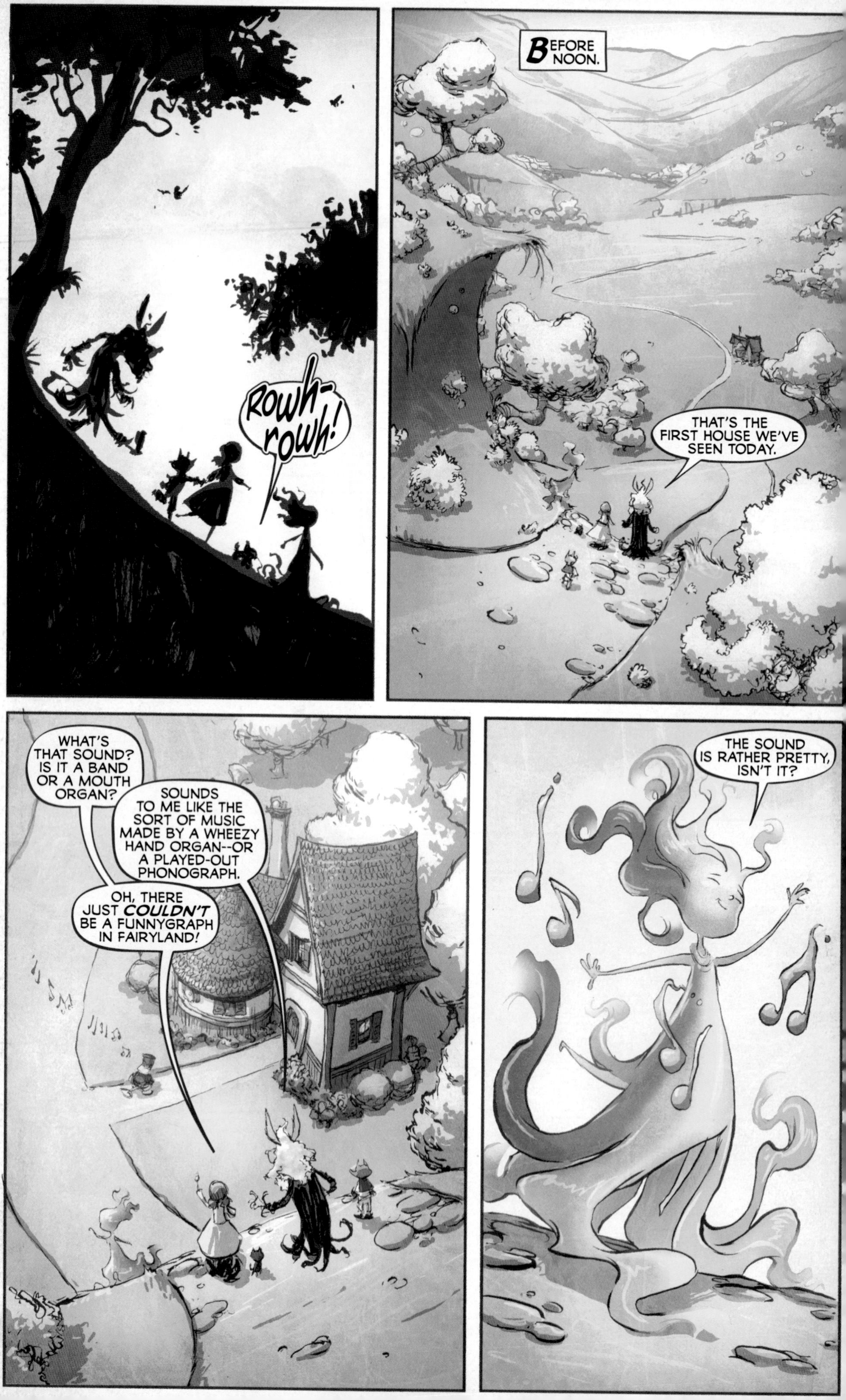
Rowh-rowh!
BEFORE NOON.
THAT'S THE FIRST HOUSE WE'VE SEEN TODAY.
WHAT'S THAT SOUND? IS IT A BAND OR A MOUTH ORGAN?
SOUNDS TO ME LIKE THE SORT OF MUSIC MADE BY A WHEEZY HAND ORGAN--OR A PLAYED-OUT PHONOGRAPH.
OH, THERE JUST COULDN'T BE A FUNNYGRAPH IN FAIRYLAND!
THE SOUND IS RATHER PRETTY, ISN'T IT?

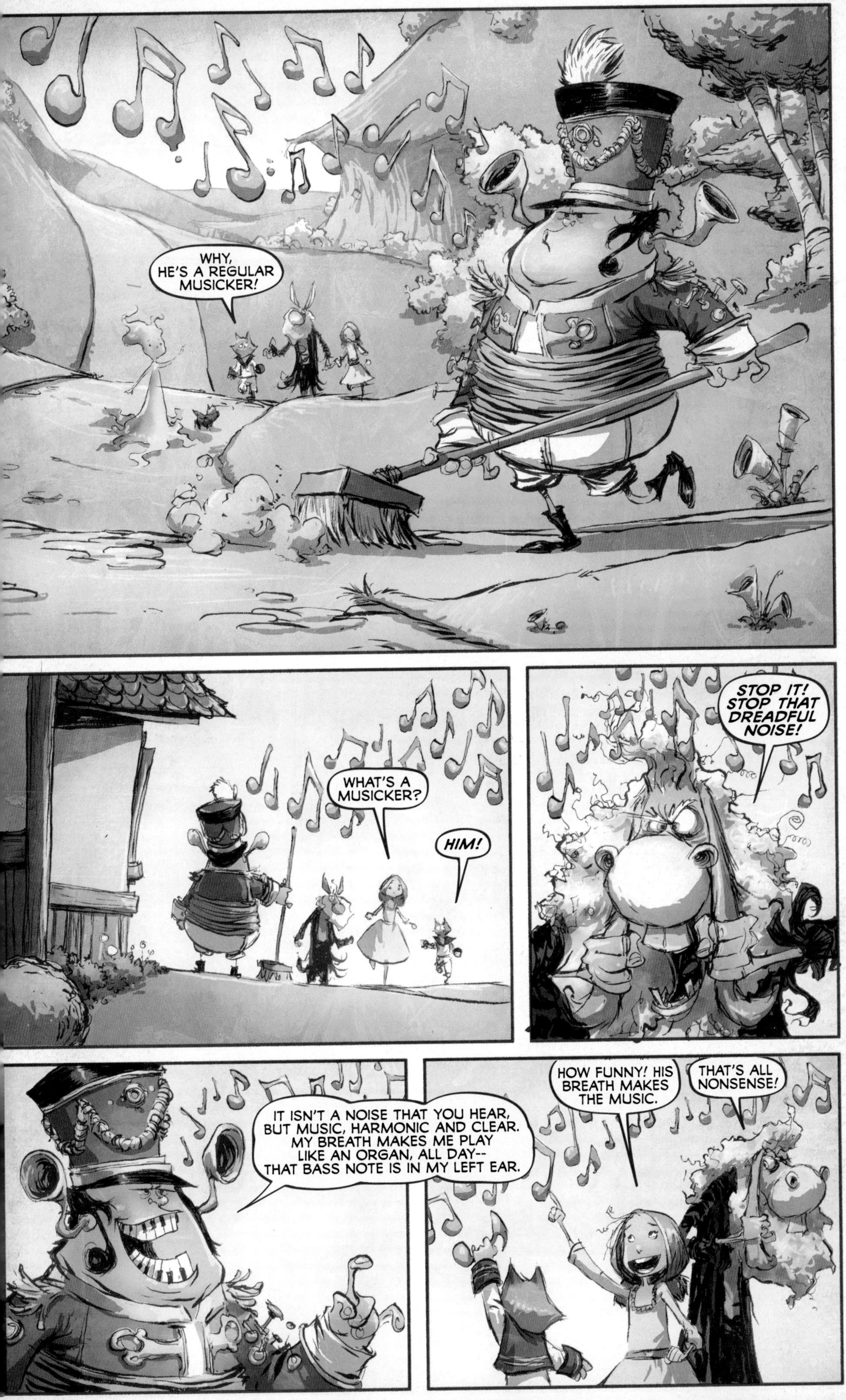
WHY, HE'S A REGULAR MUSICKER!
WHAT'S A MUSICKER?
HIM!
STOP IT! STOP THAT DREADFUL NOISE!
IT ISN'T A NOISE THAT YOU HEAR, BUT MUSIC, HARMONIC AND CLEAR. MY BREATH MAKES ME PLAY LIKE AN ORGAN, ALL DAY-- THAT BASS NOTE IS IN MY LEFT EAR.
HOW FUNNY! HIS BREATH MAKES THE MUSIC.
THAT'S ALL NONSENSE!

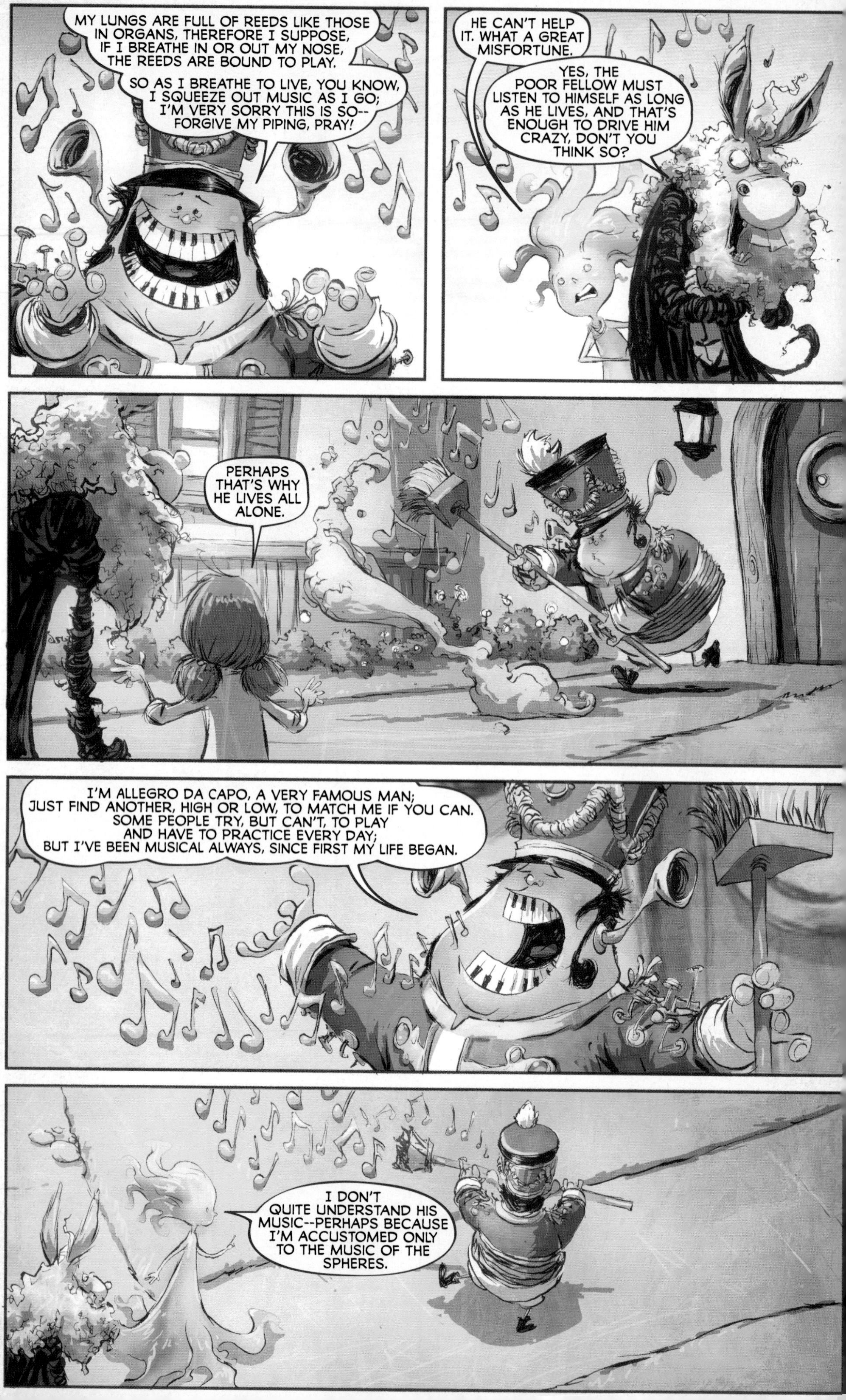
MY LUNGS ARE FULL OF REEDS LIKE THOSE IN ORGANS, THEREFORE I SUPPOSE, IF I BREATHE IN OR OUT MY NOSE, THE REEDS ARE BOUND TO PLAY.
SO AS I BREATHE TO LIVE, YOU KNOW, I SQUEEZE OUT MUSIC AS I GO; I'M VERY SORRY THIS IS SO-- FORGIVE MY PIPING, PRAY!
HE CAN'T HELP IT. WHAT A GREAT MISFORTUNE.
YES, THE POOR FELLOW MUST LISTEN TO HIMSELF AS LONG AS HE LIVES, AND THAT'S ENOUGH TO DRIVE HIM CRAZY, DON'T YOU THINK SO?
PERHAPS THAT'S WHY HE LIVES ALL ALONE.
I'M ALLEGRO DA CAPO, A VERY FAMOUS MAN; JUST FIND ANOTHER, HIGH OR LOW, TO MATCH ME IF YOU CAN. SOME PEOPLE TRY, BUT CAN'T, TO PLAY AND HAVE TO PRACTICE EVERY DAY; BUT I'VE BEEN MUSICAL ALWAYS, SINCE FIRST MY LIFE BEGAN.
I DON'T QUITE UNDERSTAND HIS MUSIC--PERHAPS BECAUSE I'M ACCUSTOMED ONLY TO THE MUSIC OF THE SPHERES.

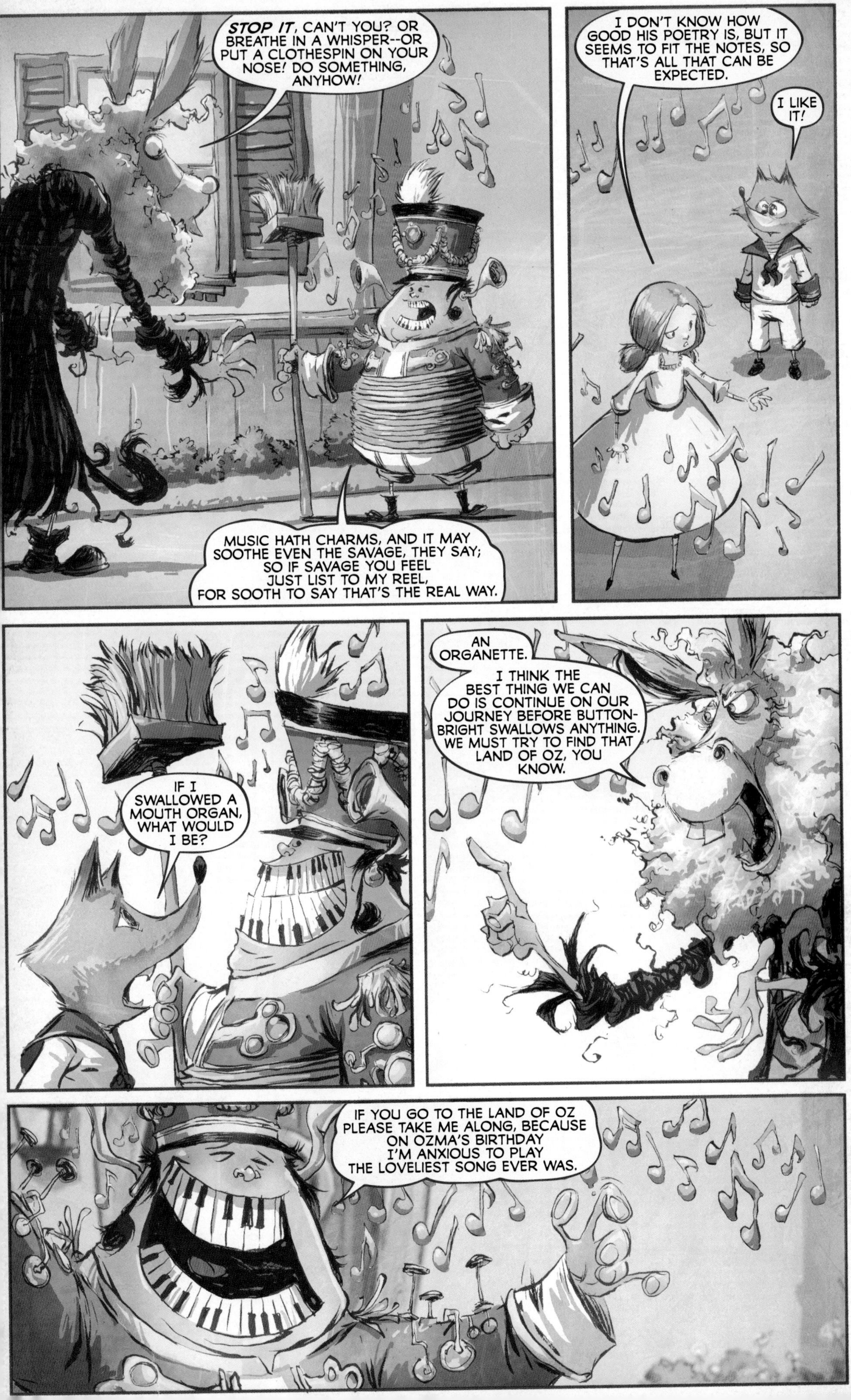
STOP IT, CAN'T YOU? OR BREATHE IN A WHISPER--OR PUT A CLOTHESPIN ON YOUR NOSE! DO SOMETHING, ANYHOW!
MUSIC HATH CHARMS, AND IT MAY SOOTHE EVEN THE SAVAGE, THEY SAY; SO IF SAVAGE YOU FEEL JUST LIST TO MY REEL, FOR SOOTH TO SAY THAT'S THE REAL WAY.
I DON'T KNOW HOW GOOD HIS POETRY IS, BUT IT SEEMS TO FIT THE NOTES, SO THAT'S ALL THAT CAN BE EXPECTED.
I LIKE IT!
IF I SWALLOWED A MOUTH ORGAN, WHAT WOULD I BE?
AN ORGANETTE.
I THINK THE BEST THING WE CAN DO IS CONTINUE ON OUR JOURNEY BEFORE BUTTON-BRIGHT SWALLOWS ANYTHING. WE MUST TRY TO FIND THAT LAND OF OZ, YOU KNOW.
IF YOU GO TO THE LAND OF OZ PLEASE TAKE ME ALONG, BECAUSE ON OZMA'S BIRTHDAY I'M ANXIOUS TO PLAY THE LOVELIEST SONG EVER WAS.

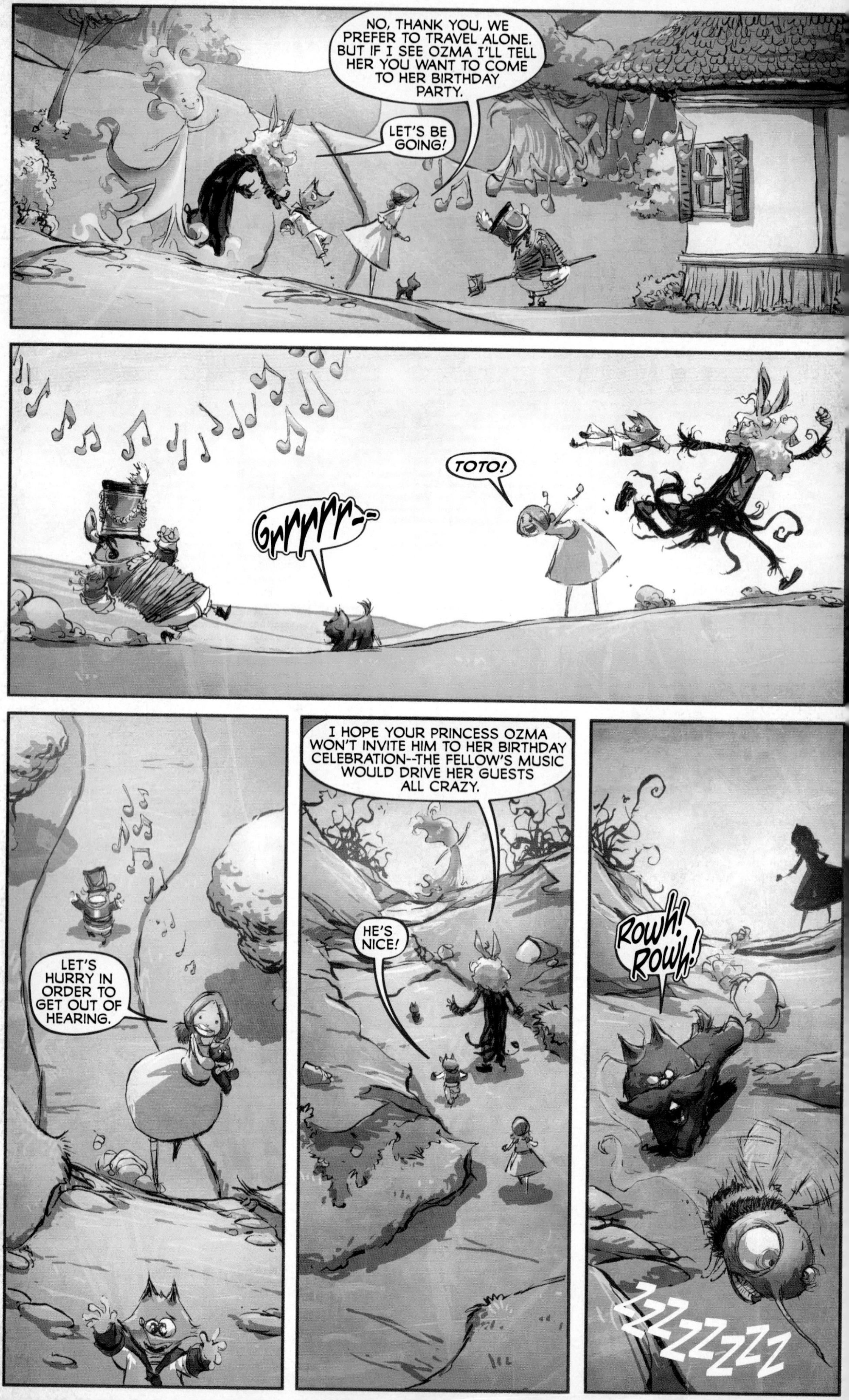
NO, THANK YOU, WE PREFER TO TRAVEL ALONE. BUT IF I SEE OZMA I'LL TELL HER YOU WANT TO COME TO HER BIRTHDAY PARTY.
LET'S BE GOING!
TOTO!
GRRRRR--
LET'S HURRY IN ORDER TO GET OUT OF HEARING.
I HOPE YOUR PRINCESS OZMA WON'T INVITE HIM TO HER BIRTHDAY CELEBRATION--THE FELLOW'S MUSIC WOULD DRIVE HER GUESTS ALL CRAZY.
HE'S NICE!
ROWH! ROWH!
ZZZZZZZ

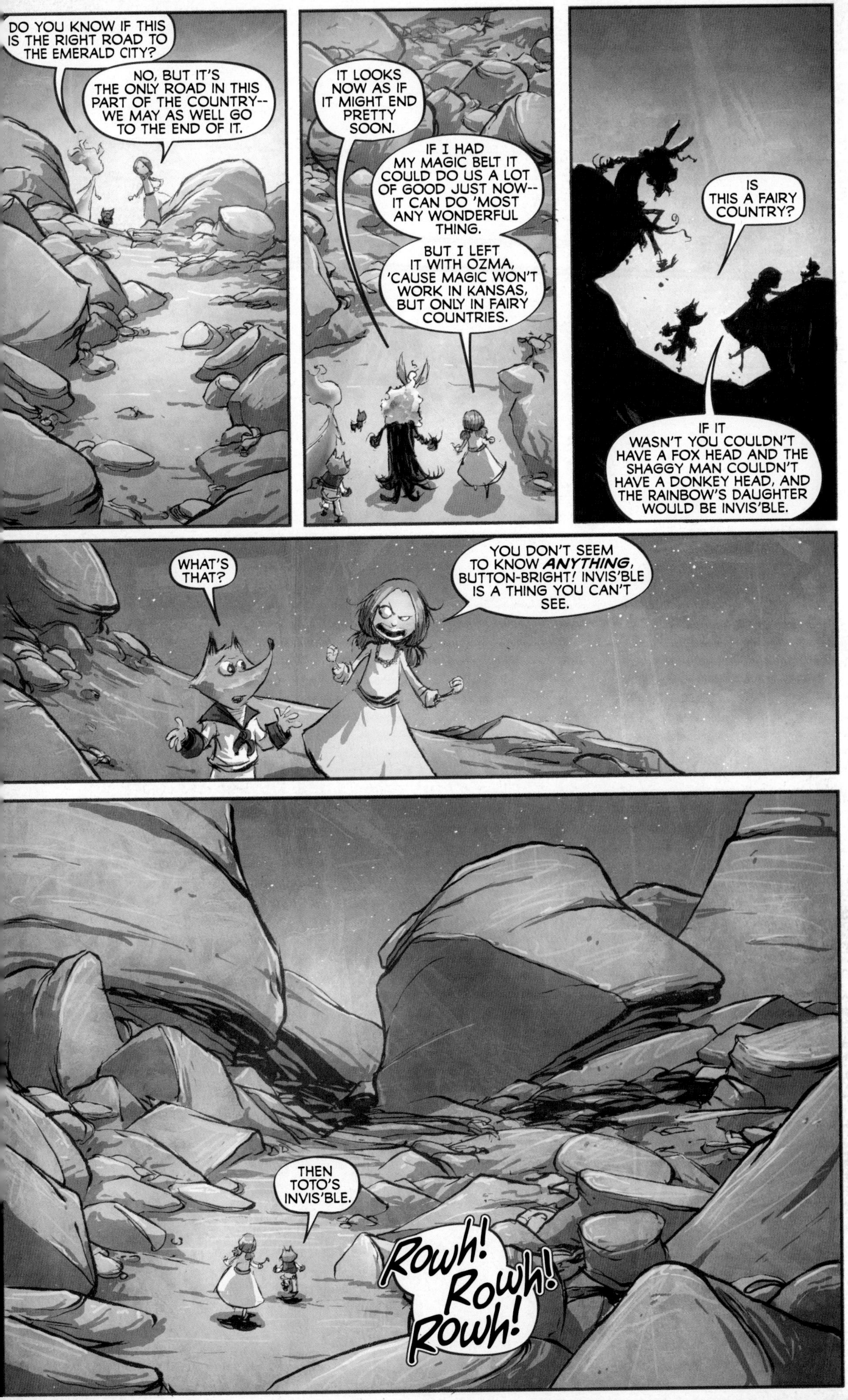
DO YOU KNOW IF THIS IS THE RIGHT ROAD TO THE EMERALD CITY?
NO, BUT IT'S THE ONLY ROAD IN THIS PART OF THE COUNTRY-- WE MAY AS WELL GO TO THE END OF IT.
IT LOOKS NOW AS IF IT MIGHT END PRETTY SOON.
IF I HAD MY MAGIC BELT IT COULD DO US A LOT OF GOOD JUST NOW-- IT CAN DO 'MOST ANY WONDERFUL THING.
BUT I LEFT IT WITH OZMA, 'CAUSE MAGIC WON'T WORK IN KANSAS, BUT ONLY IN FAIRY COUNTRIES.
IS THIS A FAIRY COUNTRY?
IF IT WASN'T YOU COULDN'T HAVE A FOX HEAD AND THE SHAGGY MAN COULDN'T HAVE A DONKEY HEAD, AND THE RAINBOW'S DAUGHTER WOULD BE INVIS'BLE.
WHAT'S THAT?
YOU DON'T SEEM TO KNOW ANYTHING, BUTTON-BRIGHT! INVIS'BLE IS A THING YOU CAN'T SEE.
THEN TOTO'S INVIS'BLE.
ROWH! ROWH! ROWH!

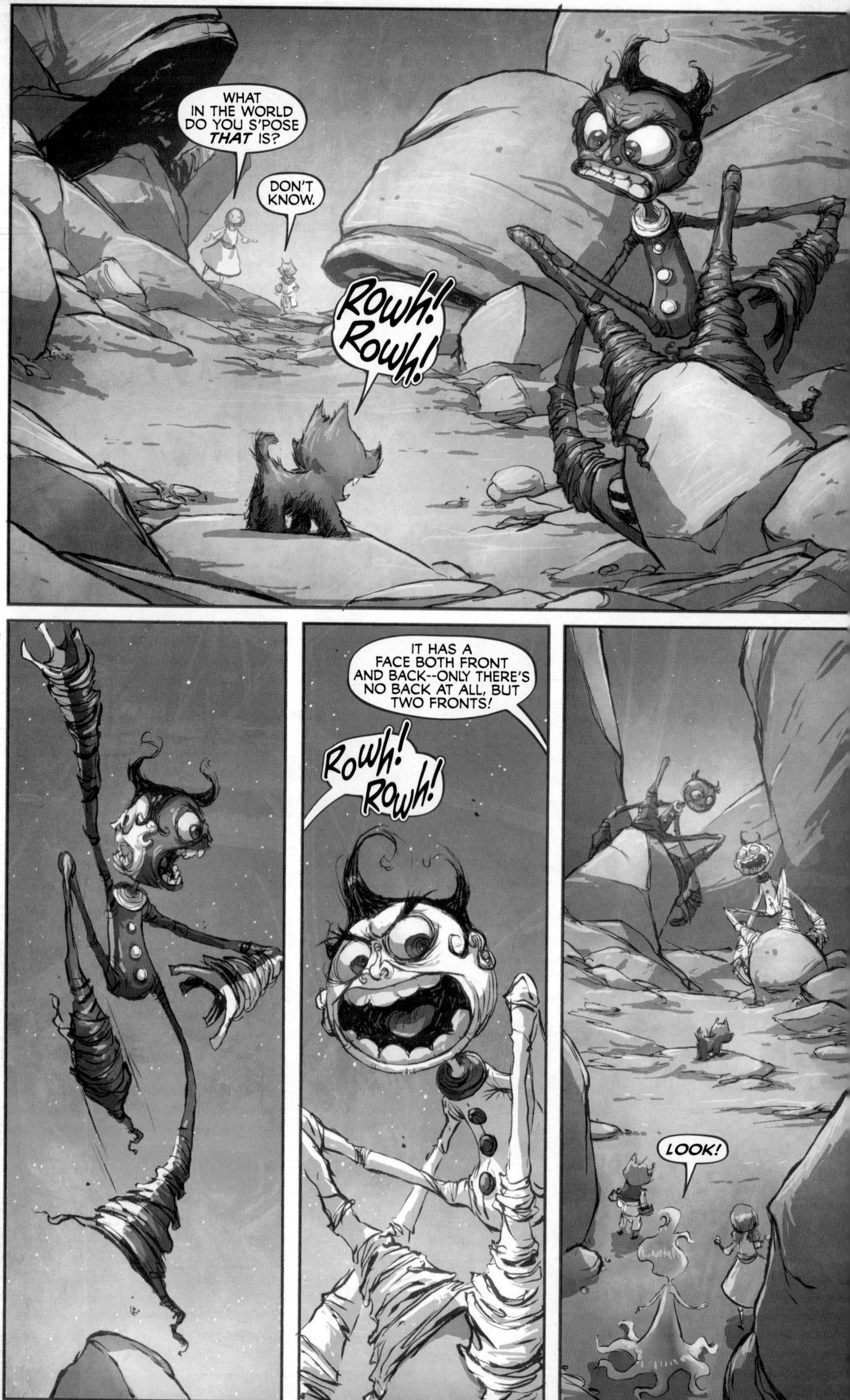
WHAT IN THE WORLD DO YOU S'POSE *THAT* IS?
DON'T KNOW.
Rowh! Rowh!
IT HAS A FACE BOTH FRONT AND BACK--ONLY THERE'S NO BACK AT ALL, BUT TWO FRONTS!
Rowh! Rowh!
LOOK!

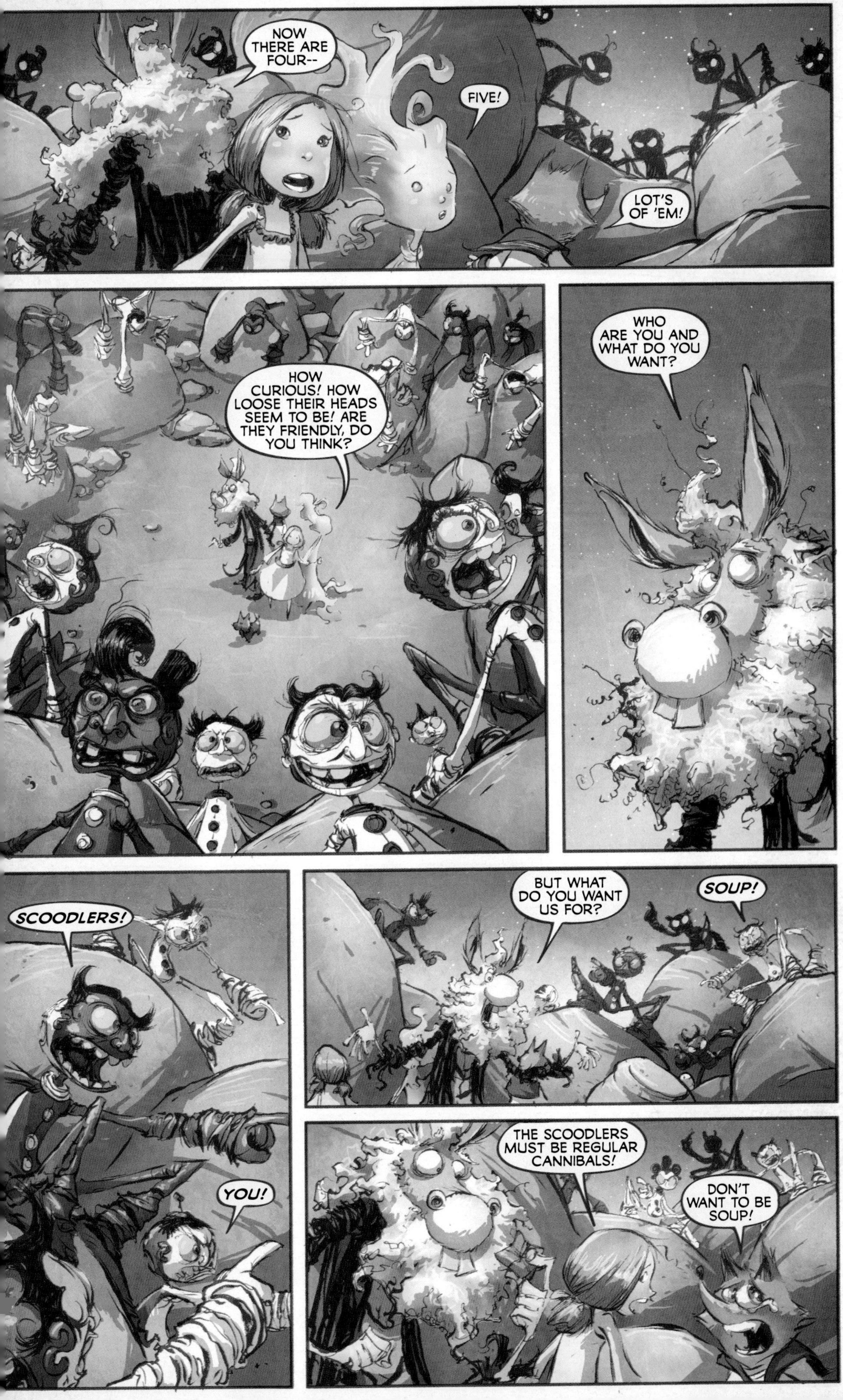
NOW THERE ARE FOUR--
FIVE!
LOT'S OF 'EM!
HOW CURIOUS! HOW LOOSE THEIR HEADS SEEM TO BE! ARE THEY FRIENDLY, DO YOU THINK?
WHO ARE YOU AND WHAT DO YOU WANT?
SCOODLERS!
YOU!
BUT WHAT DO YOU WANT US FOR?
SOUP!
THE SCOODLERS MUST BE REGULAR CANNIBALS!
DON'T WANT TO BE SOUP!

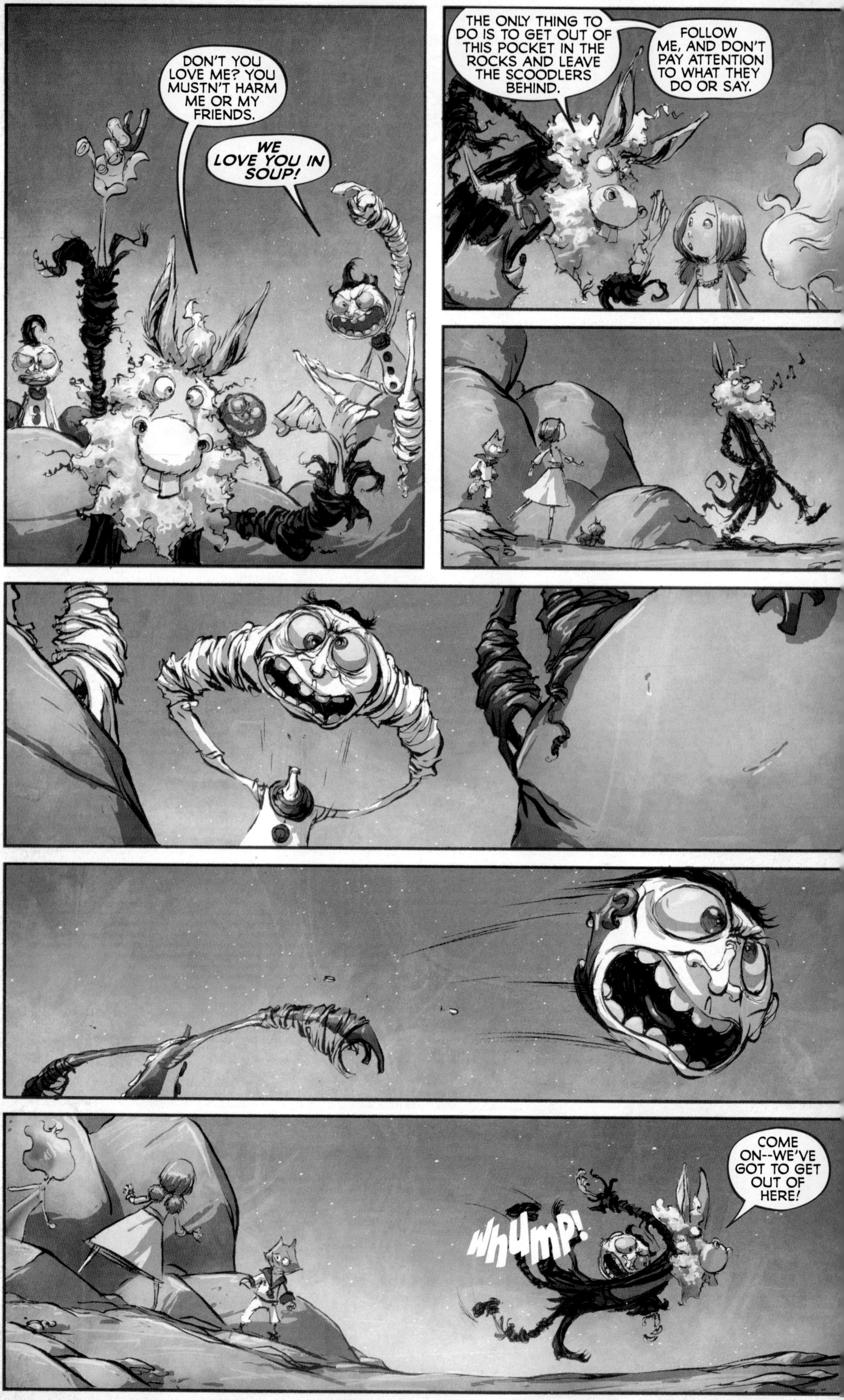
DON'T YOU LOVE ME? YOU MUSTN'T HARM ME OR MY FRIENDS.
WE LOVE YOU IN SOUP!
THE ONLY THING TO DO IS TO GET OUT OF THIS POCKET IN THE ROCKS AND LEAVE THE SCOODLERS BEHIND.
FOLLOW ME, AND DON'T PAY ATTENTION TO WHAT THEY DO OR SAY.
WHUMP!
COME ON--WE'VE GOT TO GET OUT OF HERE!

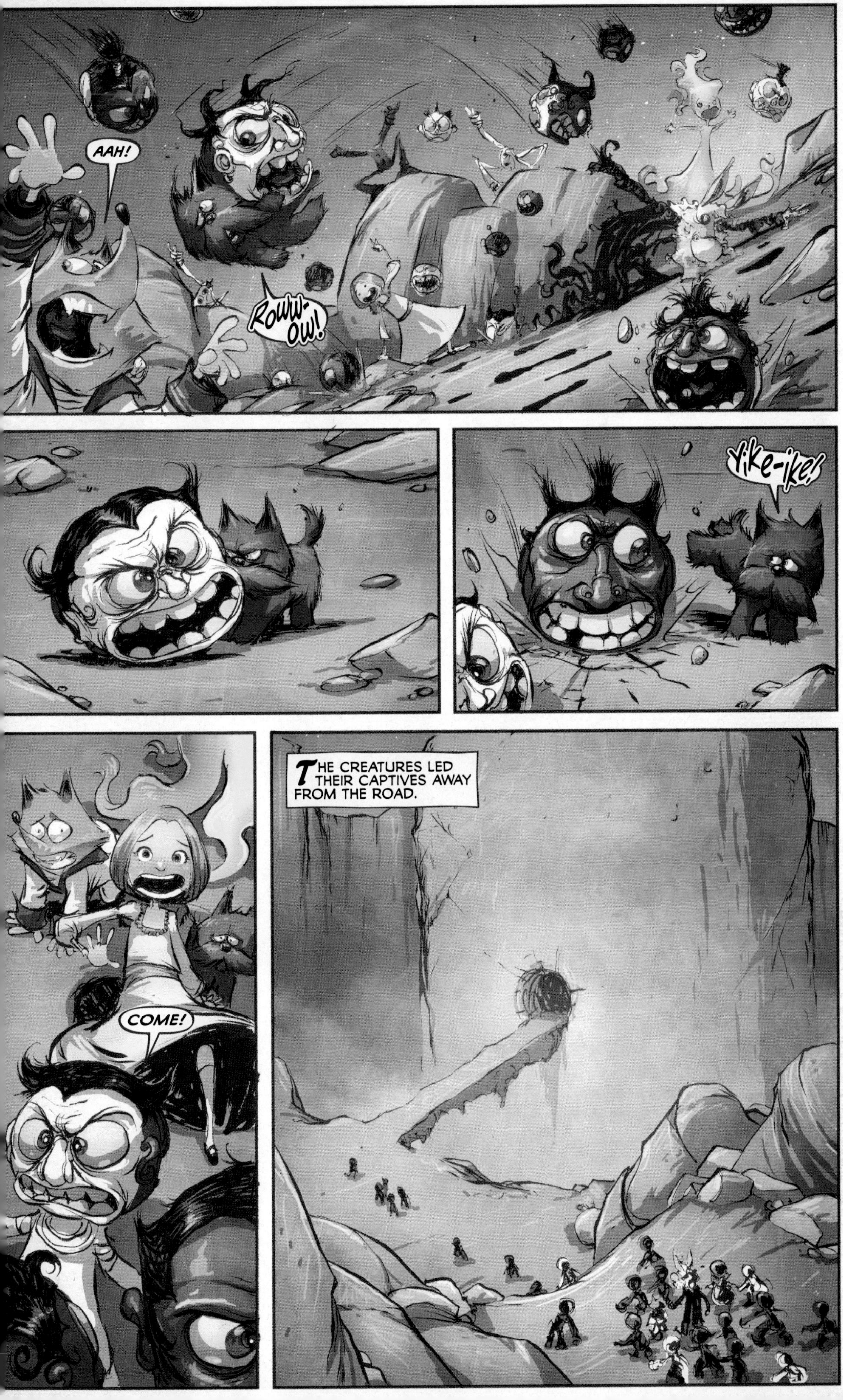
AAH!
ROWW-OW!
YIKE-IKE!
THE CREATURES LED THEIR CAPTIVES AWAY FROM THE ROAD.
COME!

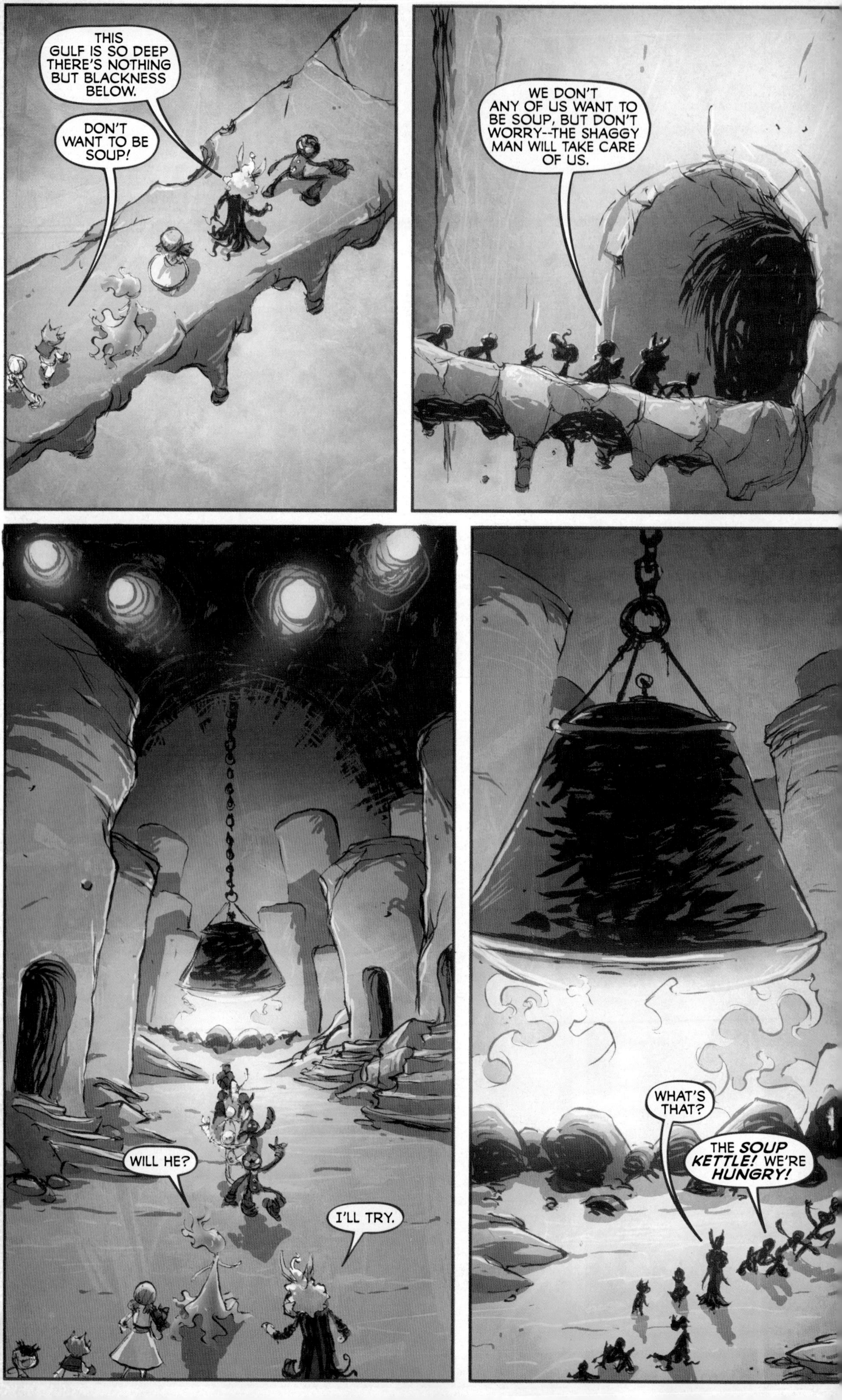
THIS GULF IS SO DEEP THERE'S NOTHING BUT BLACKNESS BELOW.
DON'T WANT TO BE SOUP!
WE DON'T ANY OF US WANT TO BE SOUP, BUT DON'T WORRY--THE SHAGGY MAN WILL TAKE CARE OF US.
WILL HE?
I'LL TRY.
WHAT'S THAT?
THE SOUP KETTLE! WE'RE HUNGRY!

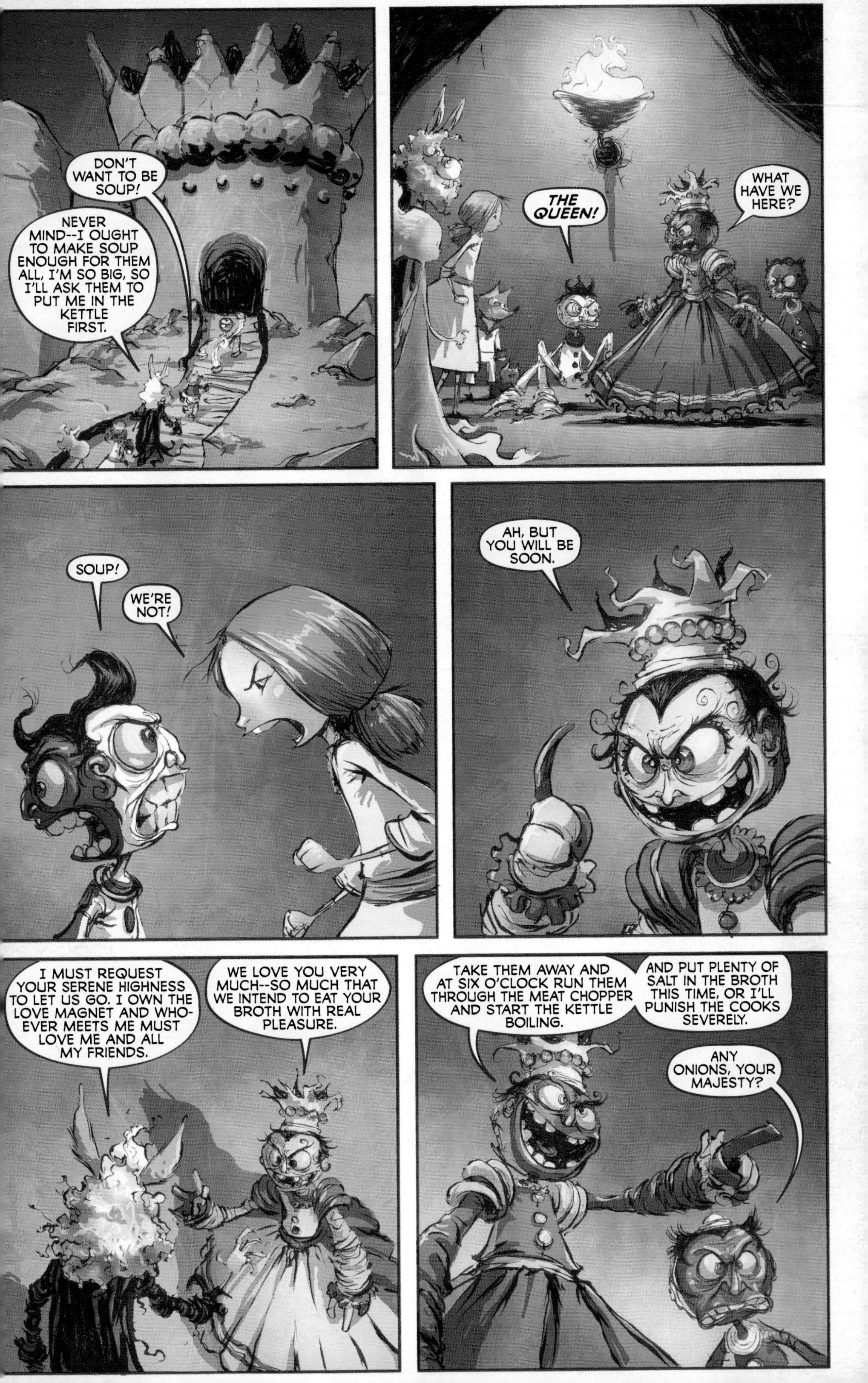
DON'T WANT TO BE SOUP!
NEVER MIND--I OUGHT TO MAKE SOUP ENOUGH FOR THEM ALL, I'M SO BIG, SO I'LL ASK THEM TO PUT ME IN THE KETTLE FIRST.
THE QUEEN!
WHAT HAVE WE HERE?
SOUP!
WE'RE NOT!
AH, BUT YOU WILL BE SOON.
I MUST REQUEST YOUR SERENE HIGHNESS TO LET US GO. I OWN THE LOVE MAGNET AND WHO-EVER MEETS ME MUST LOVE ME AND ALL MY FRIENDS.
WE LOVE YOU VERY MUCH--SO MUCH THAT WE INTEND TO EAT YOUR BROTH WITH REAL PLEASURE.
TAKE THEM AWAY AND AT SIX O'CLOCK RUN THEM THROUGH THE MEAT CHOPPER AND START THE KETTLE BOILING.
AND PUT PLENTY OF SALT IN THE BROTH THIS TIME, OR I'LL PUNISH THE COOKS SEVERELY.
ANY ONIONS, YOUR MAJESTY?

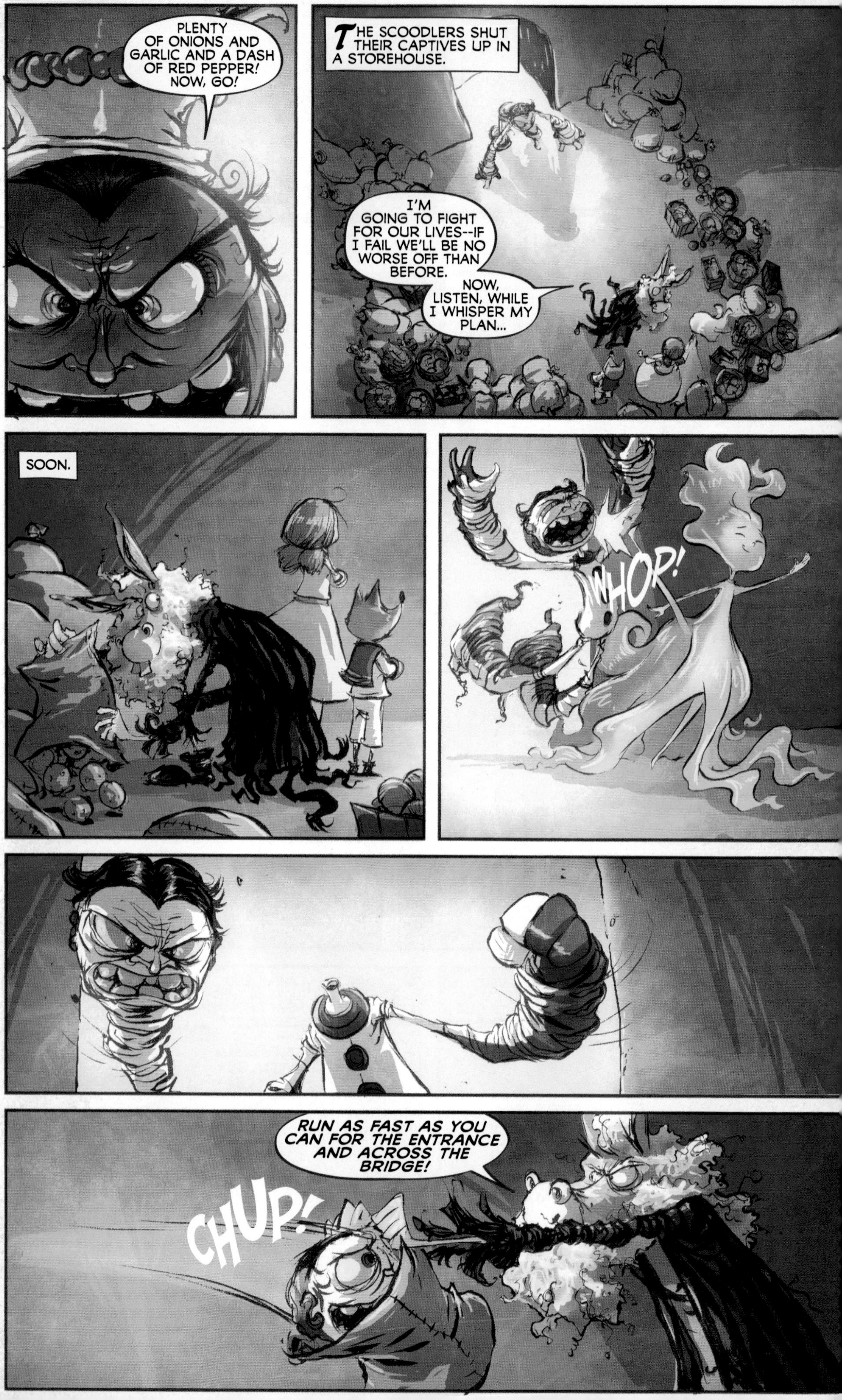
PLENTY OF ONIONS AND GARLIC AND A DASH OF RED PEPPER! NOW, GO!
THE SCOODLERS SHUT THEIR CAPTIVES UP IN A STOREHOUSE.
I'M GOING TO FIGHT FOR OUR LIVES--IF I FAIL WE'LL BE NO WORSE OFF THAN BEFORE.
NOW, LISTEN, WHILE I WHISPER MY PLAN...
SOON.
WHOP!
RUN AS FAST AS YOU CAN FOR THE ENTRANCE AND ACROSS THE BRIDGE!
CHUP!

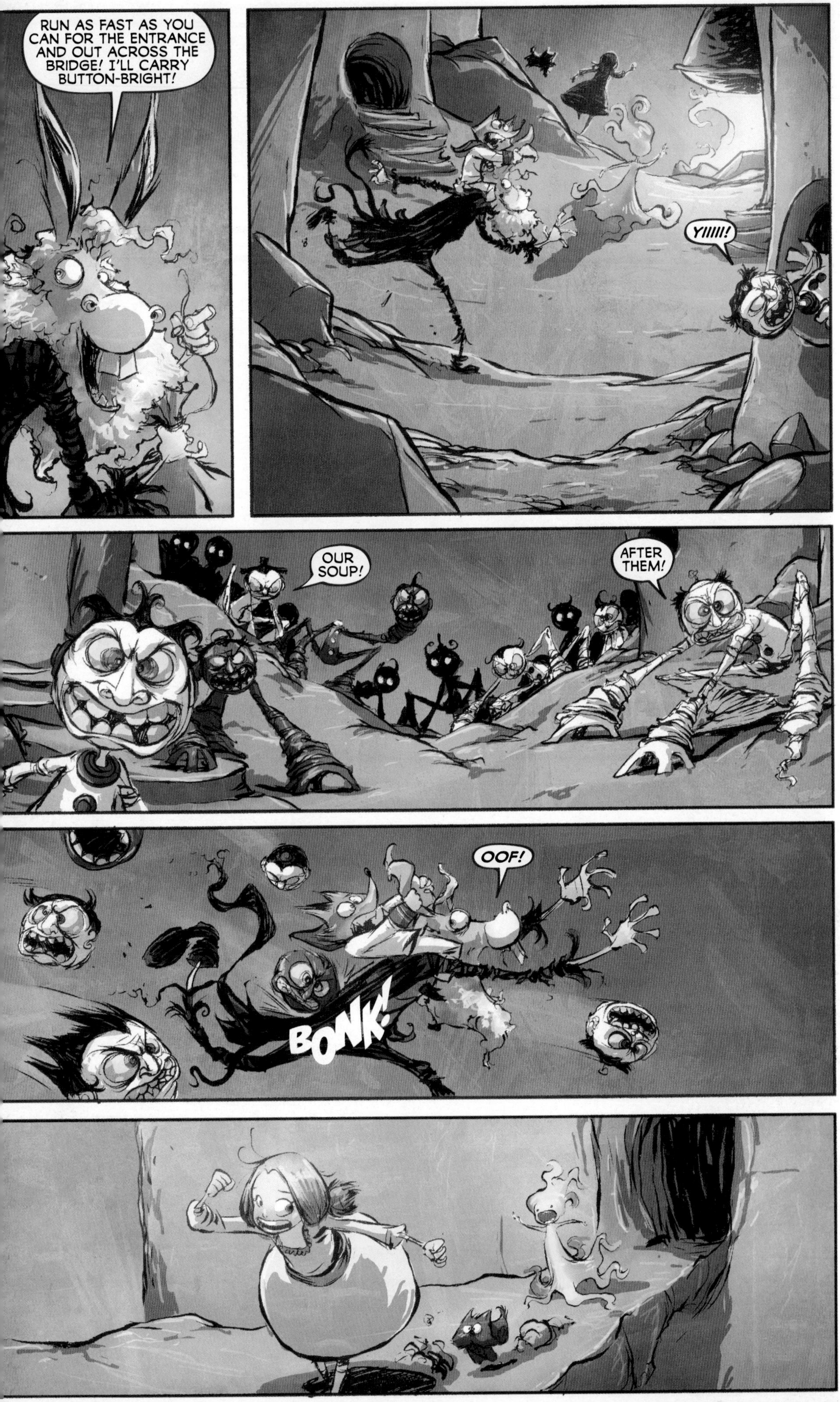
RUN AS FAST AS YOU CAN FOR THE ENTRANCE AND OUT ACROSS THE BRIDGE! I'LL CARRY BUTTON-BRIGHT!
YIIIII!
OUR SOUP!
AFTER THEM!
OOF!
BONK!

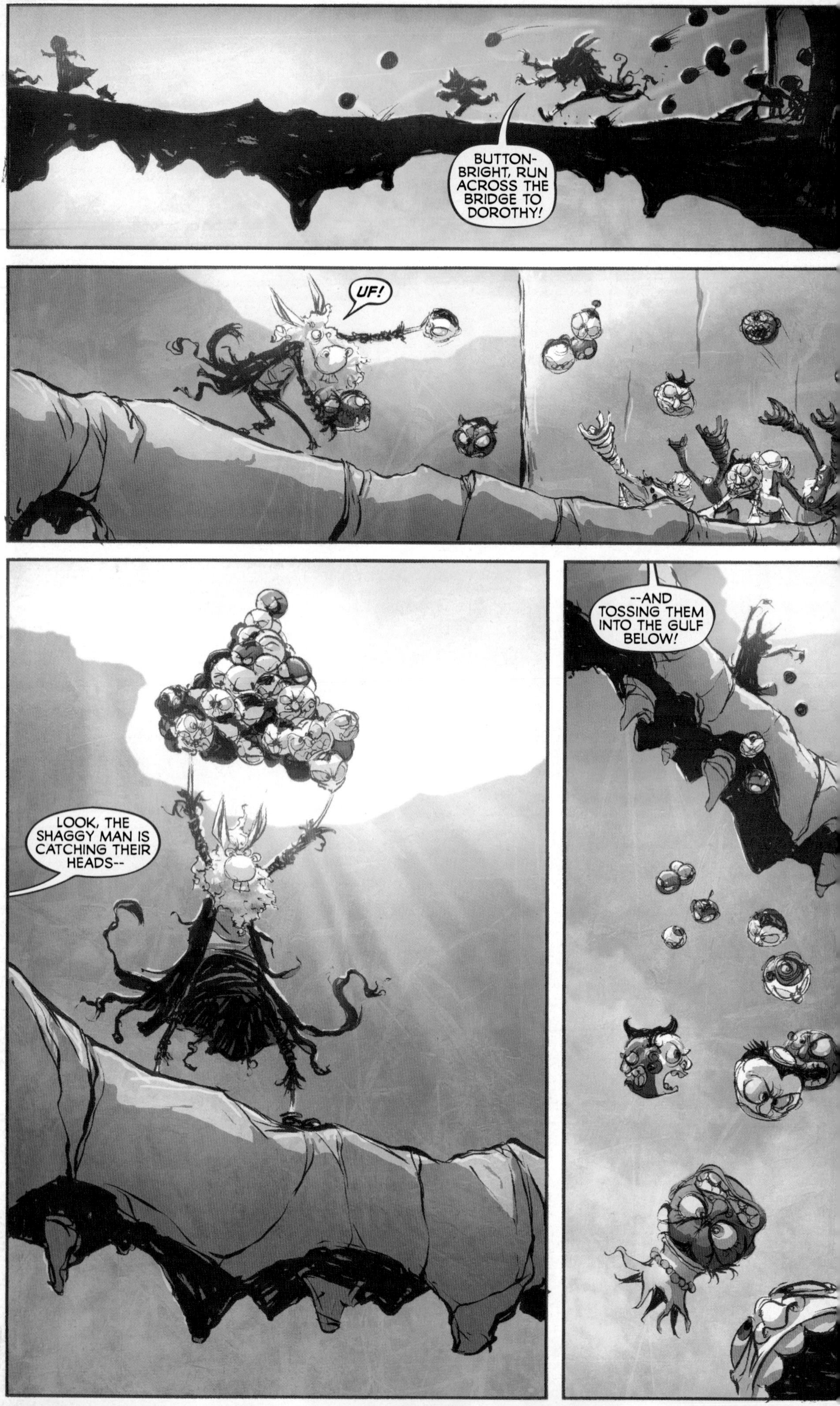
BUTTON-BRIGHT, RUN ACROSS THE BRIDGE TO DOROTHY!
UF!
LOOK, THE SHAGGY MAN IS CATCHING THEIR HEADS--
--AND TOSSING THEM INTO THE GULF BELOW!

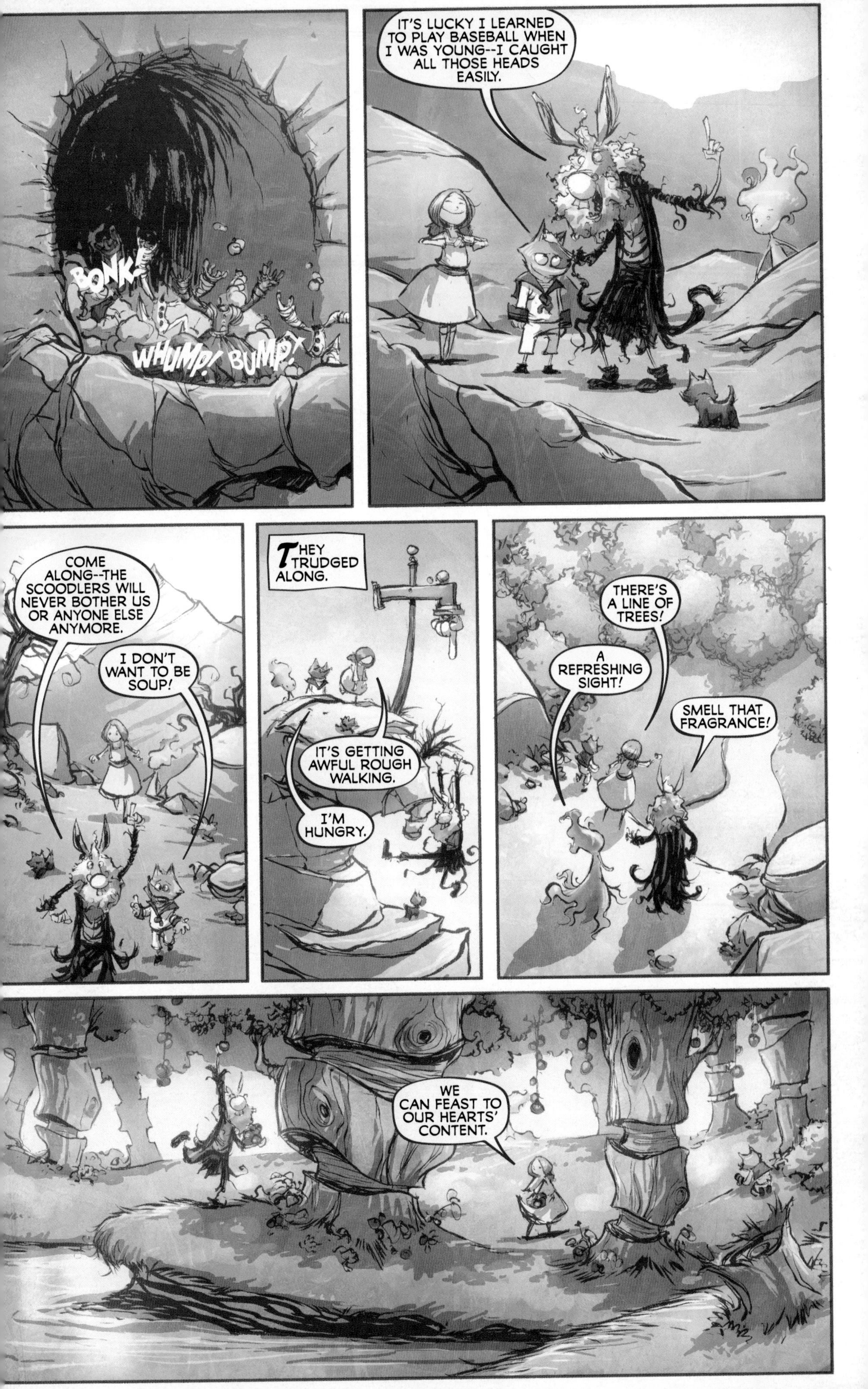
BONK
WHUMP! BUMP!
IT'S LUCKY I LEARNED TO PLAY BASEBALL WHEN I WAS YOUNG--I CAUGHT ALL THOSE HEADS EASILY.
COME ALONG--THE SCOODLERS WILL NEVER BOTHER US OR ANYONE ELSE ANYMORE.
I DON'T WANT TO BE SOUP!
THEY TRUDGED ALONG.
IT'S GETTING AWFUL ROUGH WALKING.
I'M HUNGRY.
THERE'S A LINE OF TREES!
A REFRESHING SIGHT!
SMELL THAT FRAGRANCE!
WE CAN FEAST TO OUR HEARTS' CONTENT.

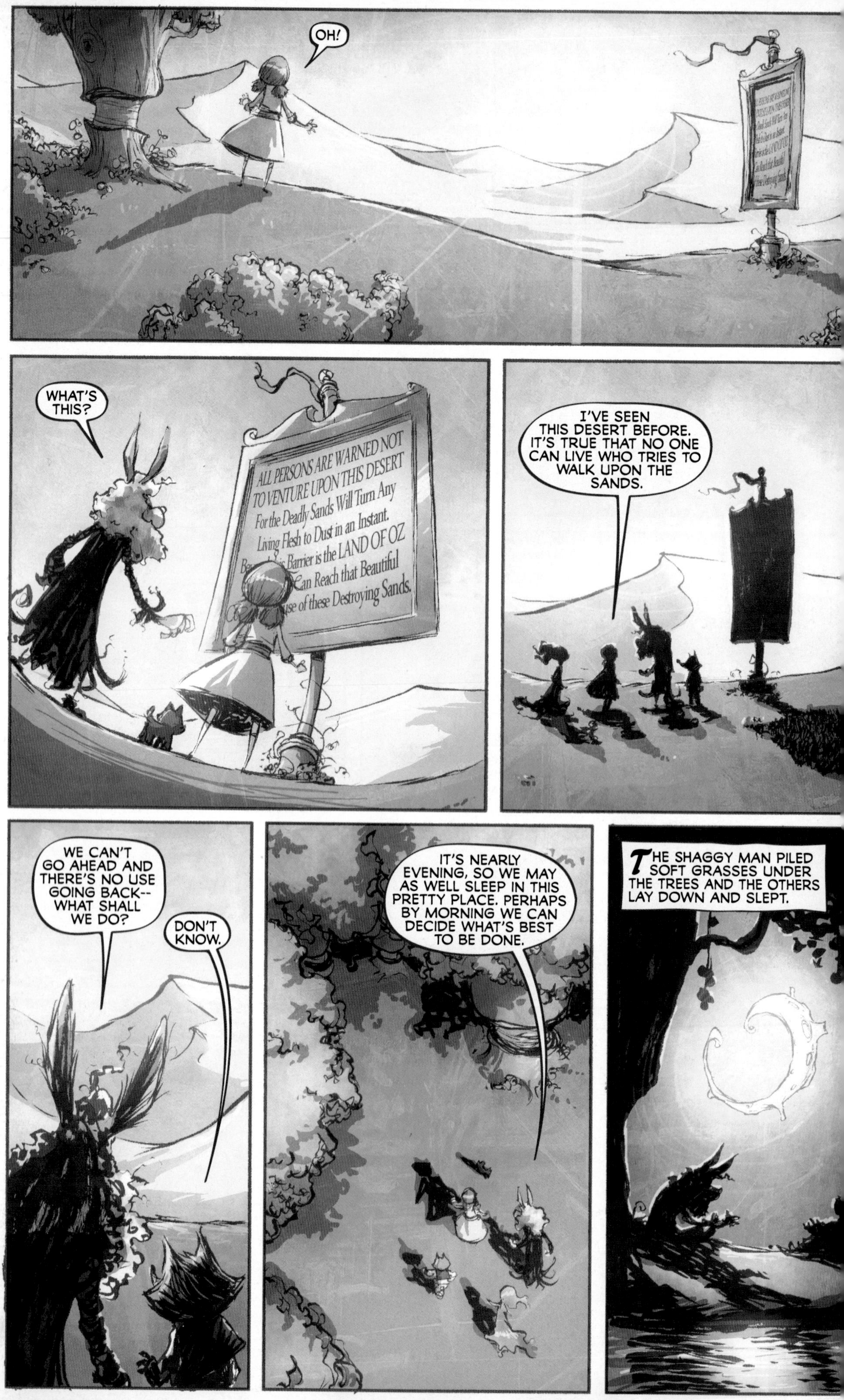
OH!
WHAT'S THIS?
ALL PERSONS ARE WARNED NOT
TO VENTURE UPON THIS DESERT
For the Deadly Sands Will Turn Any
Living Flesh to Dust in an Instant.
Barrier is the LAND OF OZ
Can Reach that Beautiful
of these Destroying Sands.
I'VE SEEN THIS DESERT BEFORE. IT'S TRUE THAT NO ONE CAN LIVE WHO TRIES TO WALK UPON THE SANDS.
WE CAN'T GO AHEAD AND THERE'S NO USE GOING BACK-- WHAT SHALL WE DO?
DON'T KNOW.
IT'S NEARLY EVENING, SO WE MAY AS WELL SLEEP IN THIS PRETTY PLACE. PERHAPS BY MORNING WE CAN DECIDE WHAT'S BEST TO BE DONE.
THE SHAGGY MAN PILED SOFT GRASSES UNDER THE TREES AND THE OTHERS LAY DOWN AND SLEPT.

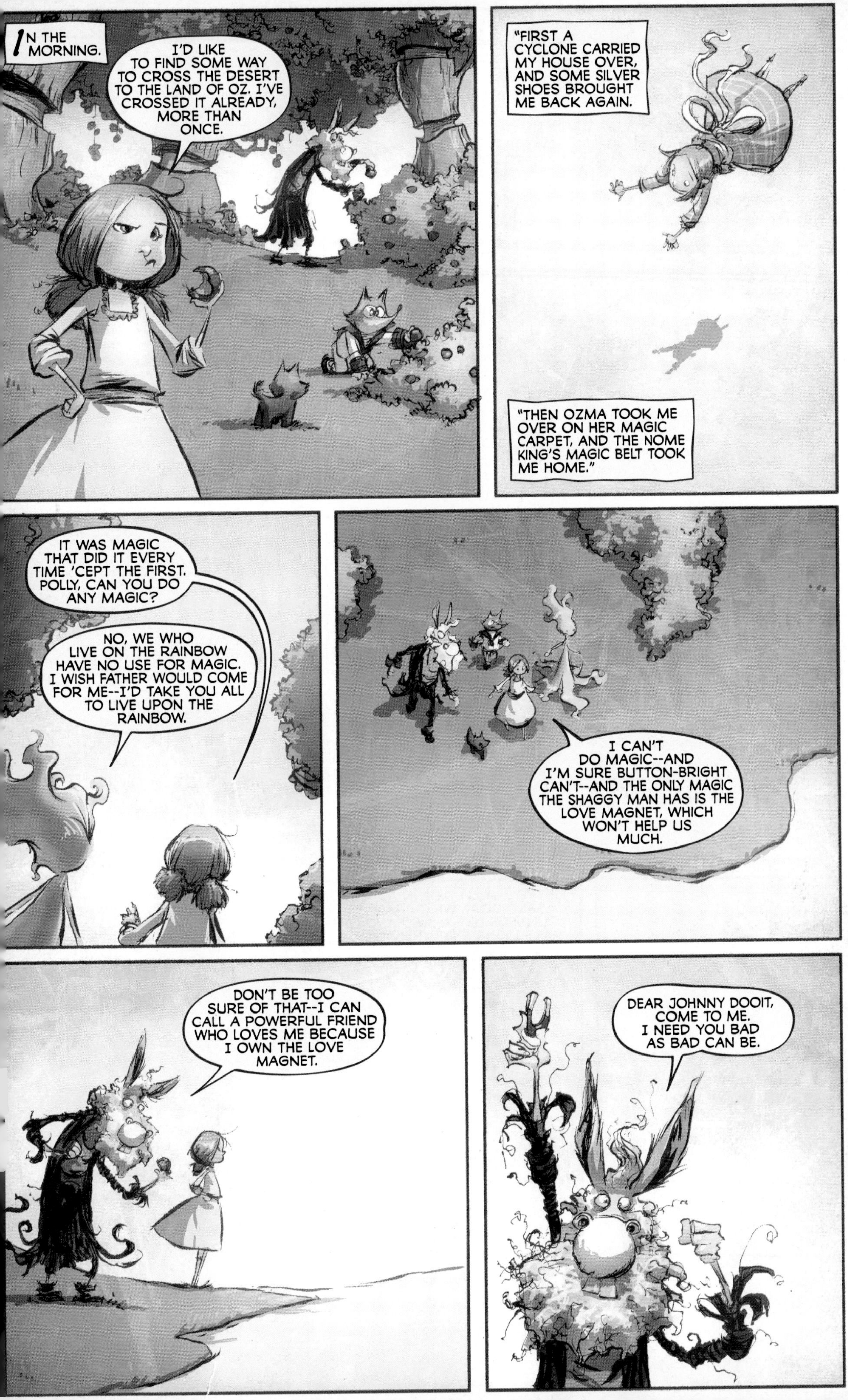
IN THE MORNING.
I'D LIKE TO FIND SOME WAY TO CROSS THE DESERT TO THE LAND OF OZ. I'VE CROSSED IT ALREADY, MORE THAN ONCE.
"FIRST A CYCLONE CARRIED MY HOUSE OVER, AND SOME SILVER SHOES BROUGHT ME BACK AGAIN.
"THEN OZMA TOOK ME OVER ON HER MAGIC CARPET, AND THE NOME KING'S MAGIC BELT TOOK ME HOME."
IT WAS MAGIC THAT DID IT EVERY TIME 'CEPT THE FIRST. POLLY, CAN YOU DO ANY MAGIC?
NO, WE WHO LIVE ON THE RAINBOW HAVE NO USE FOR MAGIC. I WISH FATHER WOULD COME FOR ME--I'D TAKE YOU ALL TO LIVE UPON THE RAINBOW.
I CAN'T DO MAGIC--AND I'M SURE BUTTON-BRIGHT CAN'T--AND THE ONLY MAGIC THE SHAGGY MAN HAS IS THE LOVE MAGNET, WHICH WON'T HELP US MUCH.
DON'T BE TOO SURE OF THAT--I CAN CALL A POWERFUL FRIEND WHO LOVES ME BECAUSE I OWN THE LOVE MAGNET.
DEAR JOHNNY DOOIT, COME TO ME. I NEED YOU BAD AS BAD CAN BE.

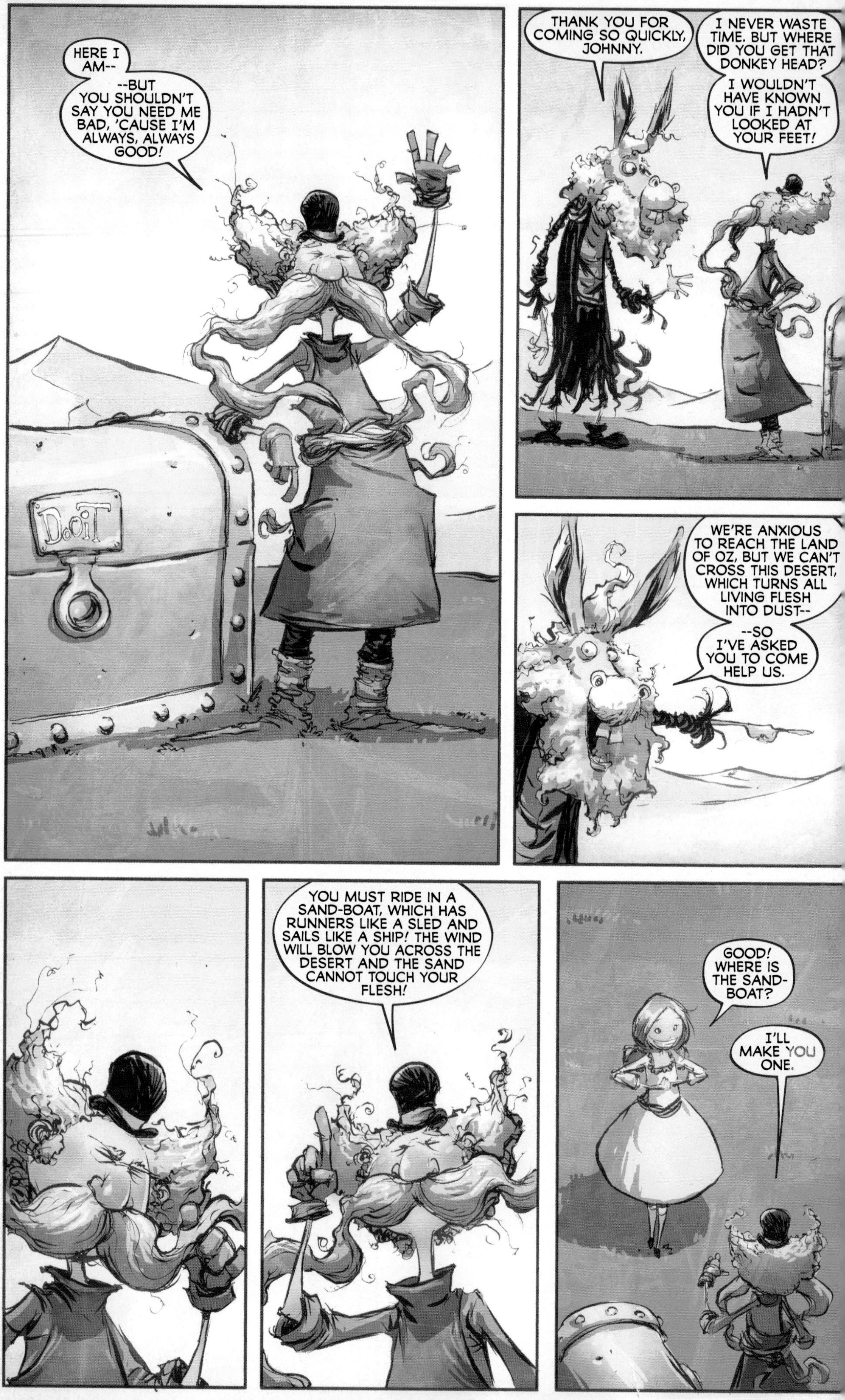
HERE I AM--
--BUT YOU SHOULDN'T SAY YOU NEED ME BAD, 'CAUSE I'M ALWAYS, ALWAYS GOOD!
DOOIT
THANK YOU FOR COMING SO QUICKLY, JOHNNY.
I NEVER WASTE TIME. BUT WHERE DID YOU GET THAT DONKEY HEAD?
I WOULDN'T HAVE KNOWN YOU IF I HADN'T LOOKED AT YOUR FEET!
WE'RE ANXIOUS TO REACH THE LAND OF OZ, BUT WE CAN'T CROSS THIS DESERT, WHICH TURNS ALL LIVING FLESH INTO DUST--
--SO I'VE ASKED YOU TO COME HELP US.
YOU MUST RIDE IN A SAND-BOAT, WHICH HAS RUNNERS LIKE A SLED AND SAILS LIKE A SHIP! THE WIND WILL BLOW YOU ACROSS THE DESERT AND THE SAND CANNOT TOUCH YOUR FLESH!
GOOD! WHERE IS THE SAND-BOAT?
I'LL MAKE YOU ONE.

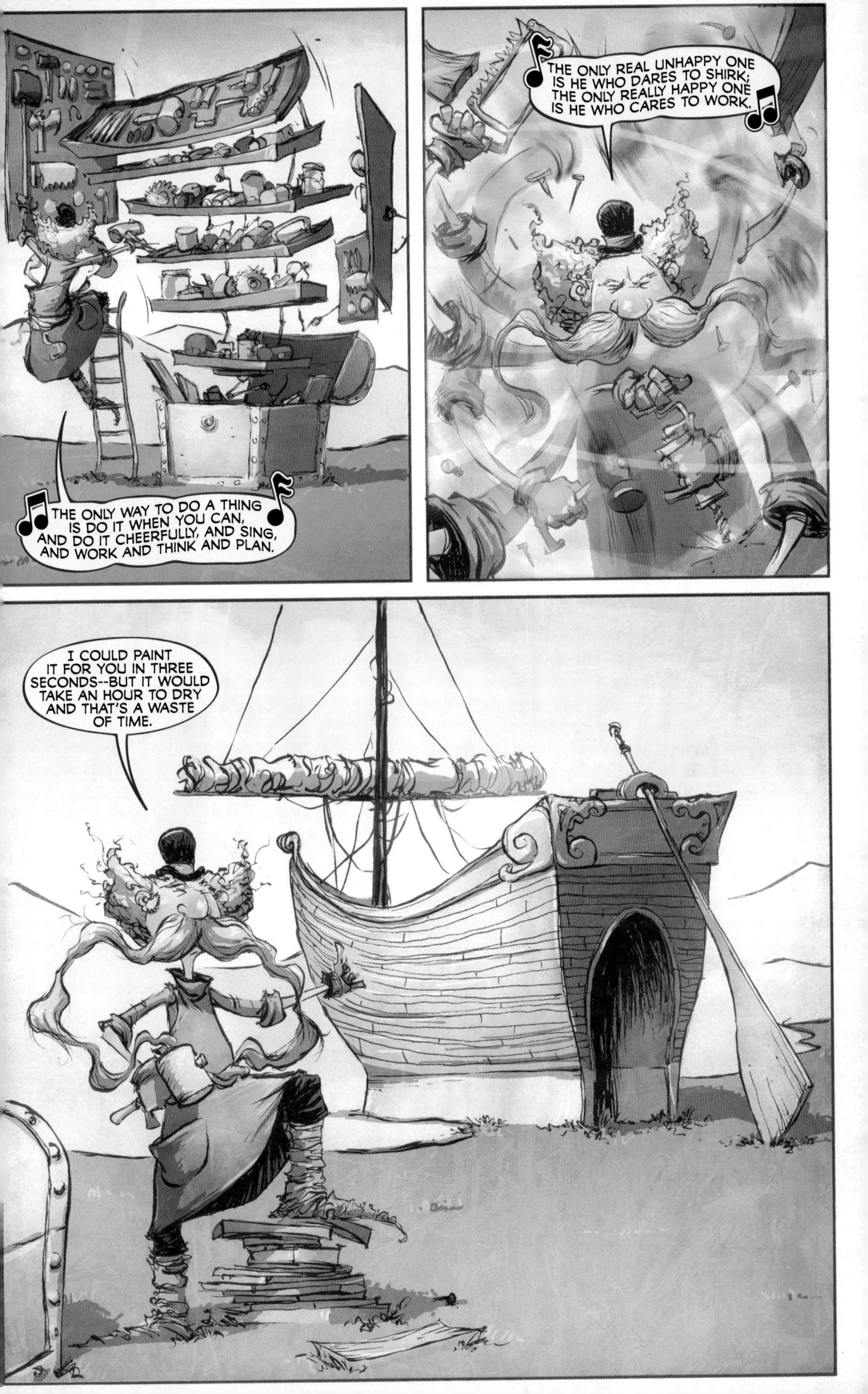
THE ONLY WAY TO DO A THING IS DO IT WHEN YOU CAN, AND DO IT CHEERFULLY, AND SING, AND WORK AND THINK AND PLAN.
THE ONLY REAL UNHAPPY ONE IS HE WHO DARES TO SHIRK; THE ONLY REALLY HAPPY ONE IS HE WHO CARES TO WORK.
I COULD PAINT IT FOR YOU IN THREE SECONDS--BUT IT WOULD TAKE AN HOUR TO DRY AND THAT'S A WASTE OF TIME.

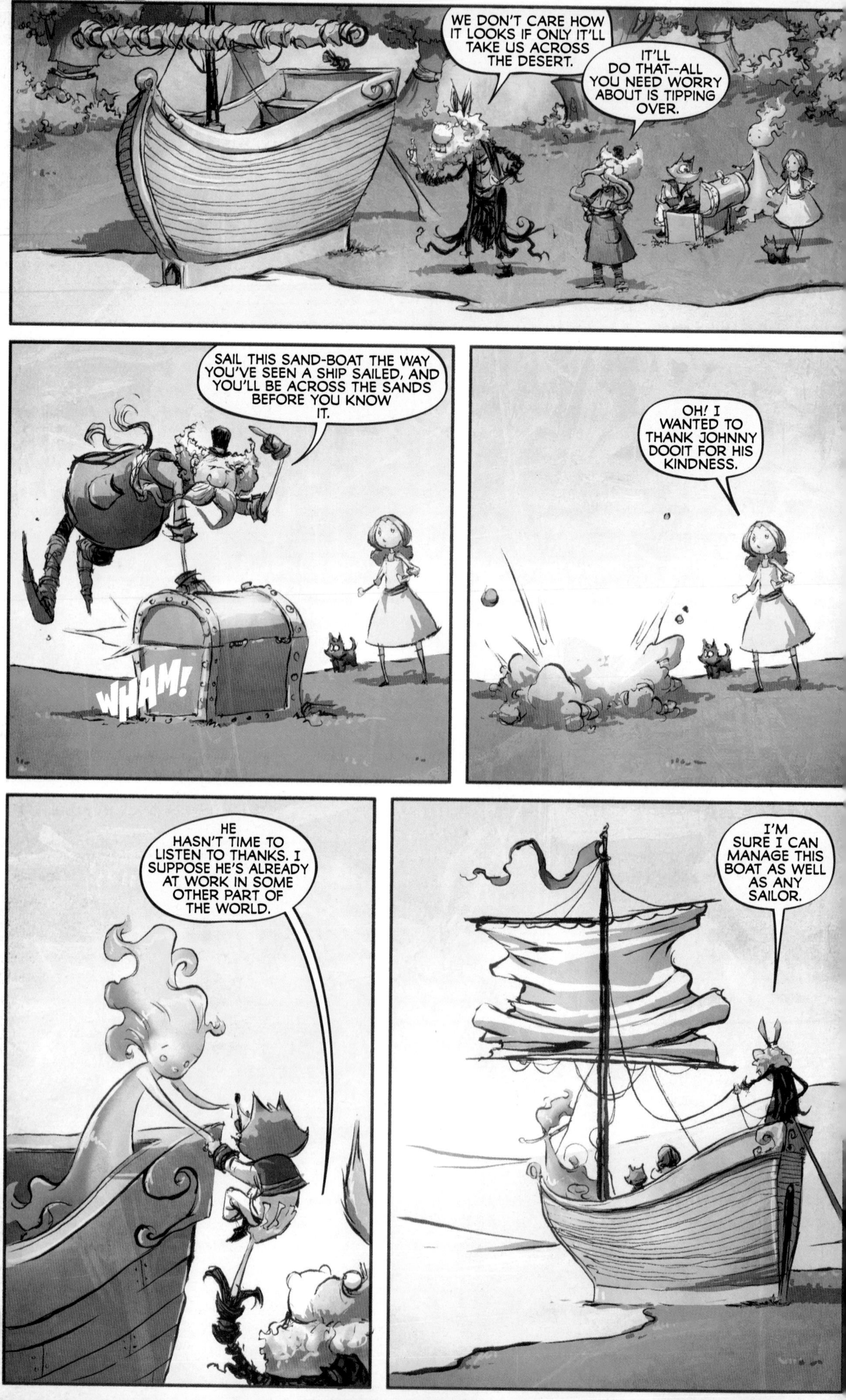
WE DON'T CARE HOW IT LOOKS IF ONLY IT'LL TAKE US ACROSS THE DESERT.
IT'LL DO THAT--ALL YOU NEED WORRY ABOUT IS TIPPING OVER.
SAIL THIS SAND-BOAT THE WAY YOU'VE SEEN A SHIP SAILED, AND YOU'LL BE ACROSS THE SANDS BEFORE YOU KNOW IT.
WHAM!
OH! I WANTED TO THANK JOHNNY DOOIT FOR HIS KINDNESS.
HE HASN'T TIME TO LISTEN TO THANKS. I SUPPOSE HE'S ALREADY AT WORK IN SOME OTHER PART OF THE WORLD.
I'M SURE I CAN MANAGE THIS BOAT AS WELL AS ANY SAILOR.

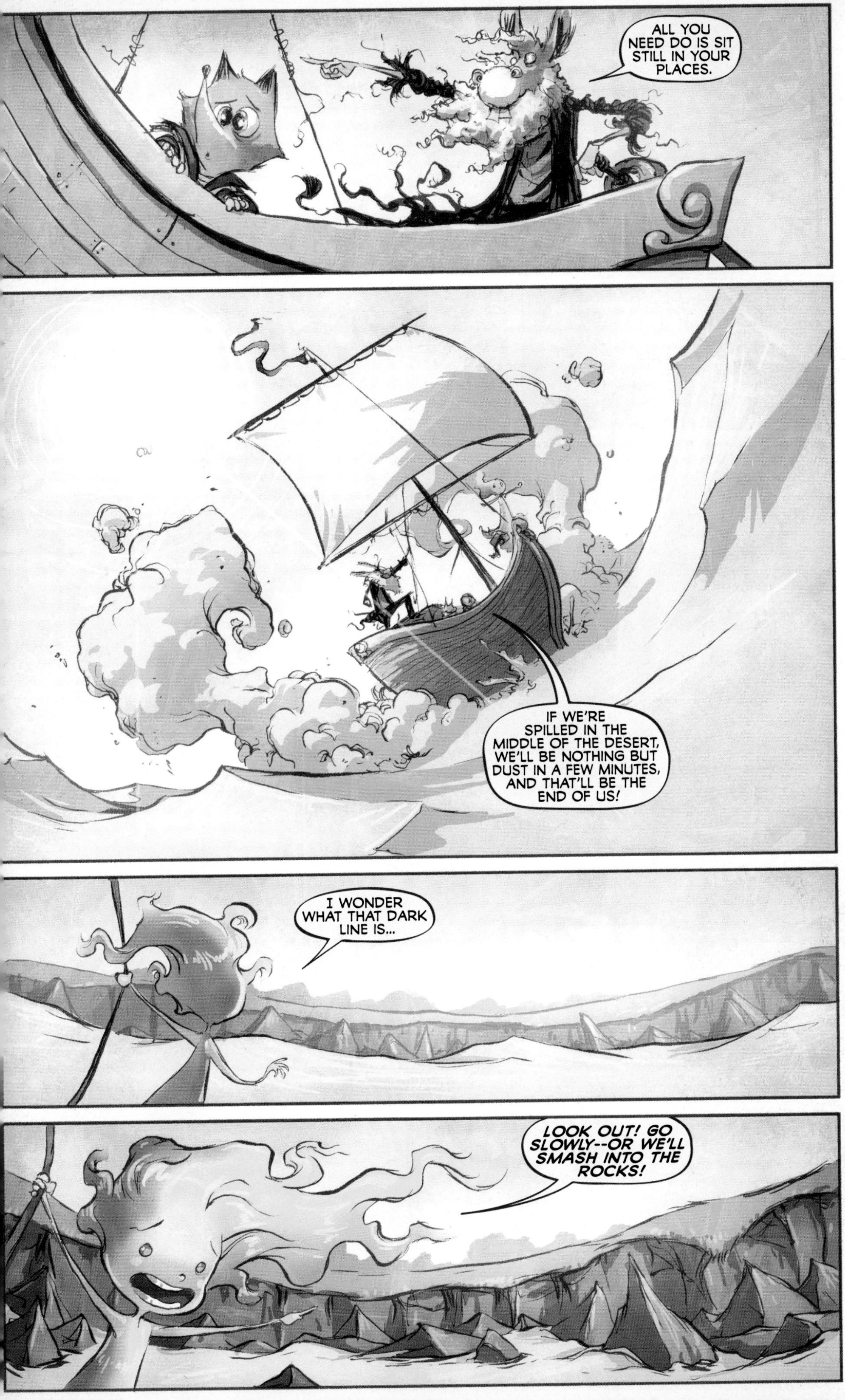
ALL YOU NEED DO IS SIT STILL IN YOUR PLACES.
IF WE'RE SPILLED IN THE MIDDLE OF THE DESERT, WE'LL BE NOTHING BUT DUST IN A FEW MINUTES, AND THAT'LL BE THE END OF US!
I WONDER WHAT THAT DARK LINE IS...
LOOK OUT! GO SLOWLY--OR WE'LL SMASH INTO THE ROCKS!

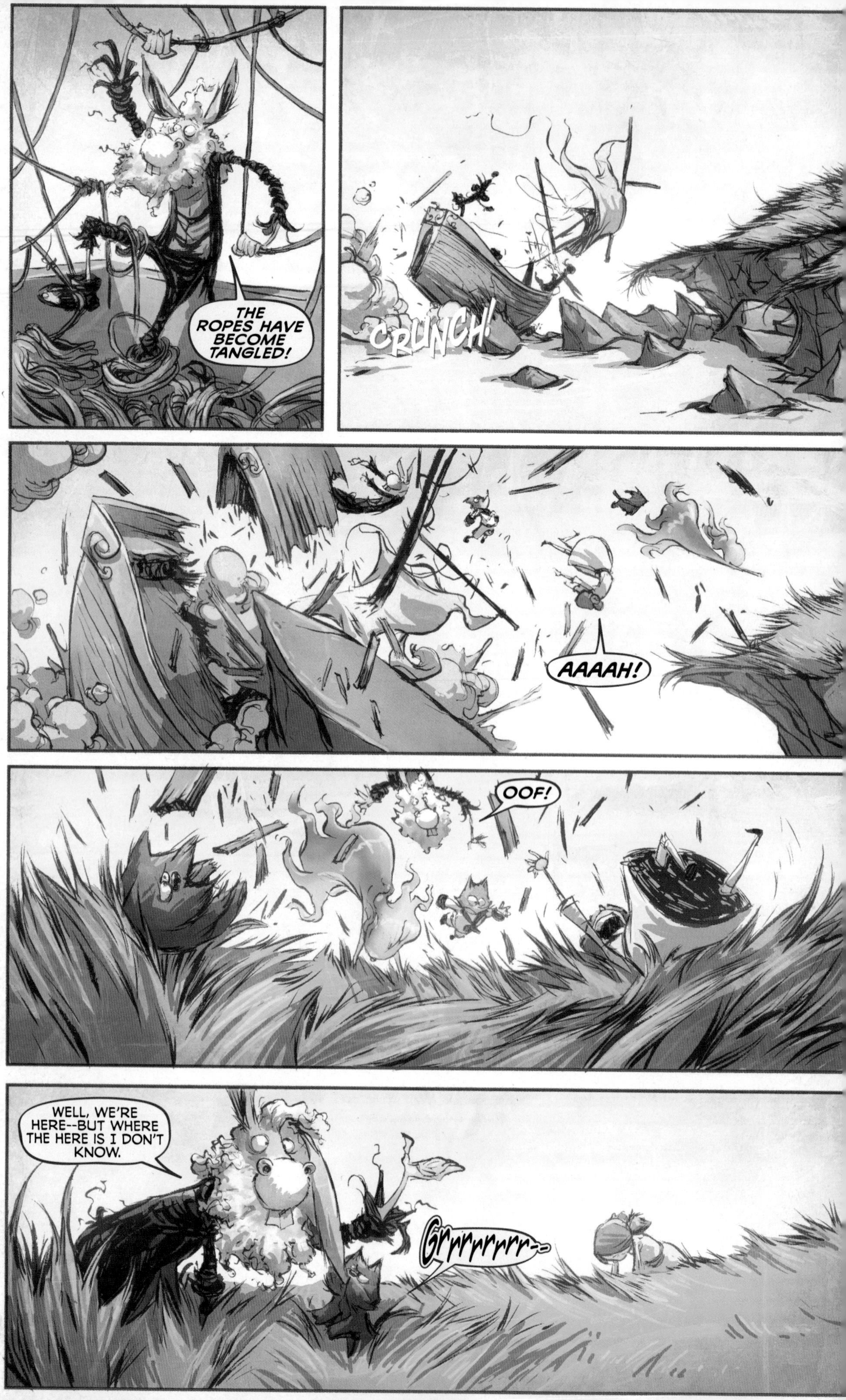

THE ROPES HAVE BECOME TANGLED!
CRUNCH!
AAAAH!
OOF!
WELL, WE'RE HERE--BUT WHERE THE HERE IS I DON'T KNOW.
Grrrrrrrr--

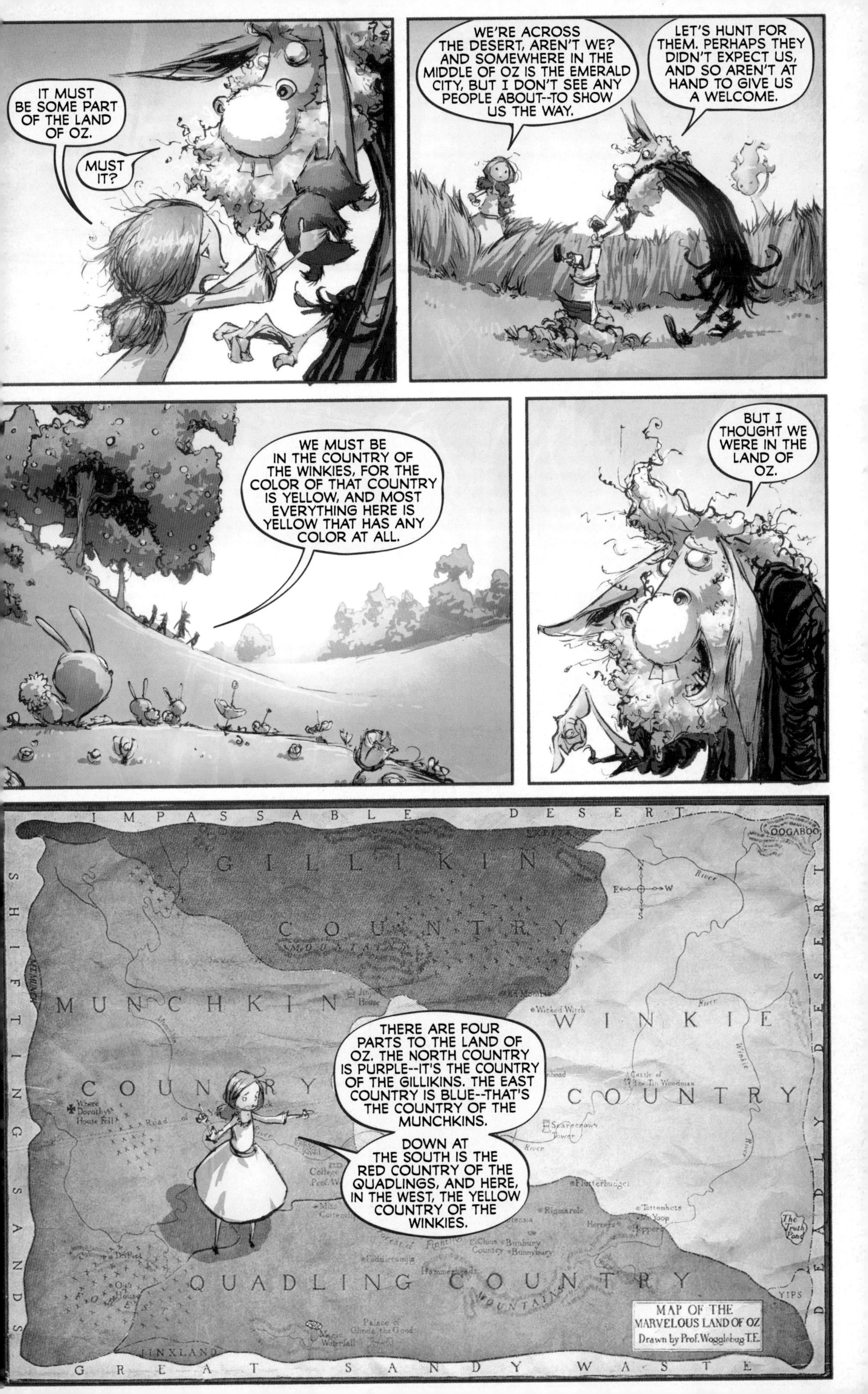
IT MUST BE SOME PART OF THE LAND OF OZ.
MUST IT?
WE'RE ACROSS THE DESERT, AREN'T WE? AND SOMEWHERE IN THE MIDDLE OF OZ IS THE EMERALD CITY, BUT I DON'T SEE ANY PEOPLE ABOUT--TO SHOW US THE WAY.
LET'S HUNT FOR THEM. PERHAPS THEY DIDN'T EXPECT US, AND SO AREN'T AT HAND TO GIVE US A WELCOME.
WE MUST BE IN THE COUNTRY OF THE WINKIES, FOR THE COLOR OF THAT COUNTRY IS YELLOW, AND MOST EVERYTHING HERE IS YELLOW THAT HAS ANY COLOR AT ALL.
BUT I THOUGHT WE WERE IN THE LAND OF OZ.
IMPASSABLE DESERT
OOGABOO
GILLIKIN COUNTRY
SHIFTING SANDS
DEADLY DESERT
MUNCHKIN COUNTRY
WINKIE COUNTRY
Wicked Witch
Castle of the Tin Woodman
Scarecrow's Tower
Where Dorothy's House Fell
THERE ARE FOUR PARTS TO THE LAND OF OZ. THE NORTH COUNTRY IS PURPLE--IT'S THE COUNTRY OF THE GILLIKINS. THE EAST COUNTRY IS BLUE--THAT'S THE COUNTRY OF THE MUNCHKINS.
DOWN AT THE SOUTH IS THE RED COUNTRY OF THE QUADLINGS, AND HERE, IN THE WEST, THE YELLOW COUNTRY OF THE WINKIES.
Flutterbudget
Rigmarole
Tottenhots
Bunbury
Bunnybury
The Truth Pond
QUADLING COUNTRY
YIPS
Palace of Glinda the Good
Magic Waterfall
JINXLAND
MAP OF THE MARVELOUS LAND OF OZ
Drawn by Prof. Wogglebug T.E.
GREAT SANDY WASTE

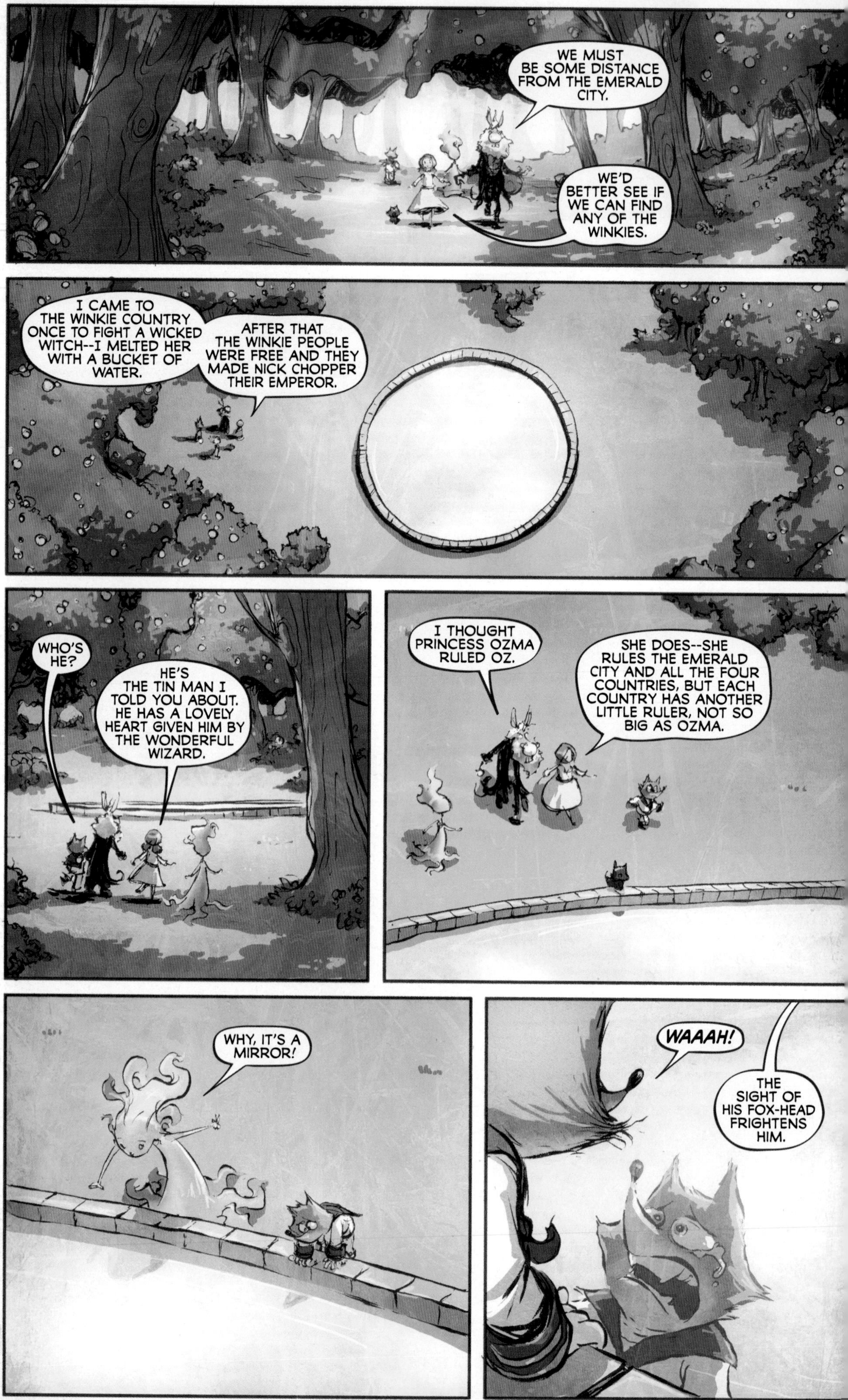
WE MUST BE SOME DISTANCE FROM THE EMERALD CITY.
WE'D BETTER SEE IF WE CAN FIND ANY OF THE WINKIES.
I CAME TO THE WINKIE COUNTRY ONCE TO FIGHT A WICKED WITCH--I MELTED HER WITH A BUCKET OF WATER.
AFTER THAT THE WINKIE PEOPLE WERE FREE AND THEY MADE NICK CHOPPER THEIR EMPEROR.
WHO'S HE?
HE'S THE TIN MAN I TOLD YOU ABOUT. HE HAS A LOVELY HEART GIVEN HIM BY THE WONDERFUL WIZARD.
I THOUGHT PRINCESS OZMA RULED OZ.
SHE DOES--SHE RULES THE EMERALD CITY AND ALL THE FOUR COUNTRIES, BUT EACH COUNTRY HAS ANOTHER LITTLE RULER, NOT SO BIG AS OZMA.
WHY, IT'S A MIRROR!
WAAAH!
THE SIGHT OF HIS FOX-HEAD FRIGHTENS HIM.

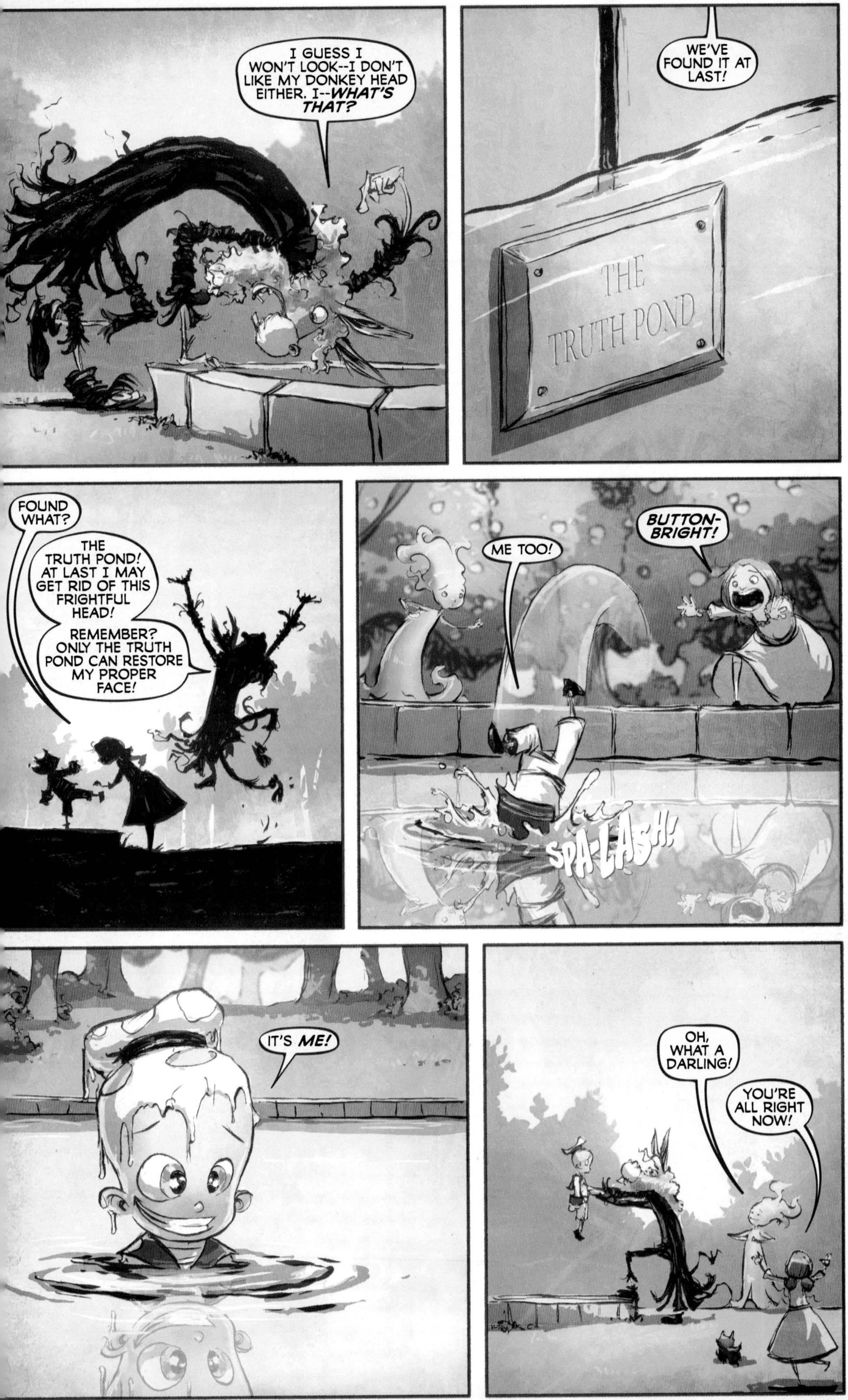
I GUESS I WON'T LOOK--I DON'T LIKE MY DONKEY HEAD EITHER. I--WHAT'S THAT?
WE'VE FOUND IT AT LAST!
THE TRUTH POND
FOUND WHAT?
THE TRUTH POND! AT LAST I MAY GET RID OF THIS FRIGHTFUL HEAD!
REMEMBER? ONLY THE TRUTH POND CAN RESTORE MY PROPER FACE!
BUTTON-BRIGHT!
ME TOO!
SPA-LASH!!
IT'S ME!
OH, WHAT A DARLING!
YOU'RE ALL RIGHT NOW!

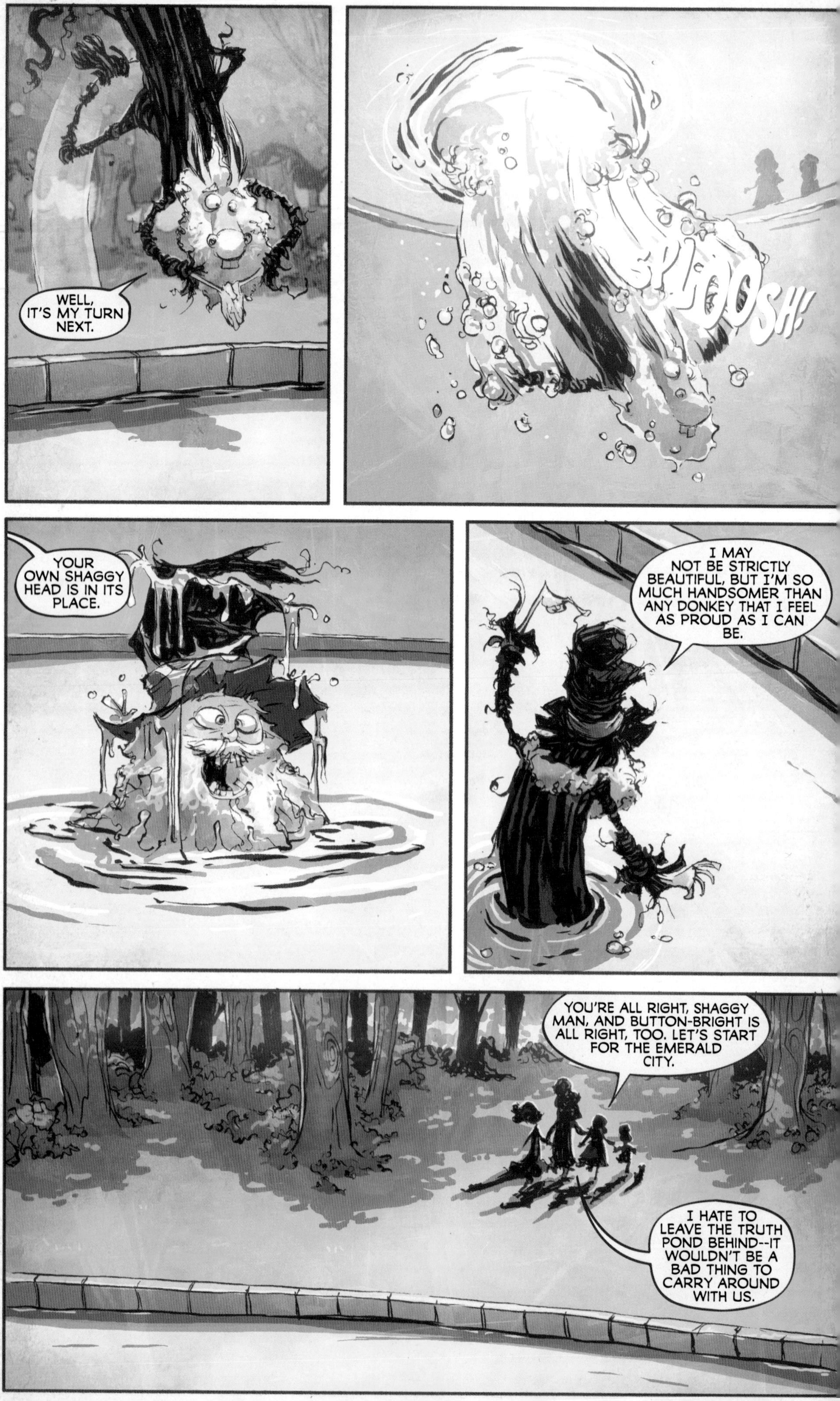
WELL, IT'S MY TURN NEXT.
SPLOOSH!
YOUR OWN SHAGGY HEAD IS IN ITS PLACE.
I MAY NOT BE STRICTLY BEAUTIFUL, BUT I'M SO MUCH HANDSOMER THAN ANY DONKEY THAT I FEEL AS PROUD AS I CAN BE.
YOU'RE ALL RIGHT, SHAGGY MAN, AND BUTTON-BRIGHT IS ALL RIGHT, TOO. LET'S START FOR THE EMERALD CITY.
I HATE TO LEAVE THE TRUTH POND BEHIND--IT WOULDN'T BE A BAD THING TO CARRY AROUND WITH US.

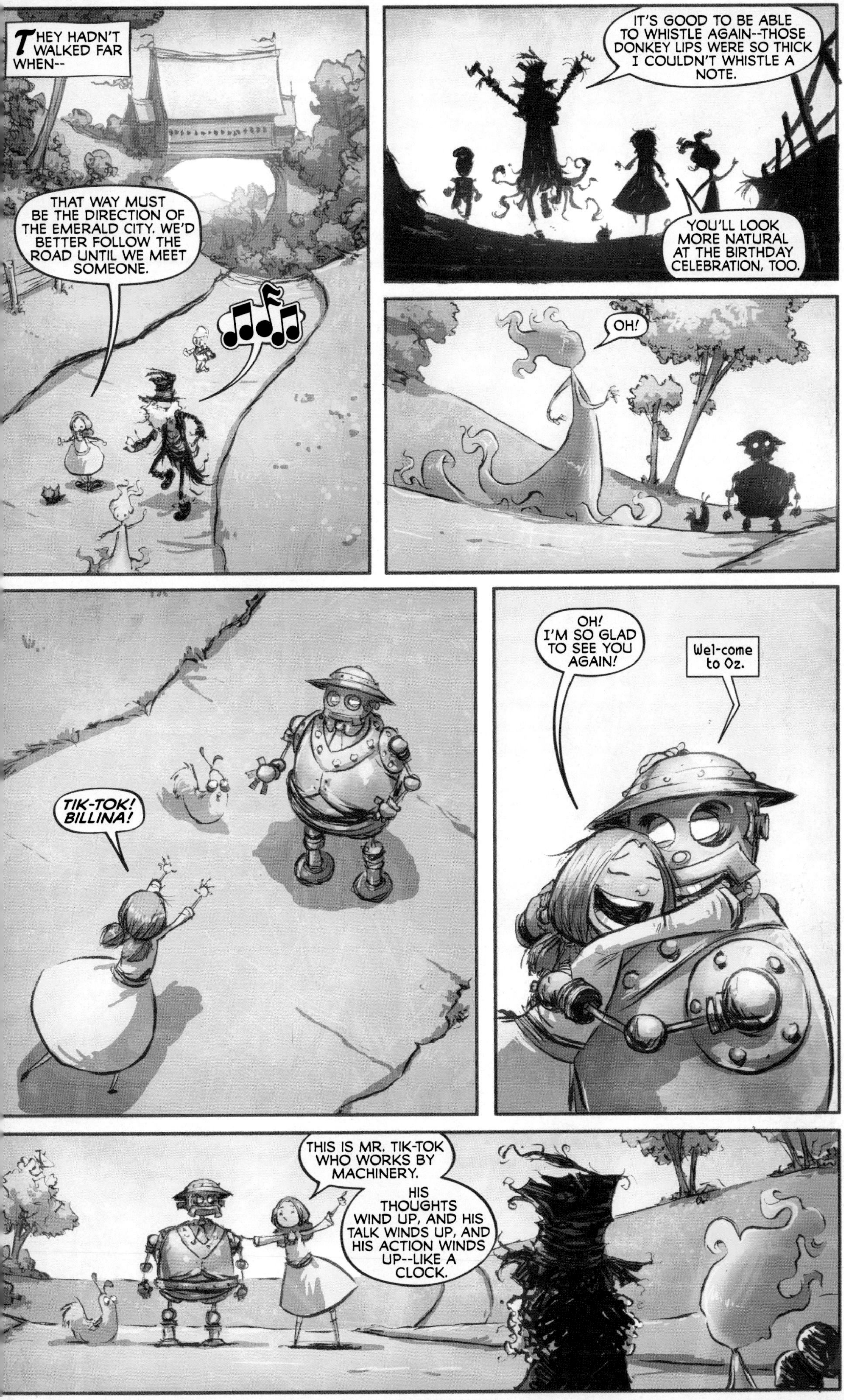

THEY HADN'T WALKED FAR WHEN--
THAT WAY MUST BE THE DIRECTION OF THE EMERALD CITY. WE'D BETTER FOLLOW THE ROAD UNTIL WE MEET SOMEONE.
IT'S GOOD TO BE ABLE TO WHISTLE AGAIN--THOSE DONKEY LIPS WERE SO THICK I COULDN'T WHISTLE A NOTE.
YOU'LL LOOK MORE NATURAL AT THE BIRTHDAY CELEBRATION, TOO.
OH!
TIK-TOK! BILLINA!
OH! I'M SO GLAD TO SEE YOU AGAIN!
Wel-come to Oz.
THIS IS MR. TIK-TOK WHO WORKS BY MACHINERY.
HIS THOUGHTS WIND UP, AND HIS TALK WINDS UP, AND HIS ACTION WINDS UP--LIKE A CLOCK.

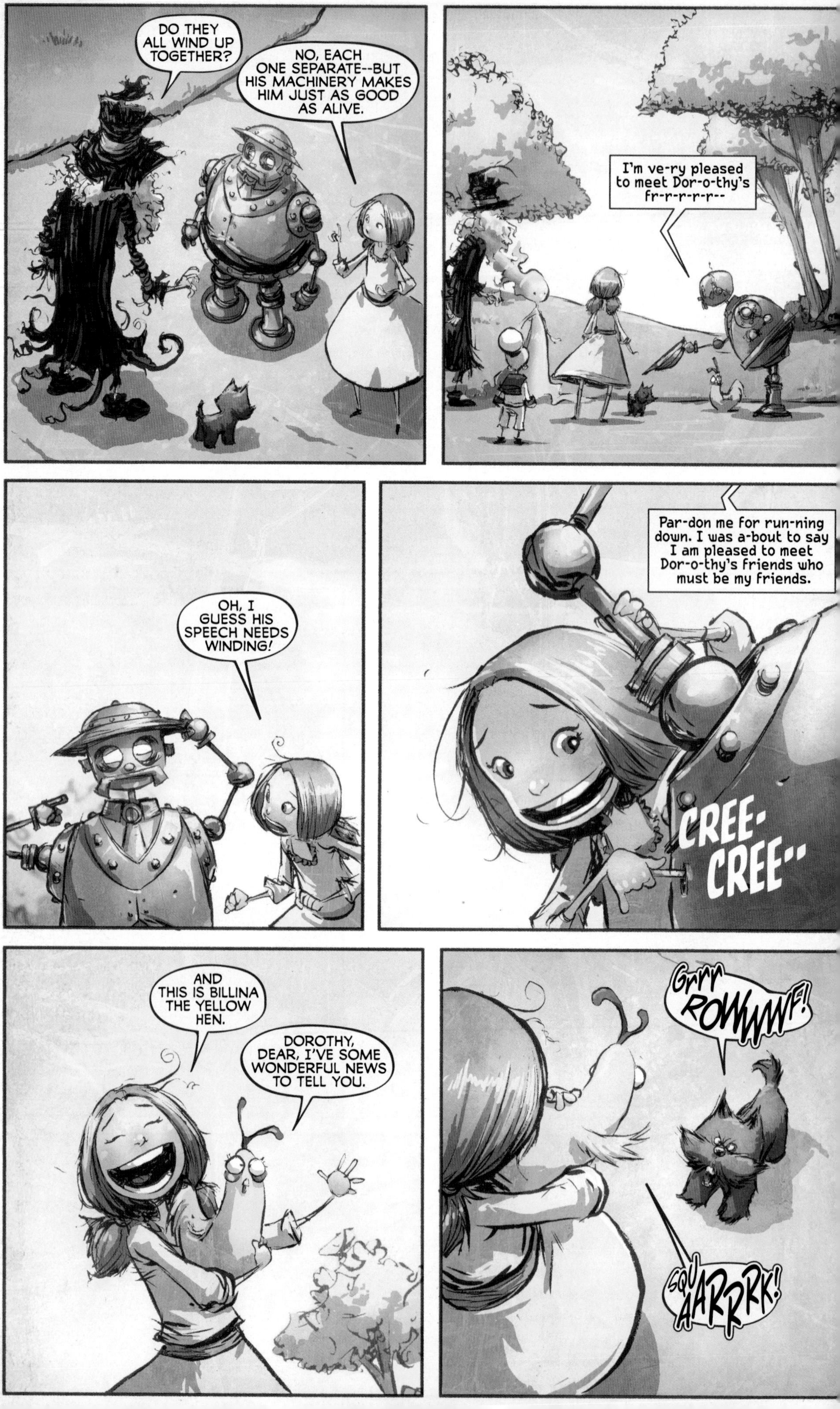

DO THEY ALL WIND UP TOGETHER?
NO, EACH ONE SEPARATE--BUT HIS MACHINERY MAKES HIM JUST AS GOOD AS ALIVE.
I'm ve-ry pleased to meet Dor-o-thy's fr-r-r-r-r--
OH, I GUESS HIS SPEECH NEEDS WINDING!
Par-don me for run-ning down. I was a-bout to say I am pleased to meet Dor-o-thy's friends who must be my friends.
CREE-CREE--
AND THIS IS BILLINA THE YELLOW HEN.
DOROTHY, DEAR, I'VE SOME WONDERFUL NEWS TO TELL YOU.
Grrr ROWWWF!
SQUAARRRK!

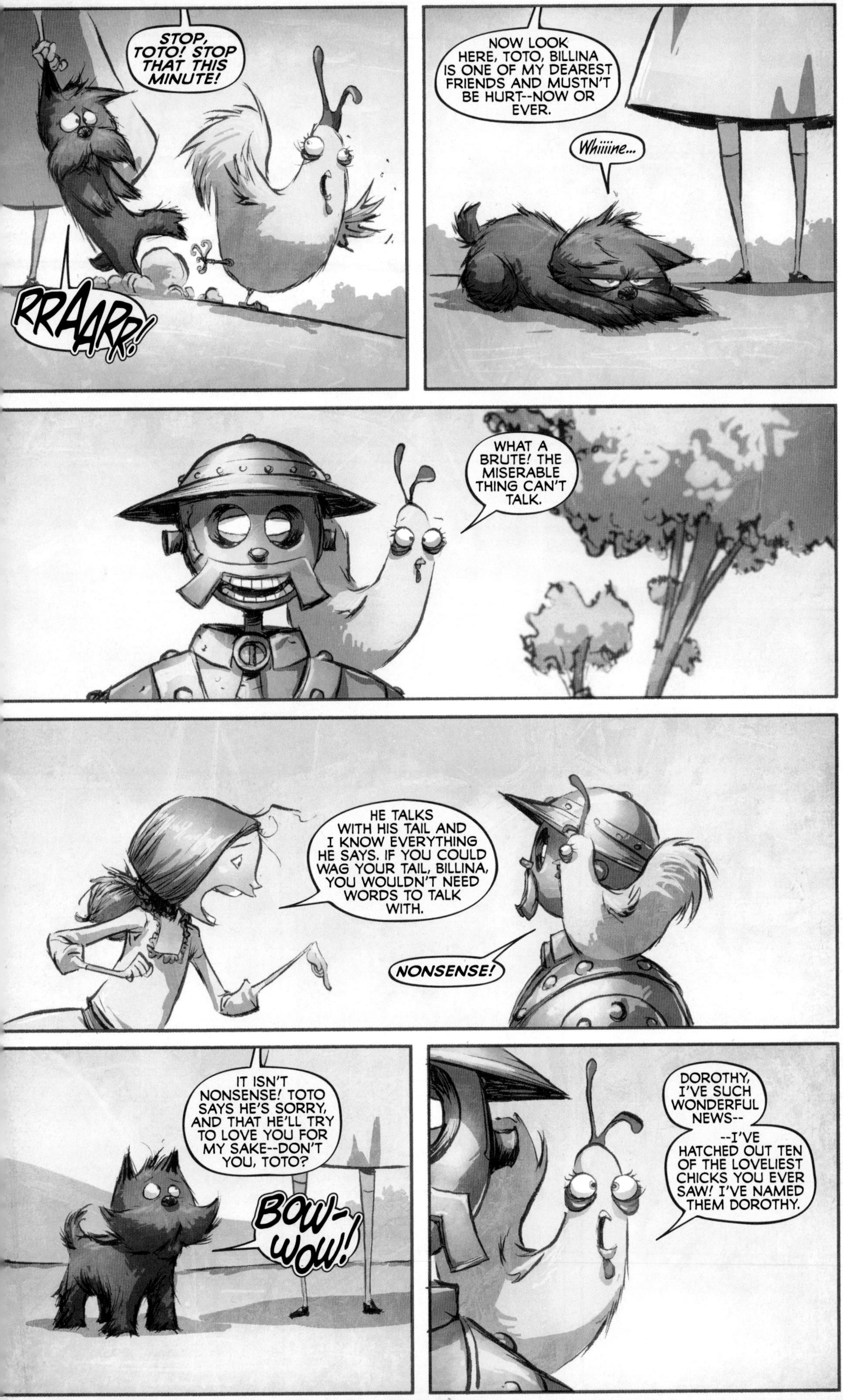
STOP, TOTO! STOP THAT THIS MINUTE!
RRAARR!
NOW LOOK HERE, TOTO, BILLINA IS ONE OF MY DEAREST FRIENDS AND MUSTN'T BE HURT--NOW OR EVER.
Whiiiine...
WHAT A BRUTE! THE MISERABLE THING CAN'T TALK.
HE TALKS WITH HIS TAIL AND I KNOW EVERYTHING HE SAYS. IF YOU COULD WAG YOUR TAIL, BILLINA, YOU WOULDN'T NEED WORDS TO TALK WITH.
NONSENSE!
IT ISN'T NONSENSE! TOTO SAYS HE'S SORRY, AND THAT HE'LL TRY TO LOVE YOU FOR MY SAKE--DON'T YOU, TOTO?
BOW-WOW!
DOROTHY, I'VE SUCH WONDERFUL NEWS--
--I'VE HATCHED OUT TEN OF THE LOVELIEST CHICKS YOU EVER SAW! I'VE NAMED THEM DOROTHY.

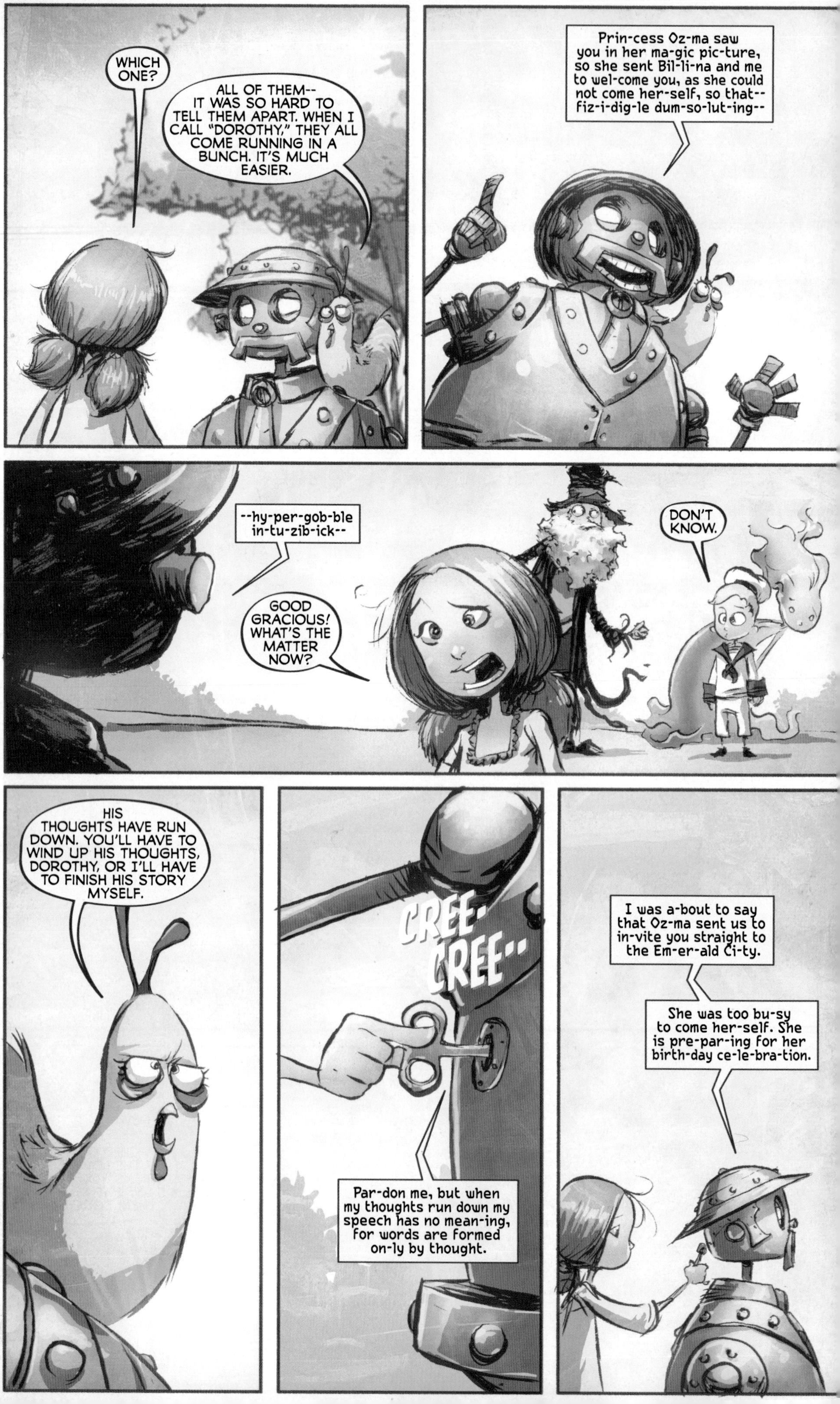
WHICH ONE?
ALL OF THEM-- IT WAS SO HARD TO TELL THEM APART. WHEN I CALL "DOROTHY," THEY ALL COME RUNNING IN A BUNCH. IT'S MUCH EASIER.
Prin-cess Oz-ma saw you in her ma-gic pic-ture, so she sent Bil-li-na and me to wel-come you, as she could not come her-self, so that-- fiz-i-dig-le dum-so-lut-ing--
--hy-per-gob-ble in-tu-zib-ick--
GOOD GRACIOUS! WHAT'S THE MATTER NOW?
DON'T KNOW.
HIS THOUGHTS HAVE RUN DOWN. YOU'LL HAVE TO WIND UP HIS THOUGHTS, DOROTHY, OR I'LL HAVE TO FINISH HIS STORY MYSELF.
CREE-CREE--
Par-don me, but when my thoughts run down my speech has no mean-ing, for words are formed on-ly by thought.
I was a-bout to say that Oz-ma sent us to in-vite you straight to the Em-er-ald Ci-ty.
She was too bu-sy to come her-self. She is pre-par-ing for her birth-day ce-le-bra-tion.

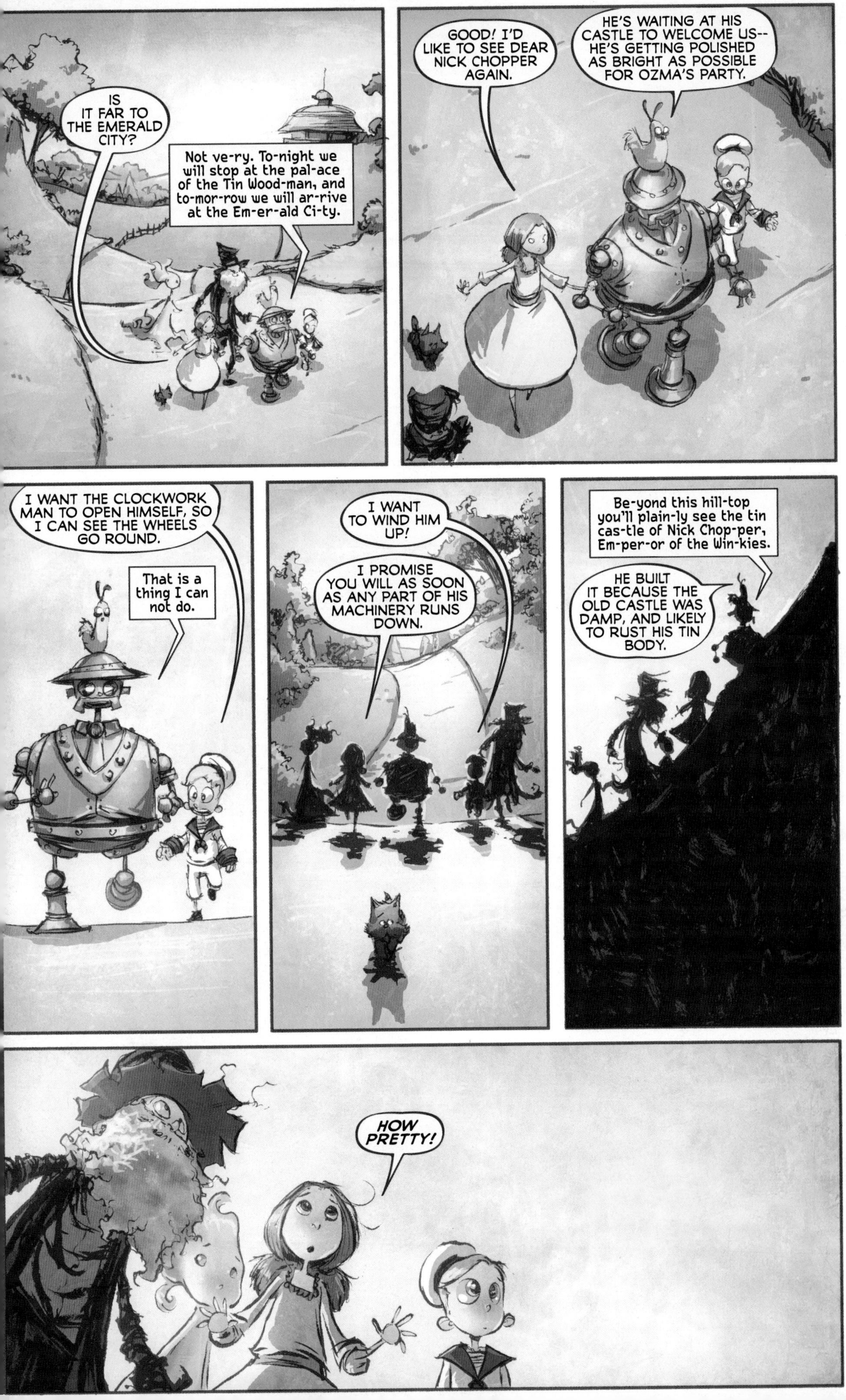
IS IT FAR TO THE EMERALD CITY?
Not ve-ry. To-night we will stop at the pal-ace of the Tin Wood-man, and to-mor-row we will ar-rive at the Em-er-ald Ci-ty.
GOOD! I'D LIKE TO SEE DEAR NICK CHOPPER AGAIN.
HE'S WAITING AT HIS CASTLE TO WELCOME US-- HE'S GETTING POLISHED AS BRIGHT AS POSSIBLE FOR OZMA'S PARTY.
I WANT THE CLOCKWORK MAN TO OPEN HIMSELF, SO I CAN SEE THE WHEELS GO ROUND.
That is a thing I can not do.
I WANT TO WIND HIM UP!
I PROMISE YOU WILL AS SOON AS ANY PART OF HIS MACHINERY RUNS DOWN.
Be-yond this hill-top you'll plain-ly see the tin cas-tle of Nick Chop-per, Em-per-or of the Win-kies.
HE BUILT IT BECAUSE THE OLD CASTLE WAS DAMP, AND LIKELY TO RUST HIS TIN BODY.
HOW PRETTY!

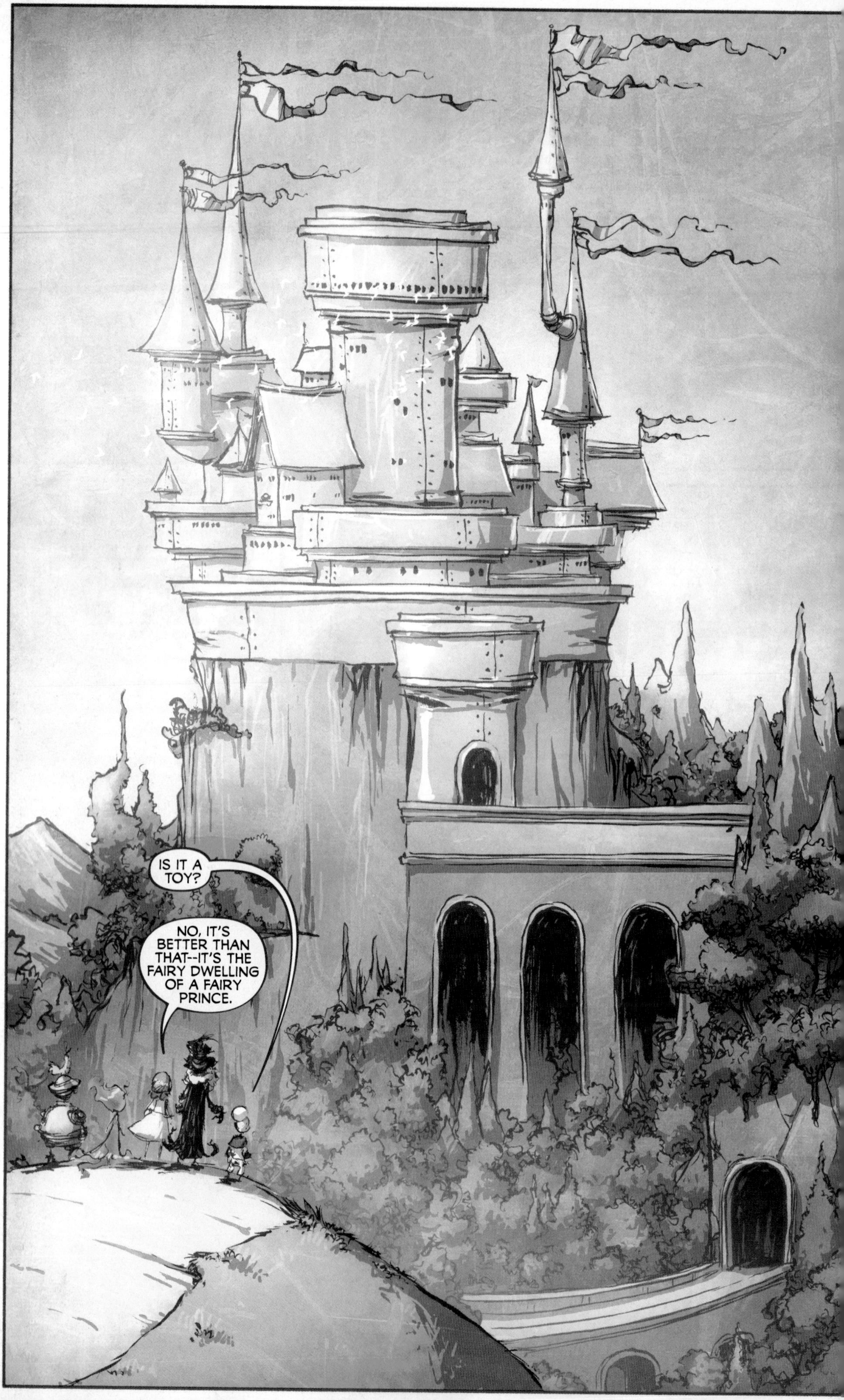
IS IT A TOY?
NO, IT'S BETTER THAN THAT--IT'S THE FAIRY DWELLING OF A FAIRY PRINCE.

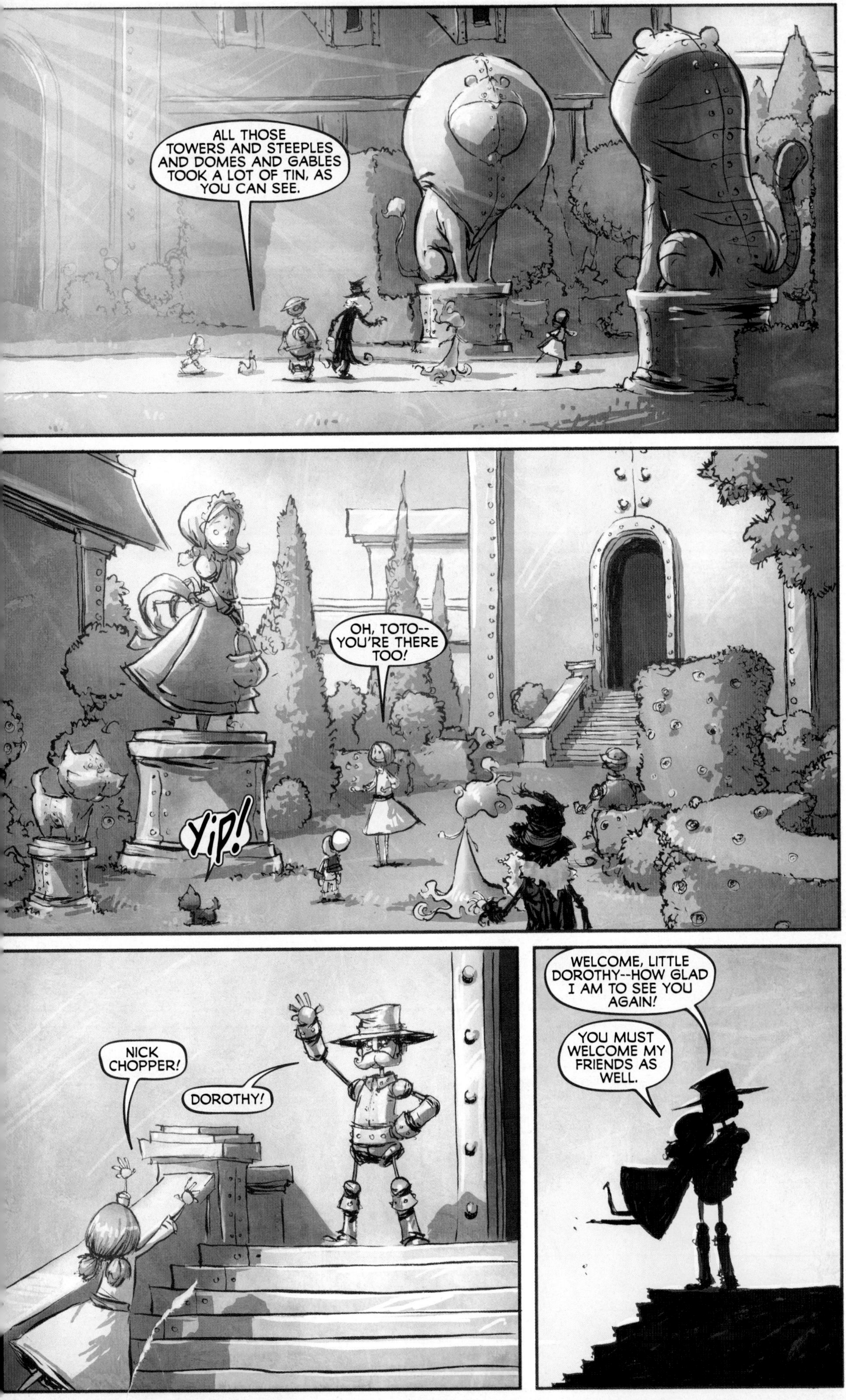
ALL THOSE TOWERS AND STEEPLES AND DOMES AND GABLES TOOK A LOT OF TIN, AS YOU CAN SEE.
OH, TOTO-- YOU'RE THERE TOO!
YIP!
NICK CHOPPER!
DOROTHY!
WELCOME, LITTLE DOROTHY--HOW GLAD I AM TO SEE YOU AGAIN!
YOU MUST WELCOME MY FRIENDS AS WELL.

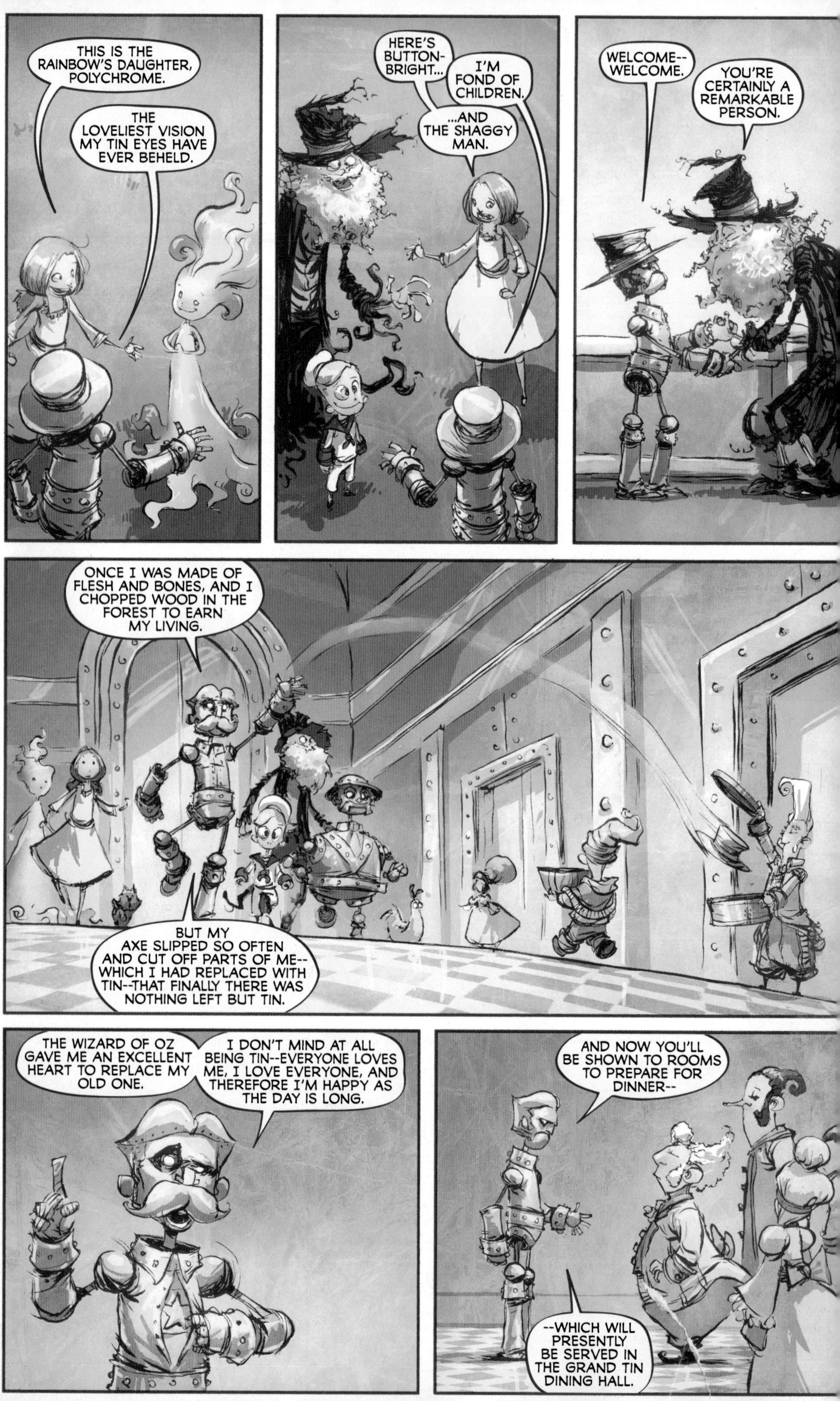
THIS IS THE RAINBOW'S DAUGHTER, POLYCHROME.
THE LOVELIEST VISION MY TIN EYES HAVE EVER BEHELD.
HERE'S BUTTON-BRIGHT...
I'M FOND OF CHILDREN.
...AND THE SHAGGY MAN.
WELCOME-- WELCOME.
YOU'RE CERTAINLY A REMARKABLE PERSON.
ONCE I WAS MADE OF FLESH AND BONES, AND I CHOPPED WOOD IN THE FOREST TO EARN MY LIVING.
BUT MY AXE SLIPPED SO OFTEN AND CUT OFF PARTS OF ME--WHICH I HAD REPLACED WITH TIN--THAT FINALLY THERE WAS NOTHING LEFT BUT TIN.
THE WIZARD OF OZ GAVE ME AN EXCELLENT HEART TO REPLACE MY OLD ONE.
I DON'T MIND AT ALL BEING TIN--EVERYONE LOVES ME, I LOVE EVERYONE, AND THEREFORE I'M HAPPY AS THE DAY IS LONG.
AND NOW YOU'LL BE SHOWN TO ROOMS TO PREPARE FOR DINNER--
--WHICH WILL PRESENTLY BE SERVED IN THE GRAND TIN DINING HALL.

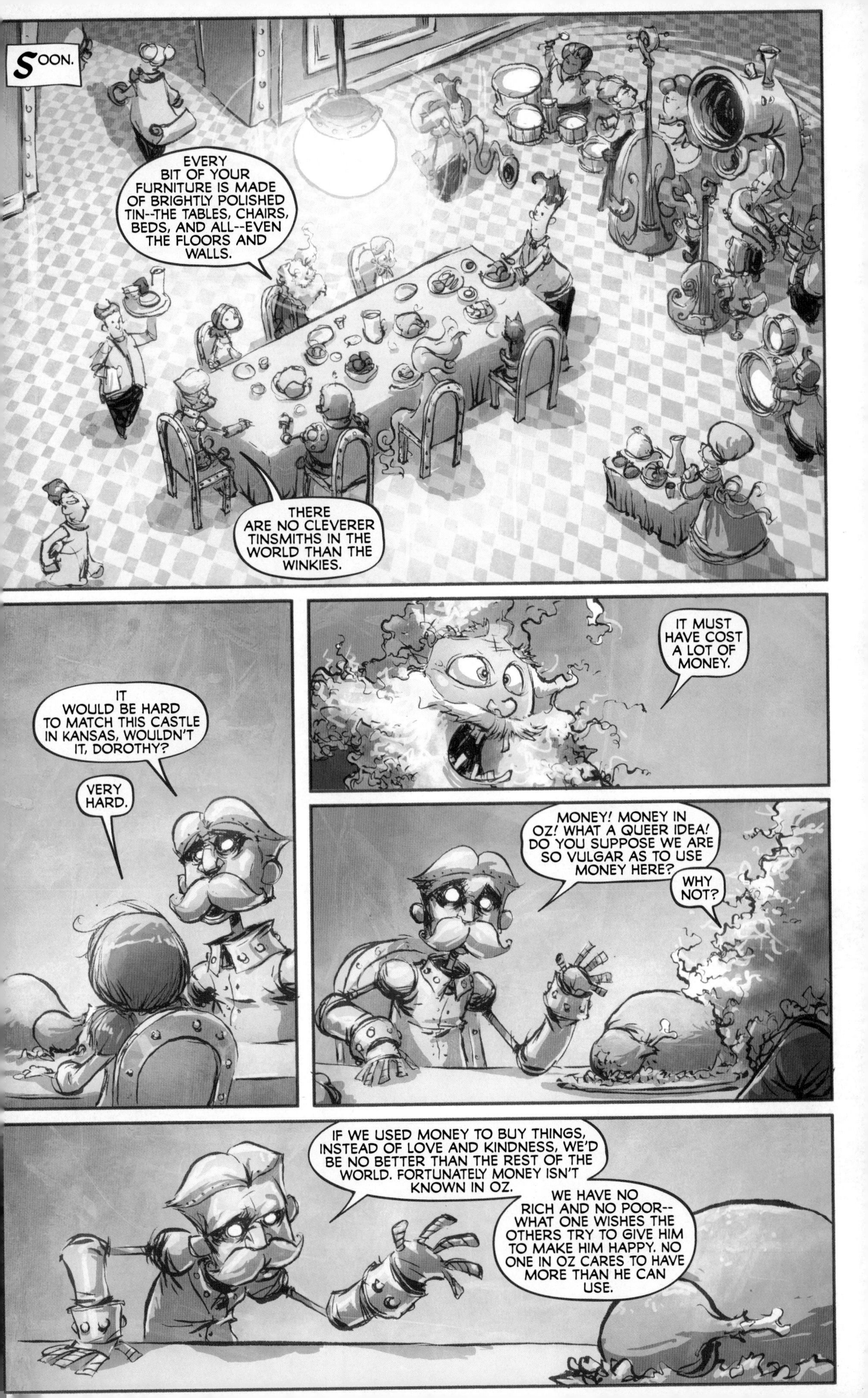
SOON.
EVERY BIT OF YOUR FURNITURE IS MADE OF BRIGHTLY POLISHED TIN--THE TABLES, CHAIRS, BEDS, AND ALL--EVEN THE FLOORS AND WALLS.
THERE ARE NO CLEVERER TINSMITHS IN THE WORLD THAN THE WINKIES.
IT WOULD BE HARD TO MATCH THIS CASTLE IN KANSAS, WOULDN'T IT, DOROTHY?
VERY HARD.
IT MUST HAVE COST A LOT OF MONEY.
MONEY! MONEY IN OZ! WHAT A QUEER IDEA! DO YOU SUPPOSE WE ARE SO VULGAR AS TO USE MONEY HERE?
WHY NOT?
IF WE USED MONEY TO BUY THINGS, INSTEAD OF LOVE AND KINDNESS, WE'D BE NO BETTER THAN THE REST OF THE WORLD. FORTUNATELY MONEY ISN'T KNOWN IN OZ.
WE HAVE NO RICH AND NO POOR--WHAT ONE WISHES THE OTHERS TRY TO GIVE HIM TO MAKE HIM HAPPY. NO ONE IN OZ CARES TO HAVE MORE THAN HE CAN USE.

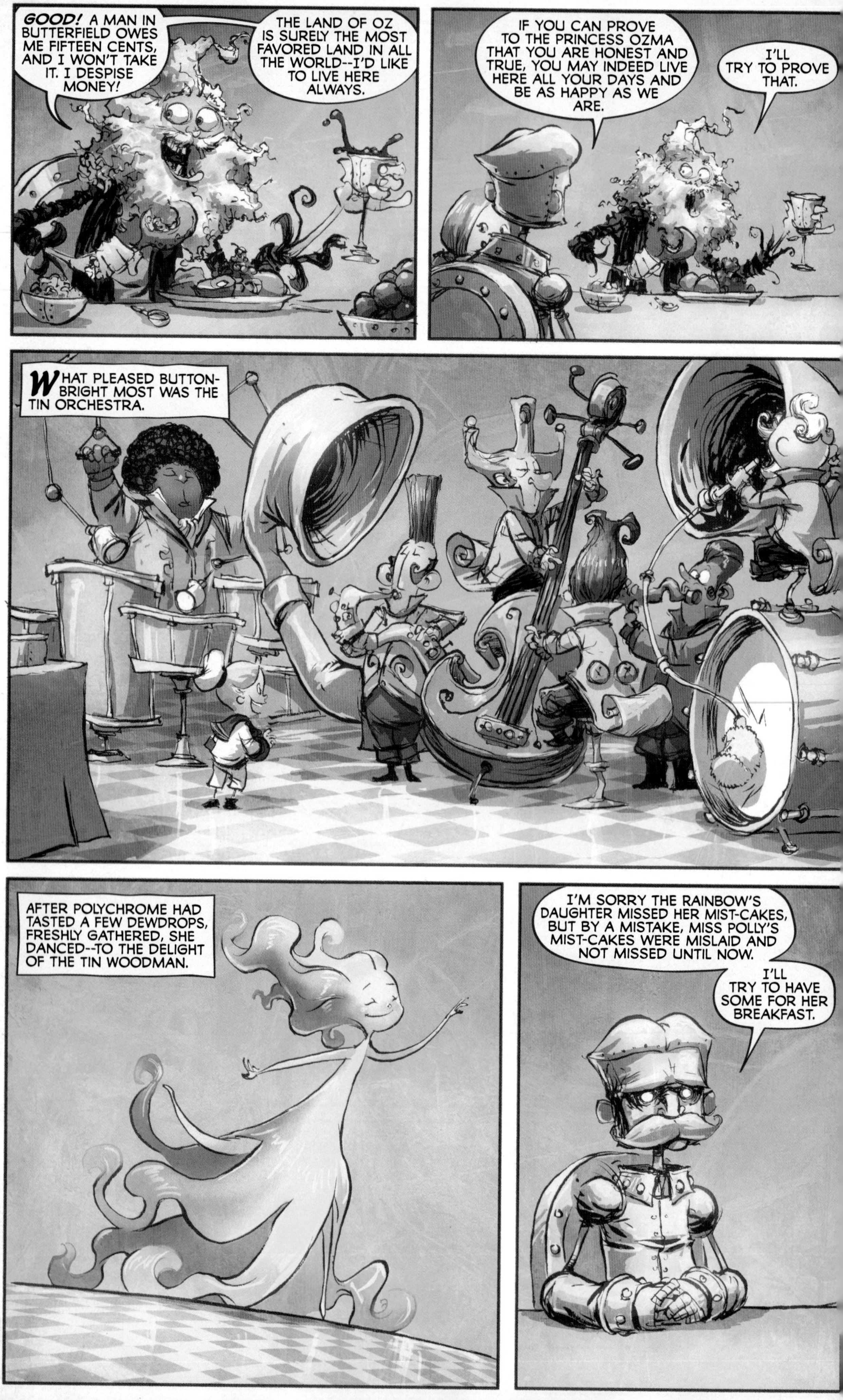
GOOD! A MAN IN BUTTERFIELD OWES ME FIFTEEN CENTS, AND I WON'T TAKE IT. I DESPISE MONEY!
THE LAND OF OZ IS SURELY THE MOST FAVORED LAND IN ALL THE WORLD--I'D LIKE TO LIVE HERE ALWAYS.
IF YOU CAN PROVE TO THE PRINCESS OZMA THAT YOU ARE HONEST AND TRUE, YOU MAY INDEED LIVE HERE ALL YOUR DAYS AND BE AS HAPPY AS WE ARE.
I'LL TRY TO PROVE THAT.
WHAT PLEASED BUTTON-BRIGHT MOST WAS THE TIN ORCHESTRA.
AFTER POLYCHROME HAD TASTED A FEW DEWDROPS, FRESHLY GATHERED, SHE DANCED--TO THE DELIGHT OF THE TIN WOODMAN.
I'M SORRY THE RAINBOW'S DAUGHTER MISSED HER MIST-CAKES, BUT BY A MISTAKE, MISS POLLY'S MIST-CAKES WERE MISLAID AND NOT MISSED UNTIL NOW.
I'LL TRY TO HAVE SOME FOR HER BREAKFAST.

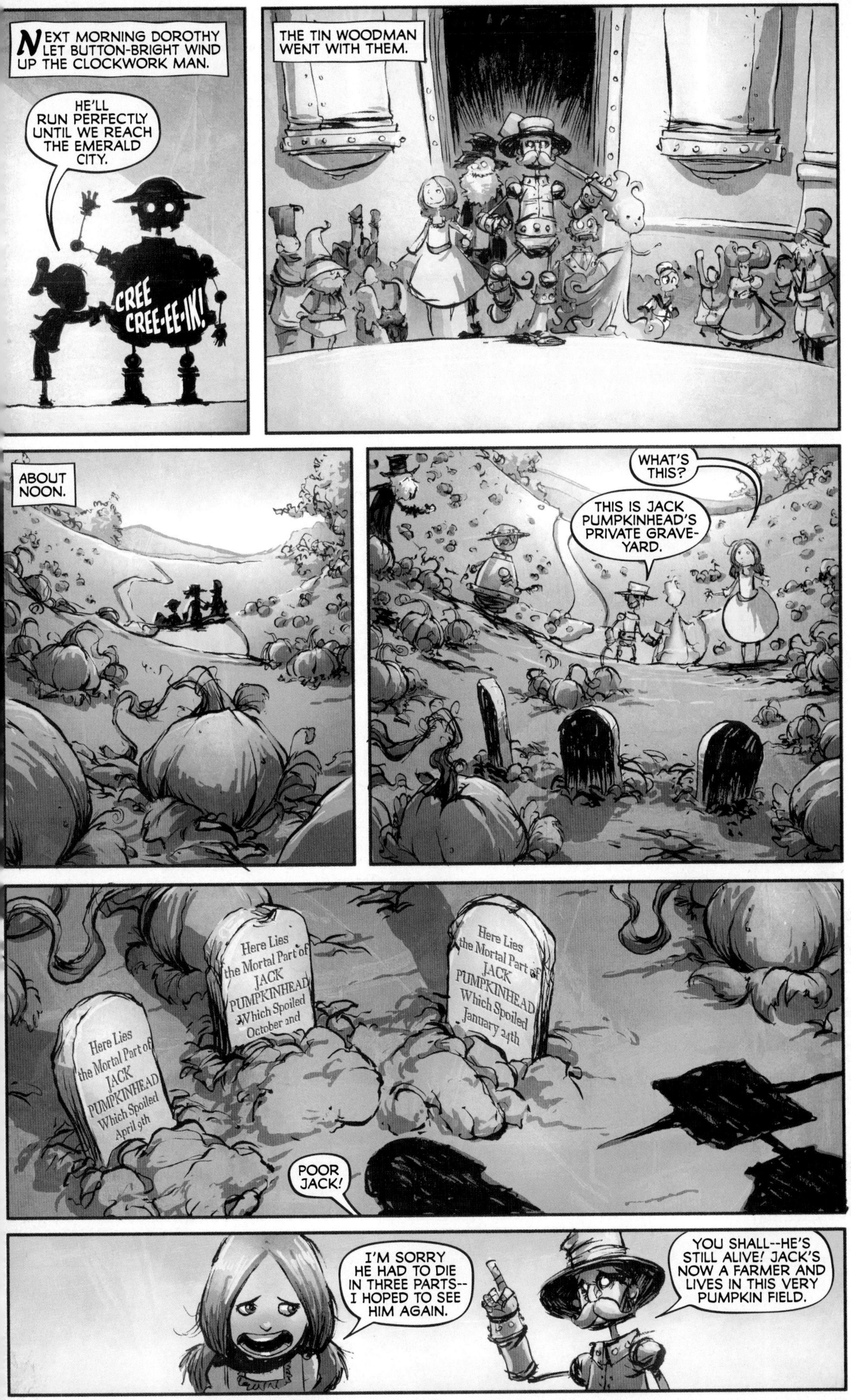
NEXT MORNING DOROTHY LET BUTTON-BRIGHT WIND UP THE CLOCKWORK MAN.
HE'LL RUN PERFECTLY UNTIL WE REACH THE EMERALD CITY.
CREE CREE-EE-IK!
THE TIN WOODMAN WENT WITH THEM.
ABOUT NOON.
WHAT'S THIS?
THIS IS JACK PUMPKINHEAD'S PRIVATE GRAVE-YARD.
Here Lies the Mortal Part of JACK PUMPKINHEAD Which Spoiled April 9th
Here Lies the Mortal Part of JACK PUMPKINHEAD Which Spoiled October 2nd
Here Lies the Mortal Part of JACK PUMPKINHEAD Which Spoiled January 24th
POOR JACK!
I'M SORRY HE HAD TO DIE IN THREE PARTS-- I HOPED TO SEE HIM AGAIN.
YOU SHALL--HE'S STILL ALIVE! JACK'S NOW A FARMER AND LIVES IN THIS VERY PUMPKIN FIELD.

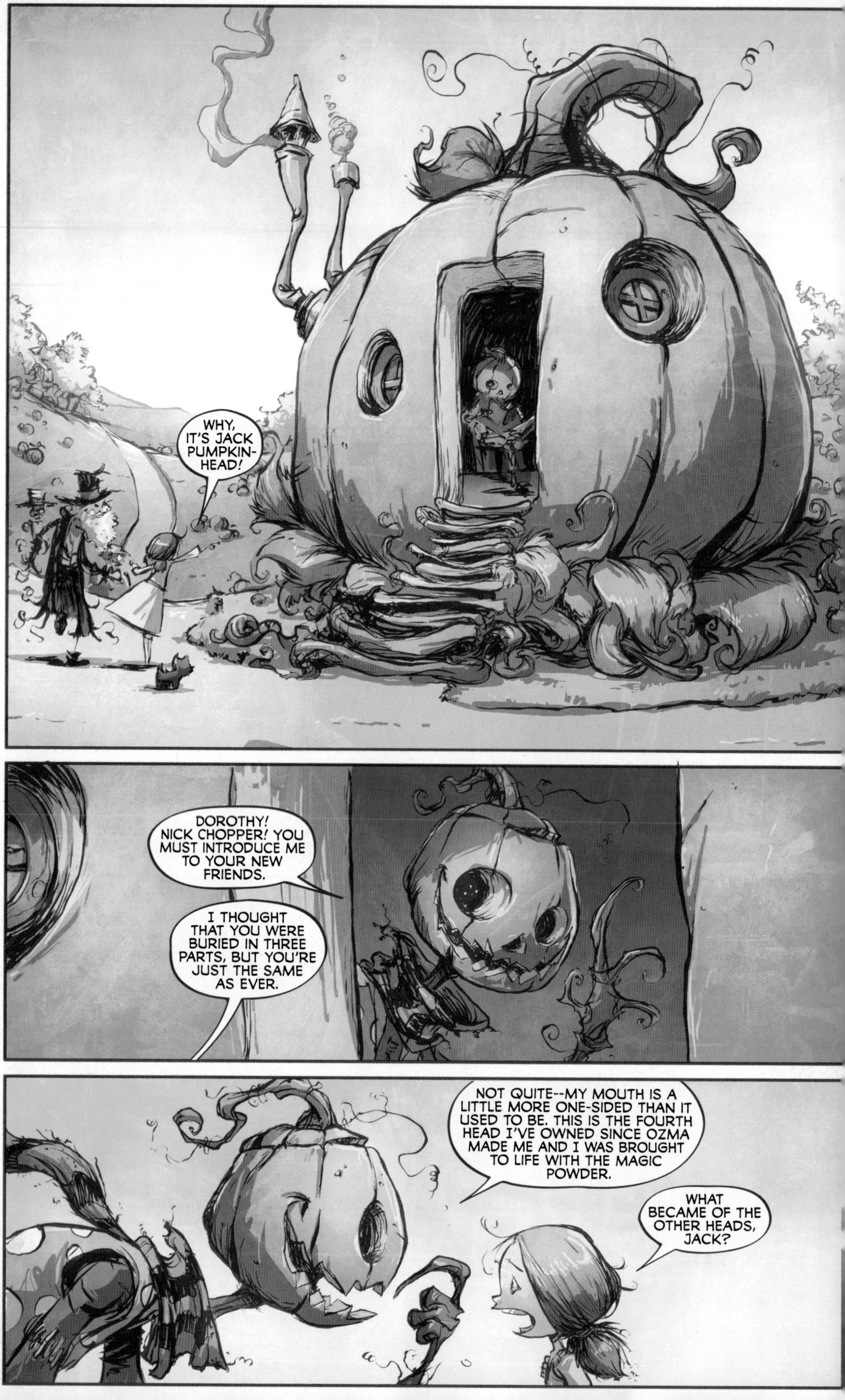
WHY, IT'S JACK PUMPKIN-HEAD!
DOROTHY! NICK CHOPPER! YOU MUST INTRODUCE ME TO YOUR NEW FRIENDS.
I THOUGHT THAT YOU WERE BURIED IN THREE PARTS, BUT YOU'RE JUST THE SAME AS EVER.
NOT QUITE--MY MOUTH IS A LITTLE MORE ONE-SIDED THAN IT USED TO BE. THIS IS THE FOURTH HEAD I'VE OWNED SINCE OZMA MADE ME AND I WAS BROUGHT TO LIFE WITH THE MAGIC POWDER.
WHAT BECAME OF THE OTHER HEADS, JACK?

"THEY SPOILED AND I BURIED THEM, FOR THEY WEREN'T EVEN FIT FOR PIES, BUT EACH TIME OZMA HAS CARVED ME A NEW HEAD."

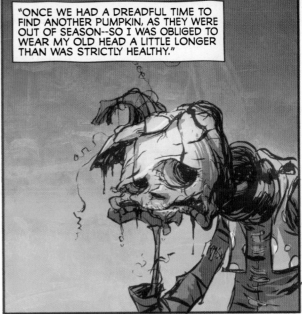

"ONCE WE HAD A DREADFUL TIME TO FIND ANOTHER PUMPKIN, AS THEY WERE OUT OF SEASON--SO I WAS OBLIGED TO WEAR MY OLD HEAD A LITTLE LONGER THAN WAS STRICTLY HEALTHY."

AFTER THIS SAD EXPERIENCE I RESOLVED TO RAISE PUMPKINS, SO AS NEVER TO BE CAUGHT WITHOUT ONE HANDY. NOW I HAVE THIS FINE FIELD.

SOME GROW PRETTY BIG, SO I DUG OUT ONE AND USE IT FOR A HOUSE.

ISN'T IT DAMP?

NOT VERY. THERE ISN'T MUCH LEFT BUT THE SHELL, AND IT WILL LAST A LONG TIME.

I THINK YOU ARE BRIGHTER THAN YOU USED TO BE, JACK. YOUR LAST HEAD WAS A STUPID ONE.

THE SEEDS IN THIS ONE ARE BETTER.

ARE YOU GOING TO OZMA'S PARTY?

I WOULDN'T MISS IT--OZMA'S MY PARENT BECAUSE SHE BUILT ME.

TODAY I HAVE TO WATER THE YOUNG VINES-- BUT TELL OZMA I'LL BE THERE TOMORROW.

*T*HEY RESUMED THEIR JOURNEY.

WHAT SORT OF MAGIC POWDER MADE THE PUMPKINHEAD LIVE?

IT WAS CALLED THE POWDER OF LIFE, INVENTED BY A CROOKED SORCERER WHO LIVED IN THE NORTH COUNTRY.

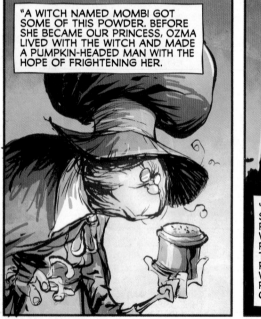

"A WITCH NAMED MOMBI GOT SOME OF THIS POWDER. BEFORE SHE BECAME OUR PRINCESS, OZMA LIVED WITH THE WITCH AND MADE A PUMPKIN-HEADED MAN WITH THE HOPE OF FRIGHTENING HER.

"BUT MOMBI SPRINKLED THE PUMPKINHEAD WITH THE MAGIC POWDER OF LIFE, TO SEE IF THE POWDER WOULD WORK, AND THE PUMPKINHEAD CAME TO LIFE.

"OZMA RAN AWAY WITH THE POWDER AND JACK. THEY FOUND A WOODEN SAWHORSE AND SPRINKLED IT WITH THE POWDER, AND USED THE LAST OF THE POWDER TO BRING THE FLYING GUMP TO LIFE."

THE POWDER OF LIFE WOULD BE A HANDY THING TO HAVE AROUND.

I'M NOT SO SURE OF THAT.

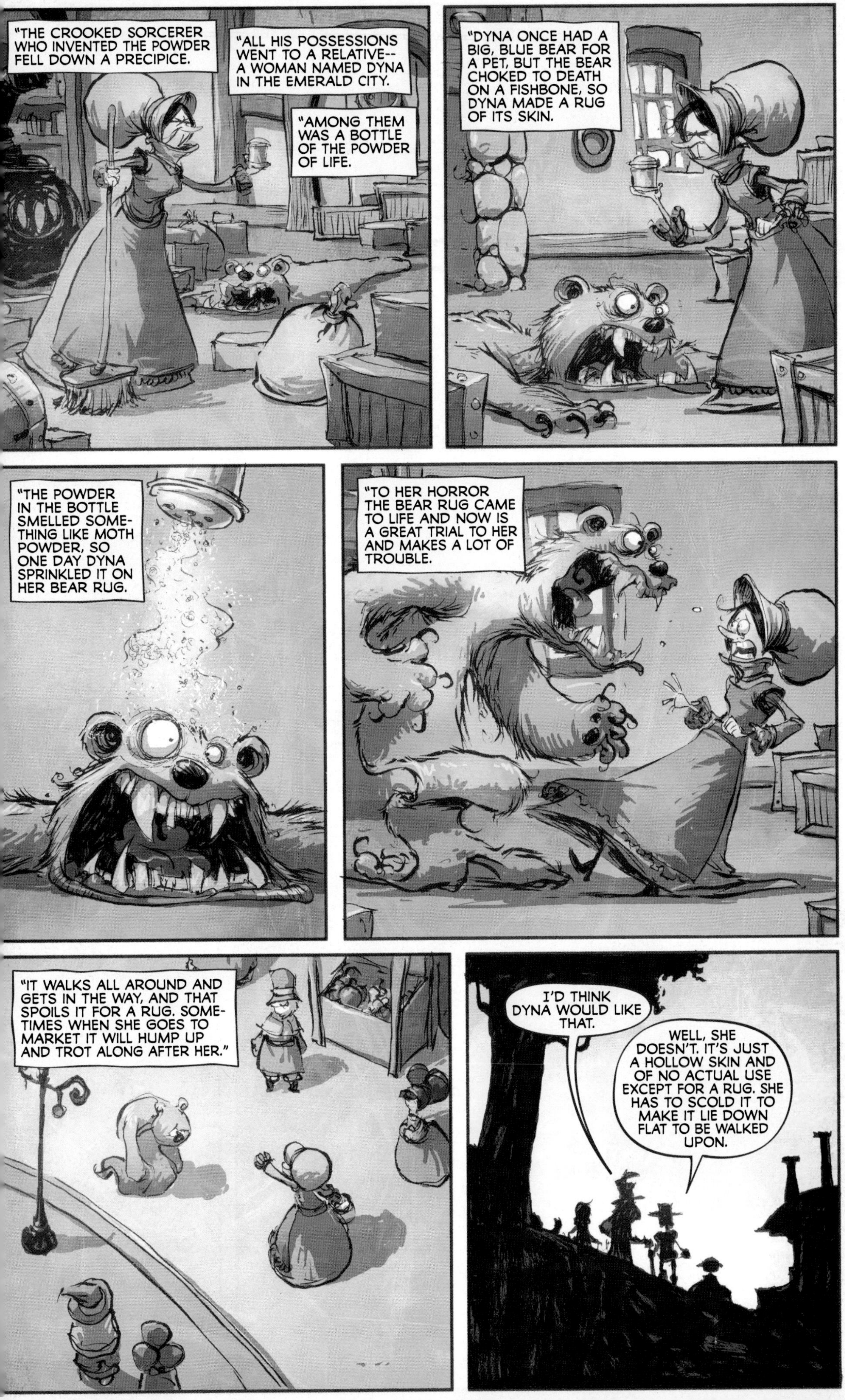
"THE CROOKED SORCERER WHO INVENTED THE POWDER FELL DOWN A PRECIPICE.
"ALL HIS POSSESSIONS WENT TO A RELATIVE-- A WOMAN NAMED DYNA IN THE EMERALD CITY.
"AMONG THEM WAS A BOTTLE OF THE POWDER OF LIFE.
"DYNA ONCE HAD A BIG, BLUE BEAR FOR A PET, BUT THE BEAR CHOKED TO DEATH ON A FISHBONE, SO DYNA MADE A RUG OF ITS SKIN.
"THE POWDER IN THE BOTTLE SMELLED SOMETHING LIKE MOTH POWDER, SO ONE DAY DYNA SPRINKLED IT ON HER BEAR RUG.
"TO HER HORROR THE BEAR RUG CAME TO LIFE AND NOW IS A GREAT TRIAL TO HER AND MAKES A LOT OF TROUBLE.
"IT WALKS ALL AROUND AND GETS IN THE WAY, AND THAT SPOILS IT FOR A RUG. SOMETIMES WHEN SHE GOES TO MARKET IT WILL HUMP UP AND TROT ALONG AFTER HER."
I'D THINK DYNA WOULD LIKE THAT.
WELL, SHE DOESN'T. IT'S JUST A HOLLOW SKIN AND OF NO ACTUAL USE EXCEPT FOR A RUG. SHE HAS TO SCOLD IT TO MAKE IT LIE DOWN FLAT TO BE WALKED UPON.

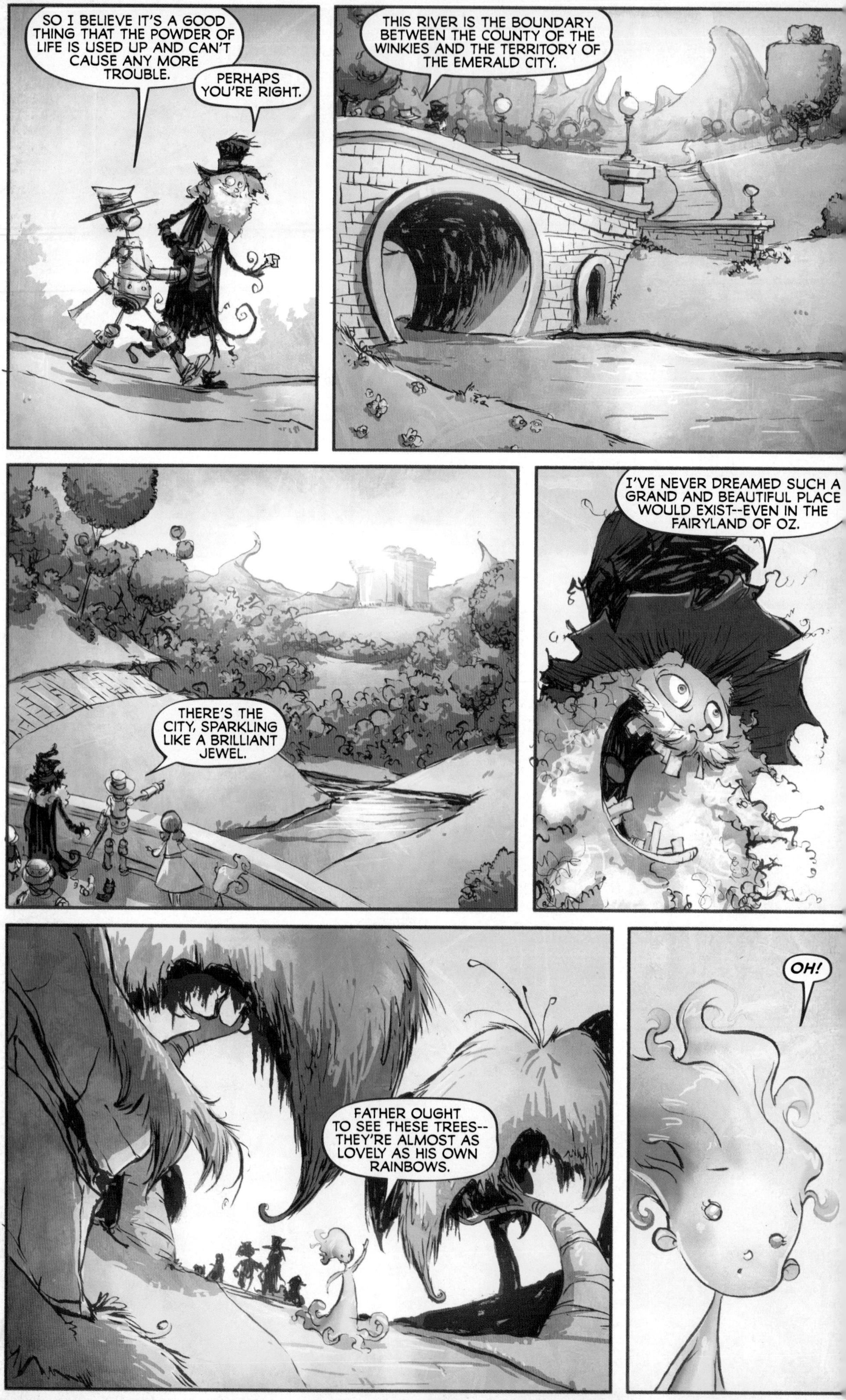

SO I BELIEVE IT'S A GOOD THING THAT THE POWDER OF LIFE IS USED UP AND CAN'T CAUSE ANY MORE TROUBLE.
PERHAPS YOU'RE RIGHT.
THIS RIVER IS THE BOUNDARY BETWEEN THE COUNTY OF THE WINKIES AND THE TERRITORY OF THE EMERALD CITY.
THERE'S THE CITY, SPARKLING LIKE A BRILLIANT JEWEL.
I'VE NEVER DREAMED SUCH A GRAND AND BEAUTIFUL PLACE WOULD EXIST--EVEN IN THE FAIRYLAND OF OZ.
FATHER OUGHT TO SEE THESE TREES-- THEY'RE ALMOST AS LOVELY AS HIS OWN RAINBOWS.
OH!

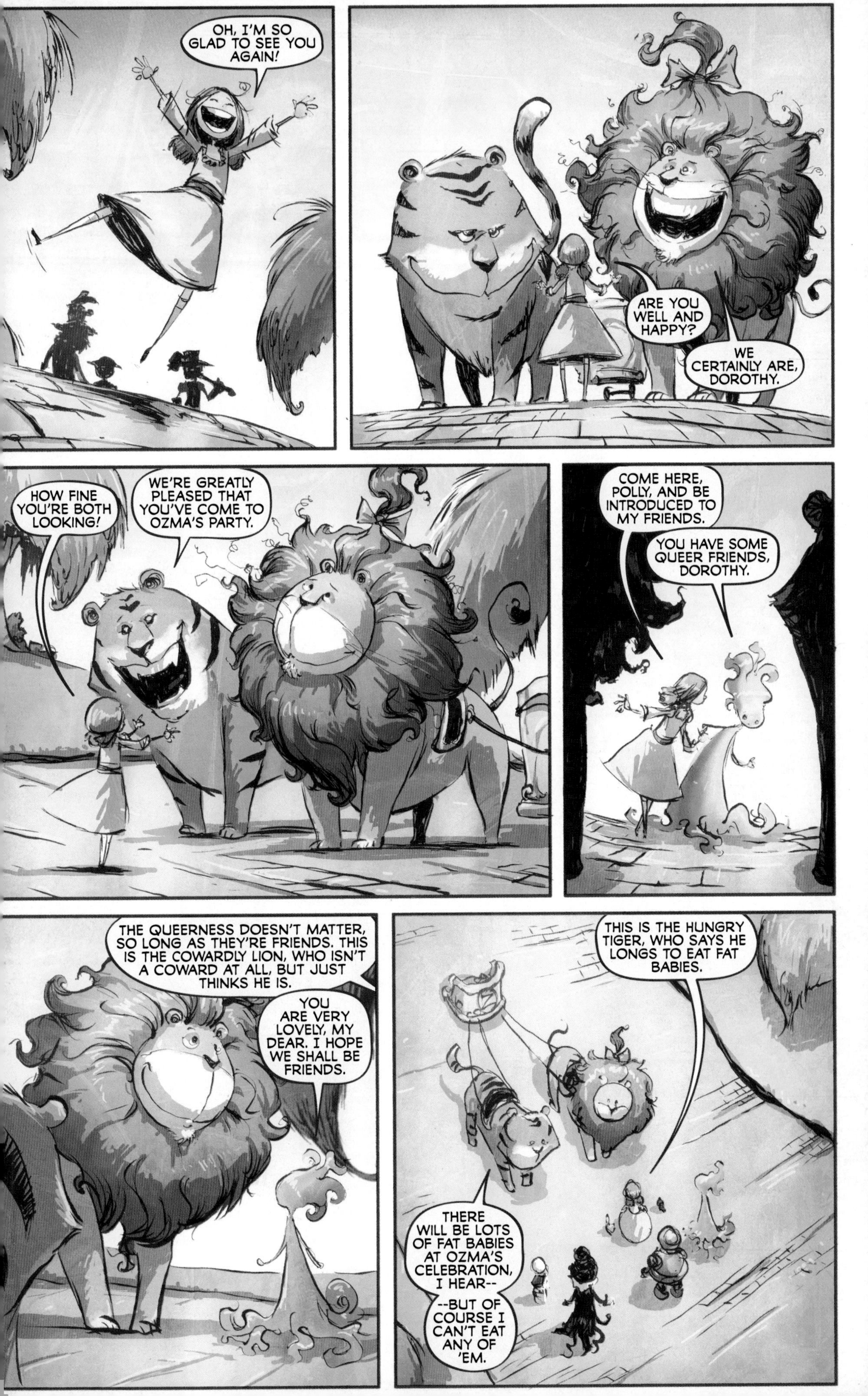
OH, I'M SO GLAD TO SEE YOU AGAIN!
ARE YOU WELL AND HAPPY?
WE CERTAINLY ARE, DOROTHY.
HOW FINE YOU'RE BOTH LOOKING!
WE'RE GREATLY PLEASED THAT YOU'VE COME TO OZMA'S PARTY.
COME HERE, POLLY, AND BE INTRODUCED TO MY FRIENDS.
YOU HAVE SOME QUEER FRIENDS, DOROTHY.
THE QUEERNESS DOESN'T MATTER, SO LONG AS THEY'RE FRIENDS. THIS IS THE COWARDLY LION, WHO ISN'T A COWARD AT ALL, BUT JUST THINKS HE IS.
YOU ARE VERY LOVELY, MY DEAR. I HOPE WE SHALL BE FRIENDS.
THIS IS THE HUNGRY TIGER, WHO SAYS HE LONGS TO EAT FAT BABIES.
THERE WILL BE LOTS OF FAT BABIES AT OZMA'S CELEBRATION, I HEAR--
--BUT OF COURSE I CAN'T EAT ANY OF 'EM.

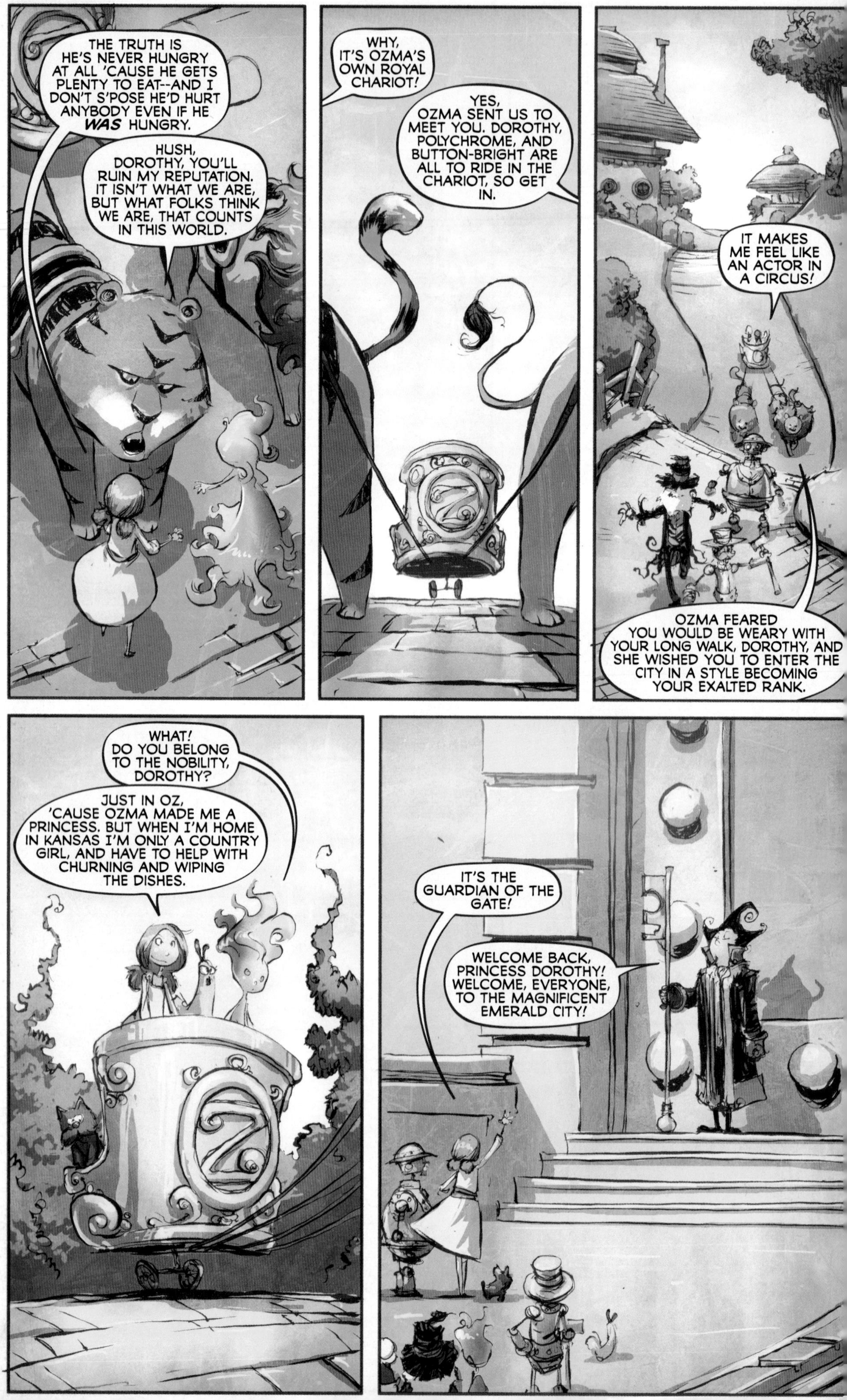
THE TRUTH IS HE'S NEVER HUNGRY AT ALL 'CAUSE HE GETS PLENTY TO EAT--AND I DON'T S'POSE HE'D HURT ANYBODY EVEN IF HE ***WAS*** HUNGRY.
HUSH, DOROTHY, YOU'LL RUIN MY REPUTATION. IT ISN'T WHAT WE ARE, BUT WHAT FOLKS THINK WE ARE, THAT COUNTS IN THIS WORLD.
WHY, IT'S OZMA'S OWN ROYAL CHARIOT!
YES, OZMA SENT US TO MEET YOU. DOROTHY, POLYCHROME, AND BUTTON-BRIGHT ARE ALL TO RIDE IN THE CHARIOT, SO GET IN.
IT MAKES ME FEEL LIKE AN ACTOR IN A CIRCUS!
OZMA FEARED YOU WOULD BE WEARY WITH YOUR LONG WALK, DOROTHY, AND SHE WISHED YOU TO ENTER THE CITY IN A STYLE BECOMING YOUR EXALTED RANK.
WHAT! DO YOU BELONG TO THE NOBILITY, DOROTHY?
JUST IN OZ, 'CAUSE OZMA MADE ME A PRINCESS. BUT WHEN I'M HOME IN KANSAS I'M ONLY A COUNTRY GIRL, AND HAVE TO HELP WITH CHURNING AND WIPING THE DISHES.
IT'S THE GUARDIAN OF THE GATE!
WELCOME BACK, PRINCESS DOROTHY! WELCOME, EVERYONE, TO THE MAGNIFICENT EMERALD CITY!

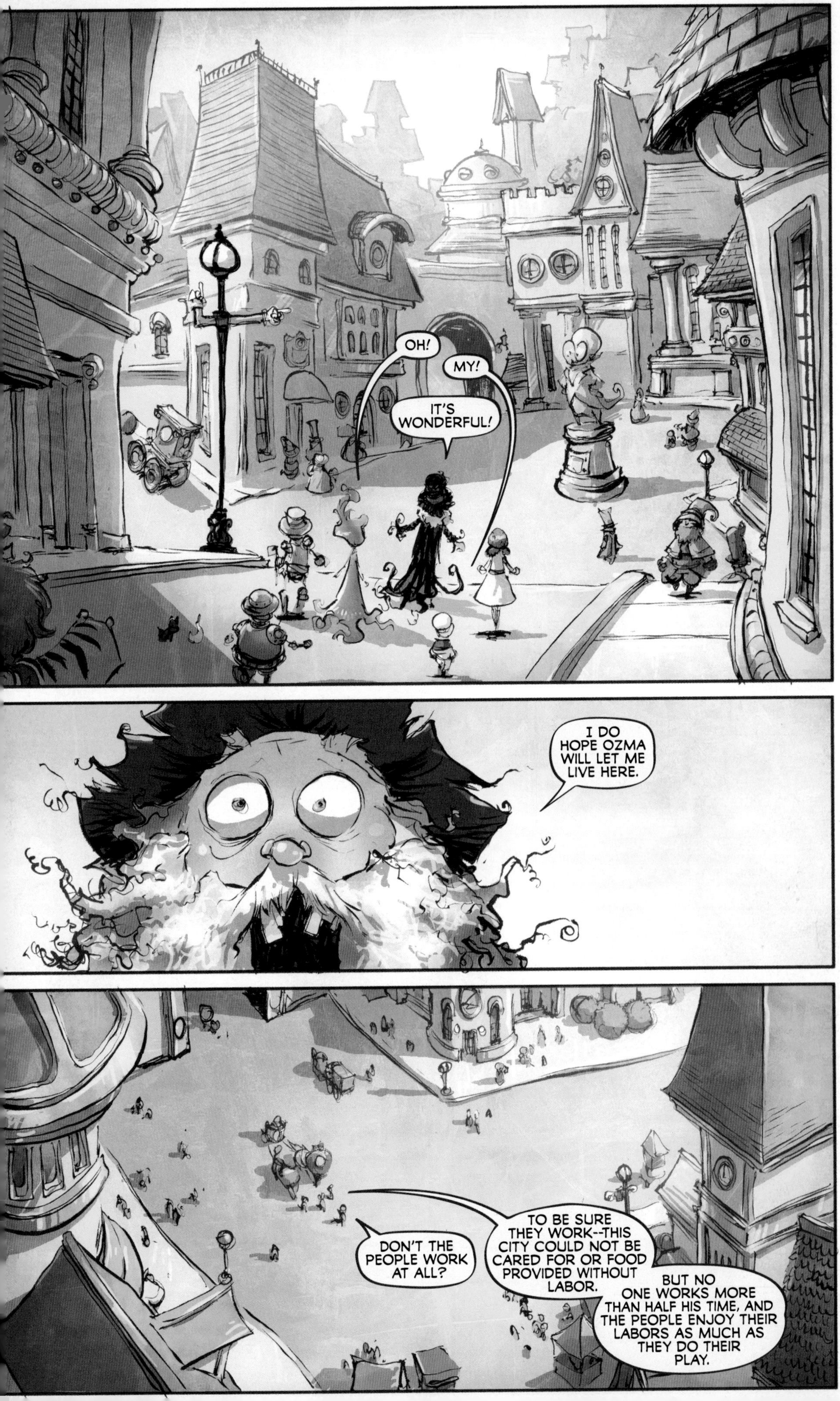
OH!
MY!
IT'S WONDERFUL!
I DO HOPE OZMA WILL LET ME LIVE HERE.
DON'T THE PEOPLE WORK AT ALL?
TO BE SURE THEY WORK--THIS CITY COULD NOT BE CARED FOR OR FOOD PROVIDED WITHOUT LABOR.
BUT NO ONE WORKS MORE THAN HALF HIS TIME, AND THE PEOPLE ENJOY THEIR LABORS AS MUCH AS THEY DO THEIR PLAY.

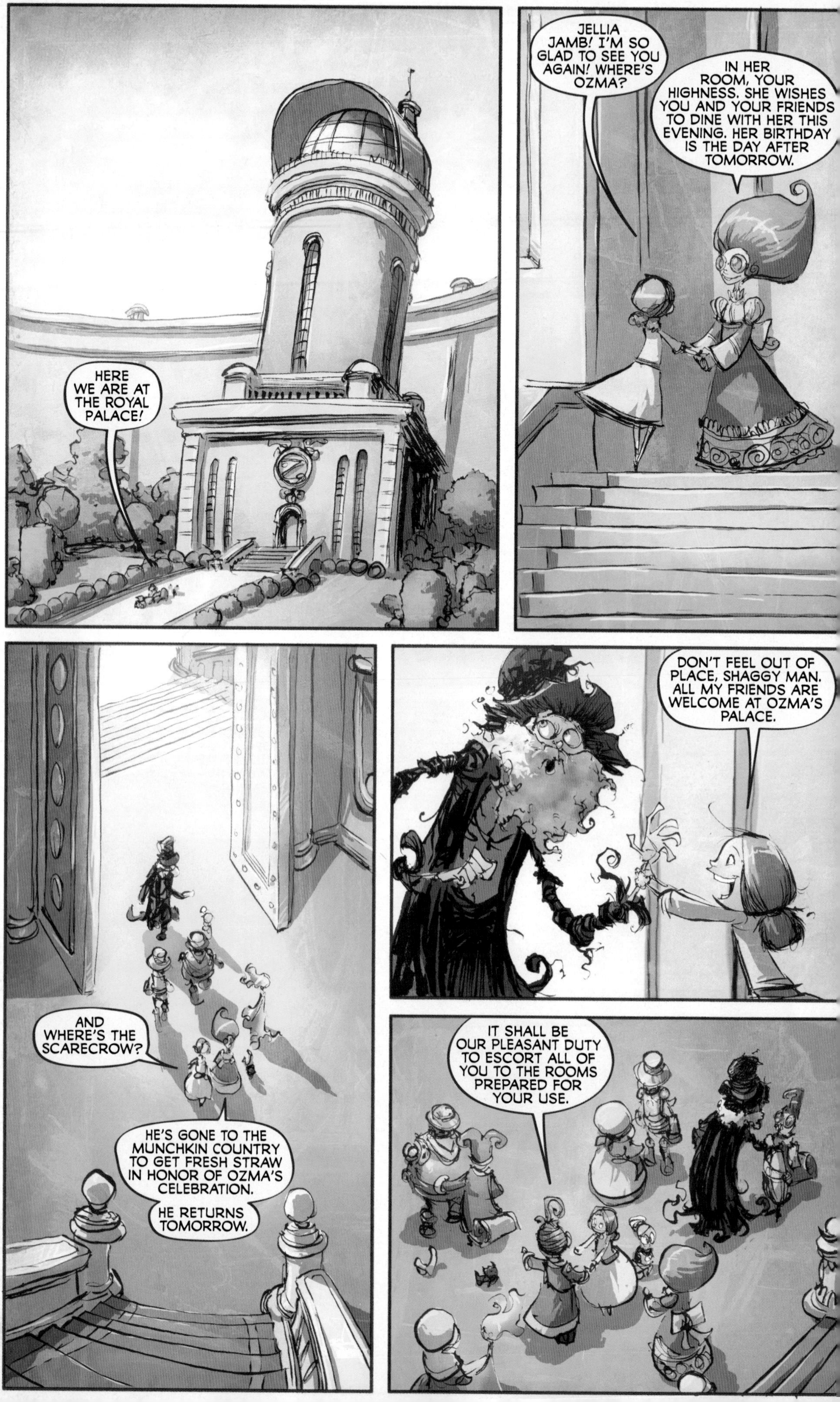
HERE WE ARE AT THE ROYAL PALACE!
JELLIA JAMB! I'M SO GLAD TO SEE YOU AGAIN! WHERE'S OZMA?
IN HER ROOM, YOUR HIGHNESS. SHE WISHES YOU AND YOUR FRIENDS TO DINE WITH HER THIS EVENING. HER BIRTHDAY IS THE DAY AFTER TOMORROW.
AND WHERE'S THE SCARECROW?
HE'S GONE TO THE MUNCHKIN COUNTRY TO GET FRESH STRAW IN HONOR OF OZMA'S CELEBRATION.
HE RETURNS TOMORROW.
DON'T FEEL OUT OF PLACE, SHAGGY MAN. ALL MY FRIENDS ARE WELCOME AT OZMA'S PALACE.
IT SHALL BE OUR PLEASANT DUTY TO ESCORT ALL OF YOU TO THE ROOMS PREPARED FOR YOUR USE.

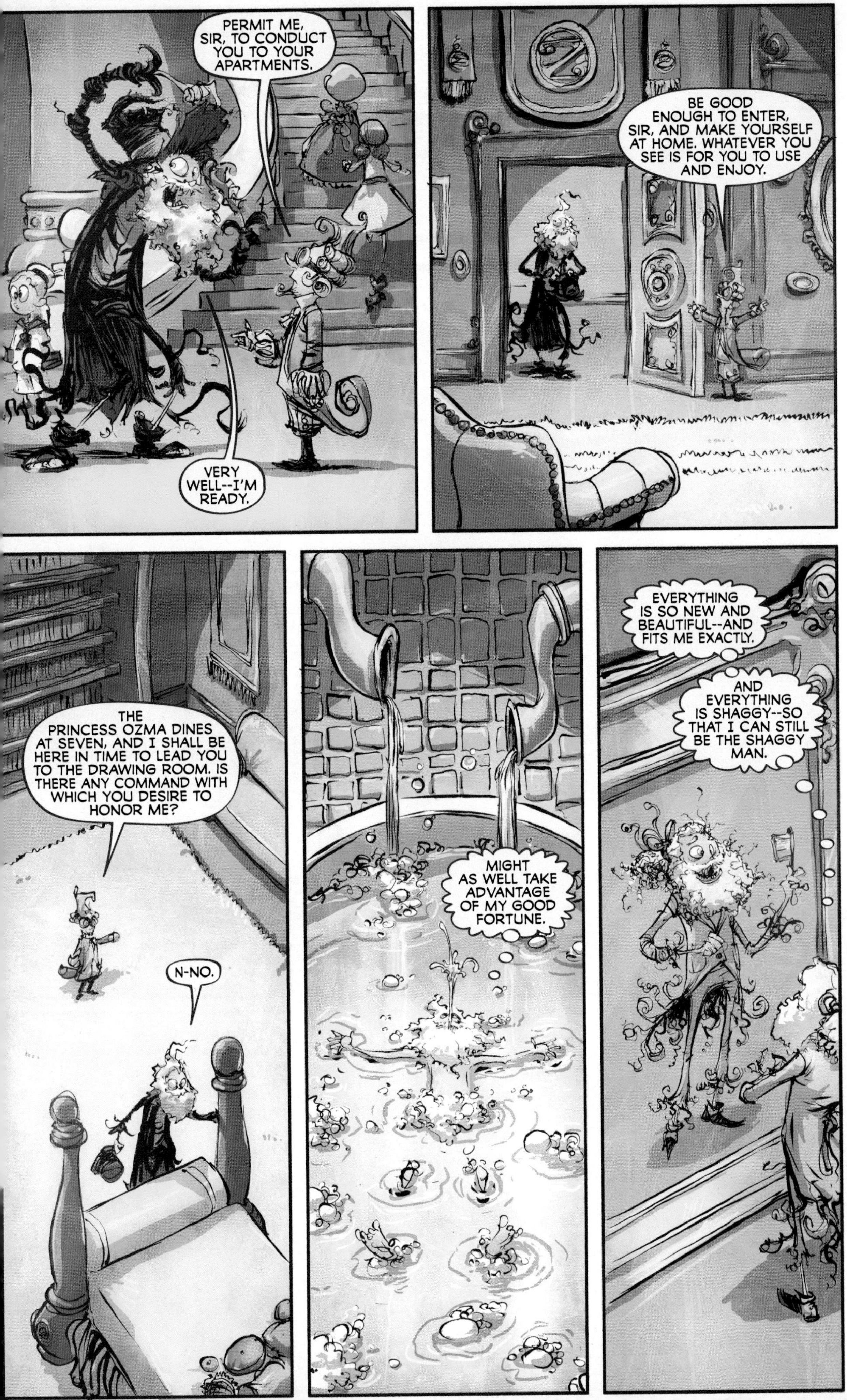
PERMIT ME, SIR, TO CONDUCT YOU TO YOUR APARTMENTS.
VERY WELL--I'M READY.
BE GOOD ENOUGH TO ENTER, SIR, AND MAKE YOURSELF AT HOME. WHATEVER YOU SEE IS FOR YOU TO USE AND ENJOY.
THE PRINCESS OZMA DINES AT SEVEN, AND I SHALL BE HERE IN TIME TO LEAD YOU TO THE DRAWING ROOM. IS THERE ANY COMMAND WITH WHICH YOU DESIRE TO HONOR ME?
N-NO.
MIGHT AS WELL TAKE ADVANTAGE OF MY GOOD FORTUNE.
EVERYTHING IS SO NEW AND BEAUTIFUL--AND FITS ME EXACTLY.
AND EVERYTHING IS SHAGGY--SO THAT I CAN STILL BE THE SHAGGY MAN.

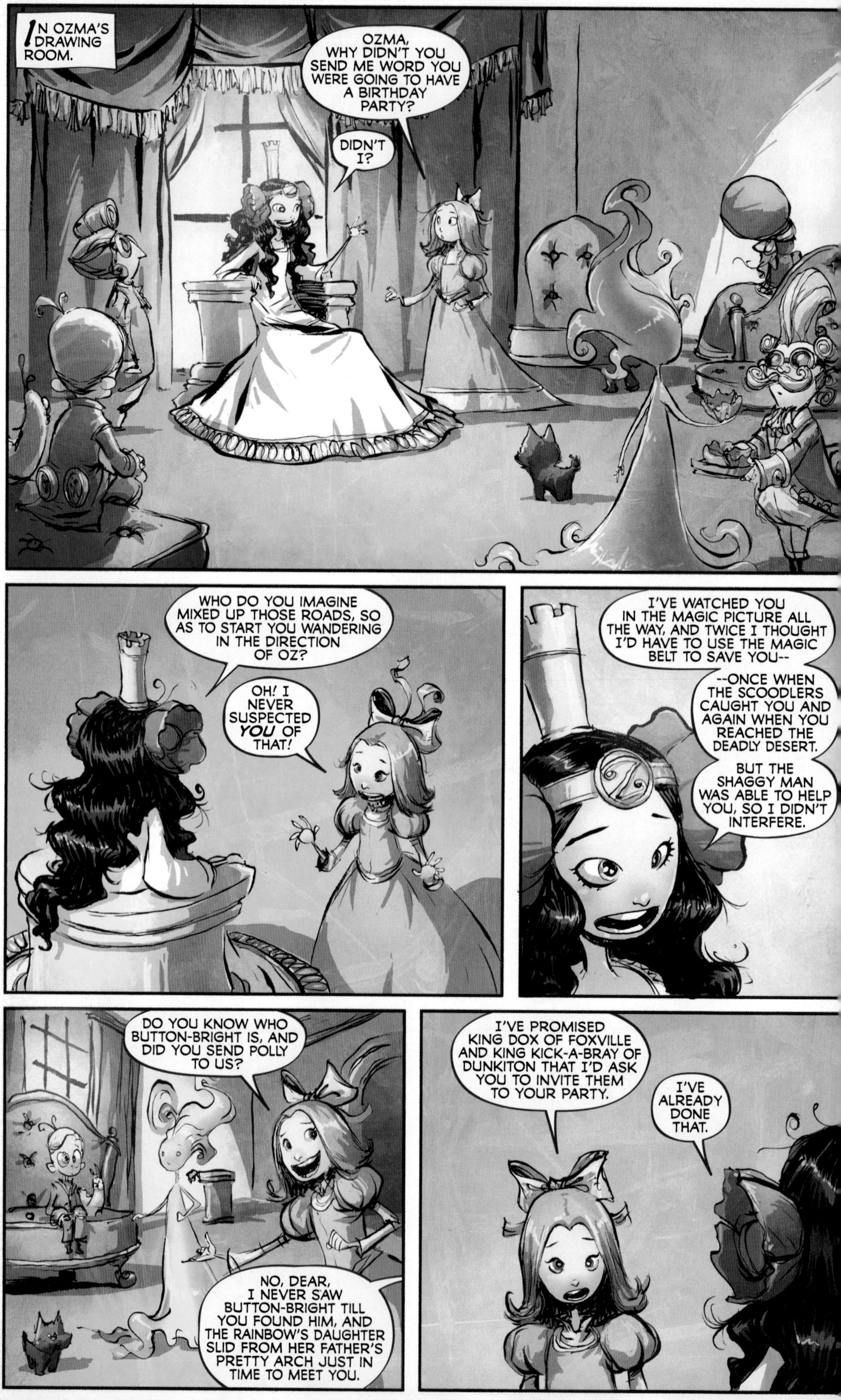
IN OZMA'S DRAWING ROOM.
OZMA, WHY DIDN'T YOU SEND ME WORD YOU WERE GOING TO HAVE A BIRTHDAY PARTY?
DIDN'T I?
WHO DO YOU IMAGINE MIXED UP THOSE ROADS, SO AS TO START YOU WANDERING IN THE DIRECTION OF OZ?
OH! I NEVER SUSPECTED *YOU* OF THAT!
I'VE WATCHED YOU IN THE MAGIC PICTURE ALL THE WAY, AND TWICE I THOUGHT I'D HAVE TO USE THE MAGIC BELT TO SAVE YOU--
--ONCE WHEN THE SCOODLERS CAUGHT YOU AND AGAIN WHEN YOU REACHED THE DEADLY DESERT.
BUT THE SHAGGY MAN WAS ABLE TO HELP YOU, SO I DIDN'T INTERFERE.
DO YOU KNOW WHO BUTTON-BRIGHT IS, AND DID YOU SEND POLLY TO US?
NO, DEAR, I NEVER SAW BUTTON-BRIGHT TILL YOU FOUND HIM, AND THE RAINBOW'S DAUGHTER SLID FROM HER FATHER'S PRETTY ARCH JUST IN TIME TO MEET YOU.
I'VE PROMISED KING DOX OF FOXVILLE AND KING KICK-A-BRAY OF DUNKITON THAT I'D ASK YOU TO INVITE THEM TO YOUR PARTY.
I'VE ALREADY DONE THAT.

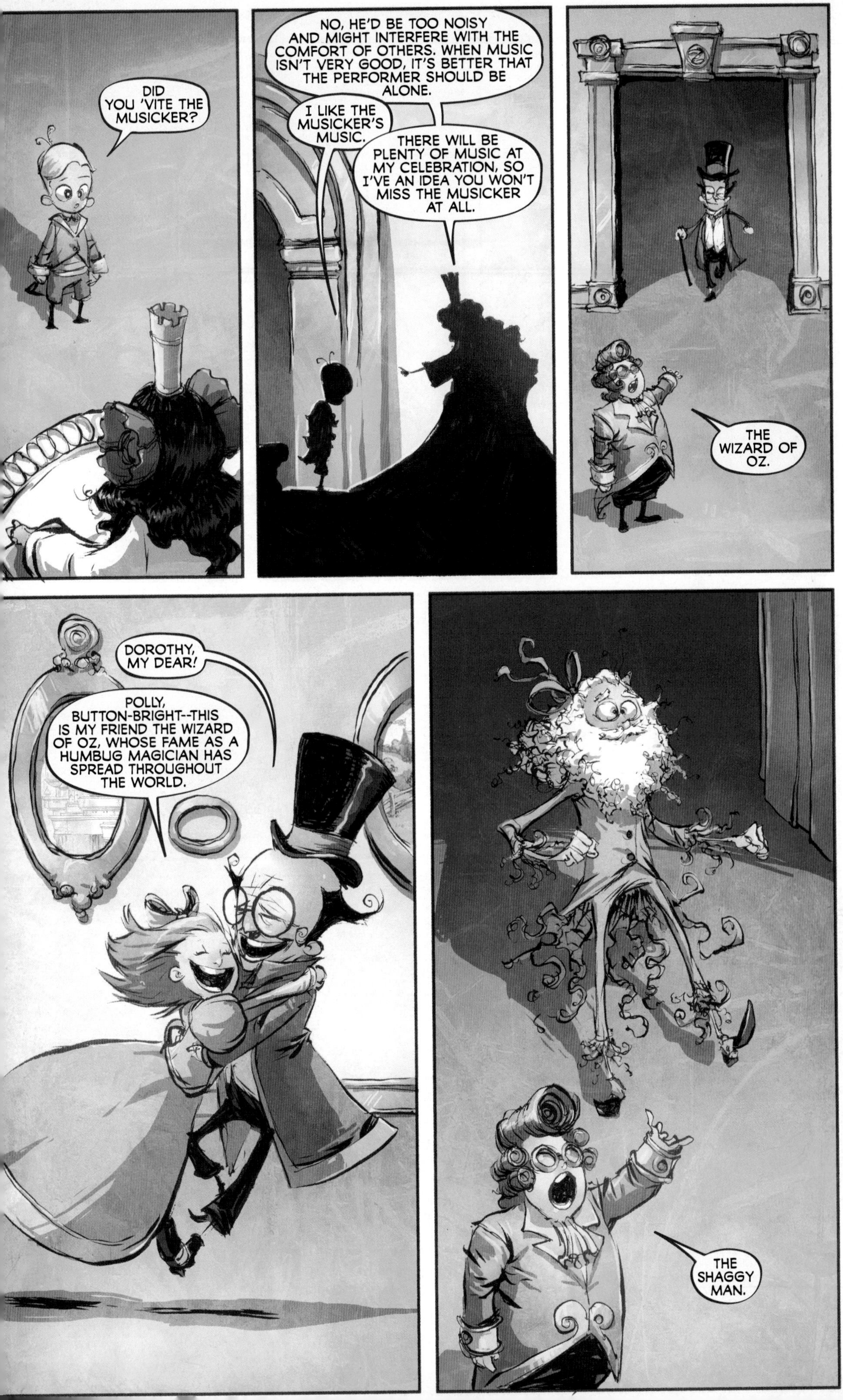
DID YOU 'VITE THE MUSICKER?
NO, HE'D BE TOO NOISY AND MIGHT INTERFERE WITH THE COMFORT OF OTHERS. WHEN MUSIC ISN'T VERY GOOD, IT'S BETTER THAT THE PERFORMER SHOULD BE ALONE.
I LIKE THE MUSICKER'S MUSIC.
THERE WILL BE PLENTY OF MUSIC AT MY CELEBRATION, SO I'VE AN IDEA YOU WON'T MISS THE MUSICKER AT ALL.
THE WIZARD OF OZ.
DOROTHY, MY DEAR!
POLLY, BUTTON-BRIGHT--THIS IS MY FRIEND THE WIZARD OF OZ, WHOSE FAME AS A HUMBUG MAGICIAN HAS SPREAD THROUGHOUT THE WORLD.
THE SHAGGY MAN.

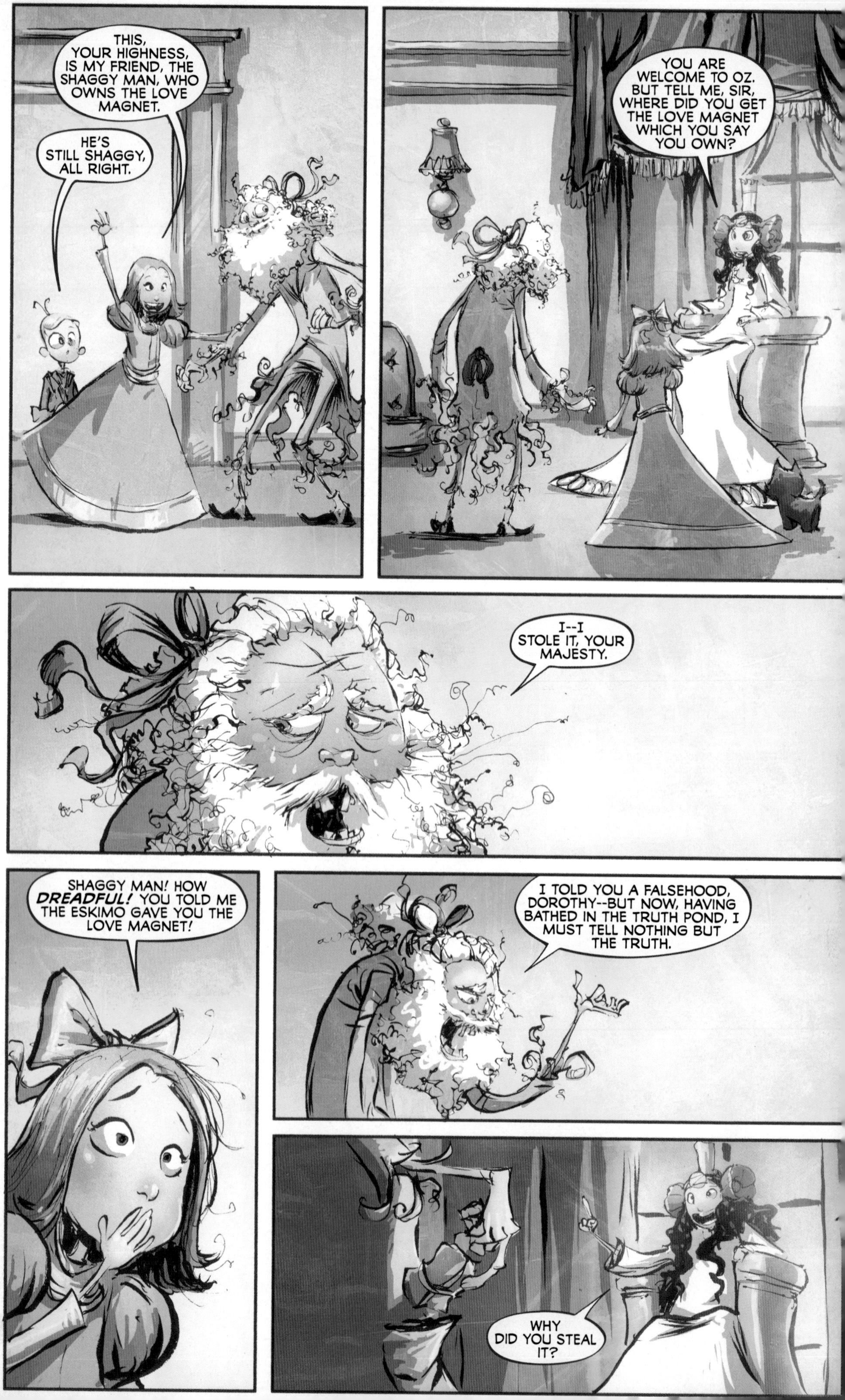
THIS, YOUR HIGHNESS, IS MY FRIEND, THE SHAGGY MAN, WHO OWNS THE LOVE MAGNET.
HE'S STILL SHAGGY, ALL RIGHT.
YOU ARE WELCOME TO OZ. BUT TELL ME, SIR, WHERE DID YOU GET THE LOVE MAGNET WHICH YOU SAY YOU OWN?
I--I STOLE IT, YOUR MAJESTY.
SHAGGY MAN! HOW *DREADFUL!* YOU TOLD ME THE ESKIMO GAVE YOU THE LOVE MAGNET!
I TOLD YOU A FALSEHOOD, DOROTHY--BUT NOW, HAVING BATHED IN THE TRUTH POND, I MUST TELL NOTHING BUT THE TRUTH.
WHY DID YOU STEAL IT?

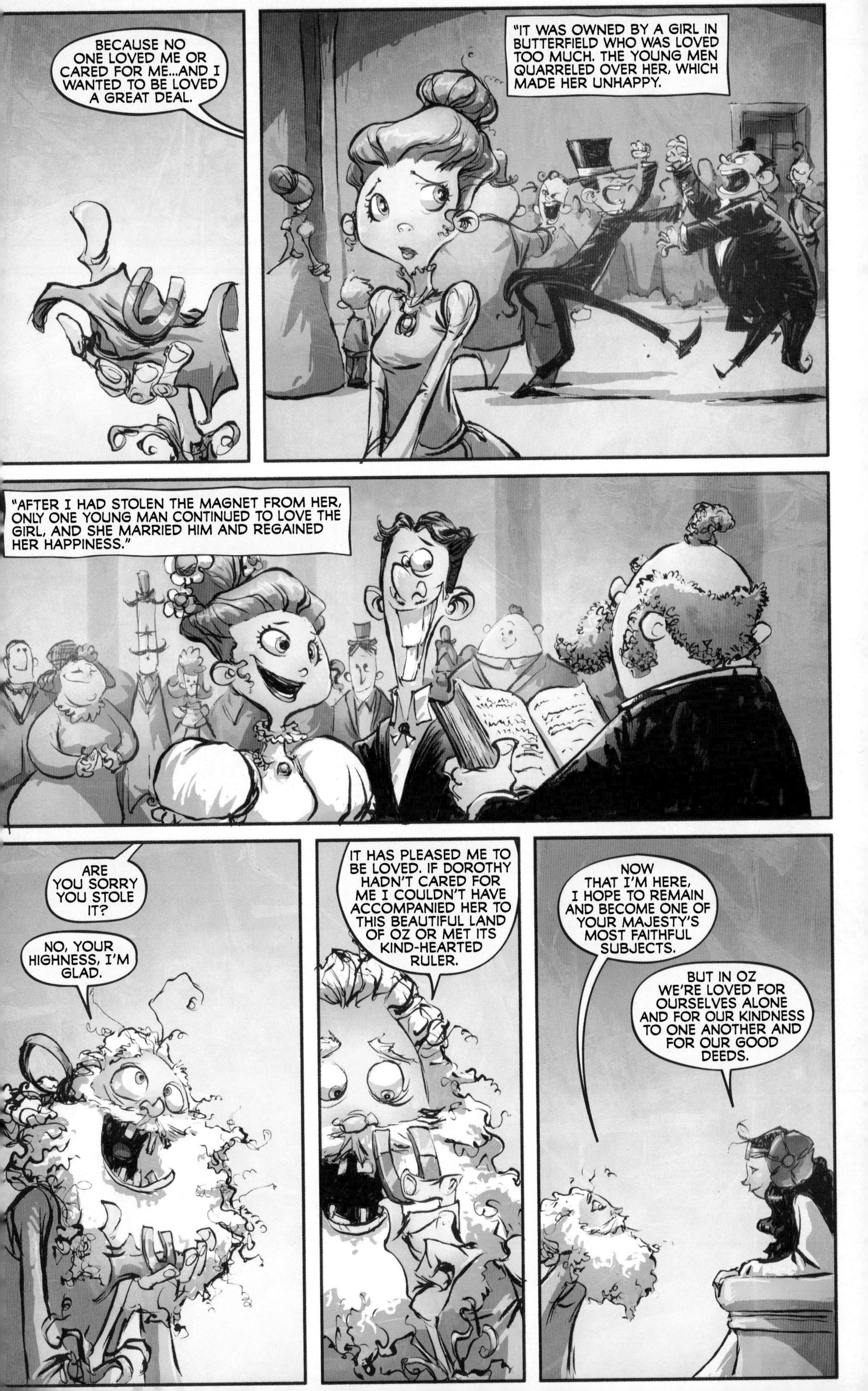
BECAUSE NO ONE LOVED ME OR CARED FOR ME...AND I WANTED TO BE LOVED A GREAT DEAL.
"IT WAS OWNED BY A GIRL IN BUTTERFIELD WHO WAS LOVED TOO MUCH. THE YOUNG MEN QUARRELED OVER HER, WHICH MADE HER UNHAPPY.
"AFTER I HAD STOLEN THE MAGNET FROM HER, ONLY ONE YOUNG MAN CONTINUED TO LOVE THE GIRL, AND SHE MARRIED HIM AND REGAINED HER HAPPINESS."
ARE YOU SORRY YOU STOLE IT?
NO, YOUR HIGHNESS, I'M GLAD.
IT HAS PLEASED ME TO BE LOVED. IF DOROTHY HADN'T CARED FOR ME I COULDN'T HAVE ACCOMPANIED HER TO THIS BEAUTIFUL LAND OF OZ OR MET ITS KIND-HEARTED RULER.
NOW THAT I'M HERE, I HOPE TO REMAIN AND BECOME ONE OF YOUR MAJESTY'S MOST FAITHFUL SUBJECTS.
BUT IN OZ WE'RE LOVED FOR OURSELVES ALONE AND FOR OUR KINDNESS TO ONE ANOTHER AND FOR OUR GOOD DEEDS.

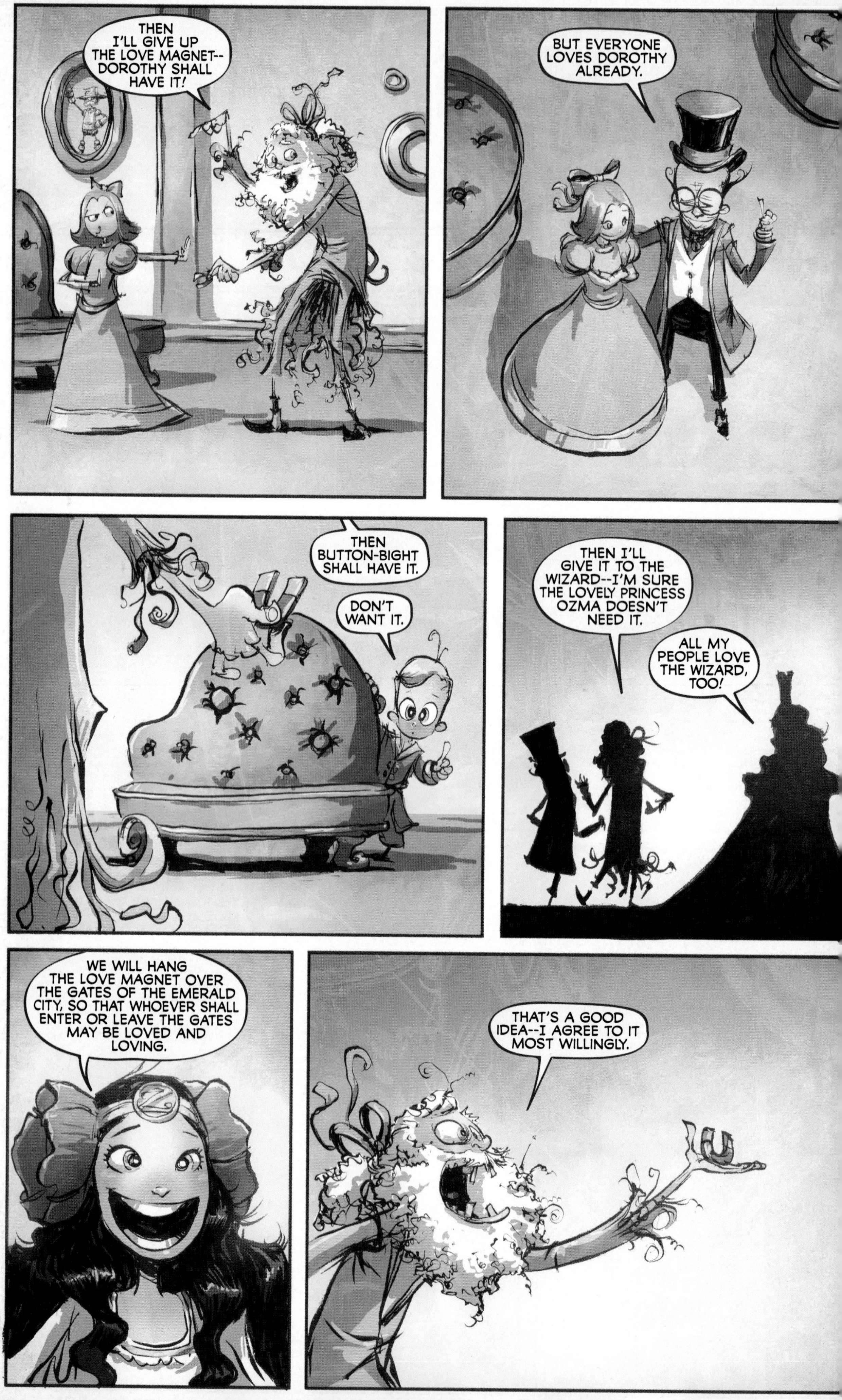
THEN I'LL GIVE UP THE LOVE MAGNET--DOROTHY SHALL HAVE IT!
BUT EVERYONE LOVES DOROTHY ALREADY.
THEN BUTTON-BIGHT SHALL HAVE IT.
DON'T WANT IT.
THEN I'LL GIVE IT TO THE WIZARD--I'M SURE THE LOVELY PRINCESS OZMA DOESN'T NEED IT.
ALL MY PEOPLE LOVE THE WIZARD, TOO!
WE WILL HANG THE LOVE MAGNET OVER THE GATES OF THE EMERALD CITY, SO THAT WHOEVER SHALL ENTER OR LEAVE THE GATES MAY BE LOVED AND LOVING.
THAT'S A GOOD IDEA--I AGREE TO IT MOST WILLINGLY.

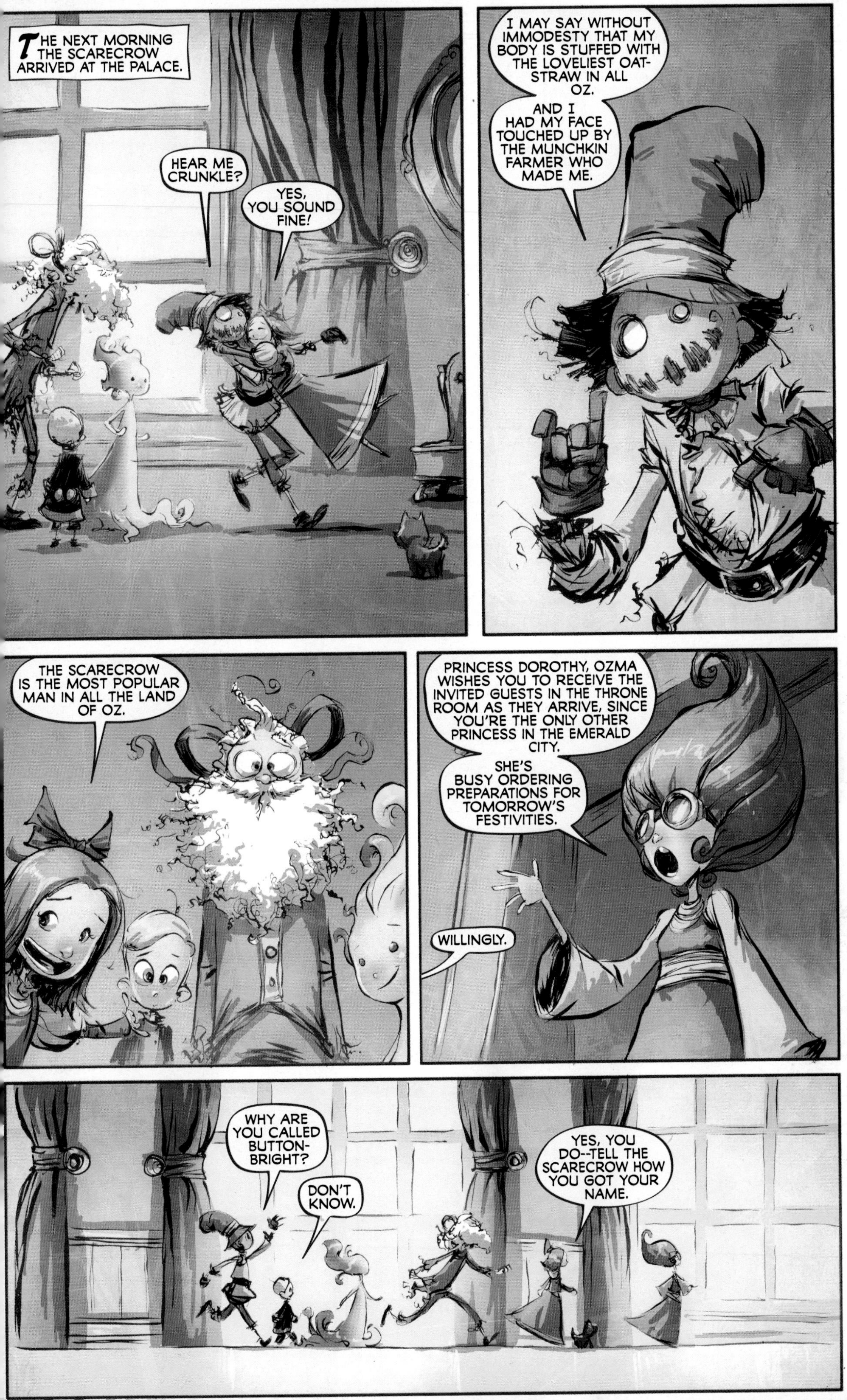
THE NEXT MORNING THE SCARECROW ARRIVED AT THE PALACE.
HEAR ME CRUNKLE?
YES, YOU SOUND FINE!
I MAY SAY WITHOUT IMMODESTY THAT MY BODY IS STUFFED WITH THE LOVELIEST OAT-STRAW IN ALL OZ.
AND I HAD MY FACE TOUCHED UP BY THE MUNCHKIN FARMER WHO MADE ME.
THE SCARECROW IS THE MOST POPULAR MAN IN ALL THE LAND OF OZ.
PRINCESS DOROTHY, OZMA WISHES YOU TO RECEIVE THE INVITED GUESTS IN THE THRONE ROOM AS THEY ARRIVE, SINCE YOU'RE THE ONLY OTHER PRINCESS IN THE EMERALD CITY.
SHE'S BUSY ORDERING PREPARATIONS FOR TOMORROW'S FESTIVITIES.
WILLINGLY.
WHY ARE YOU CALLED BUTTON-BRIGHT?
DON'T KNOW.
YES, YOU DO--TELL THE SCARECROW HOW YOU GOT YOUR NAME.

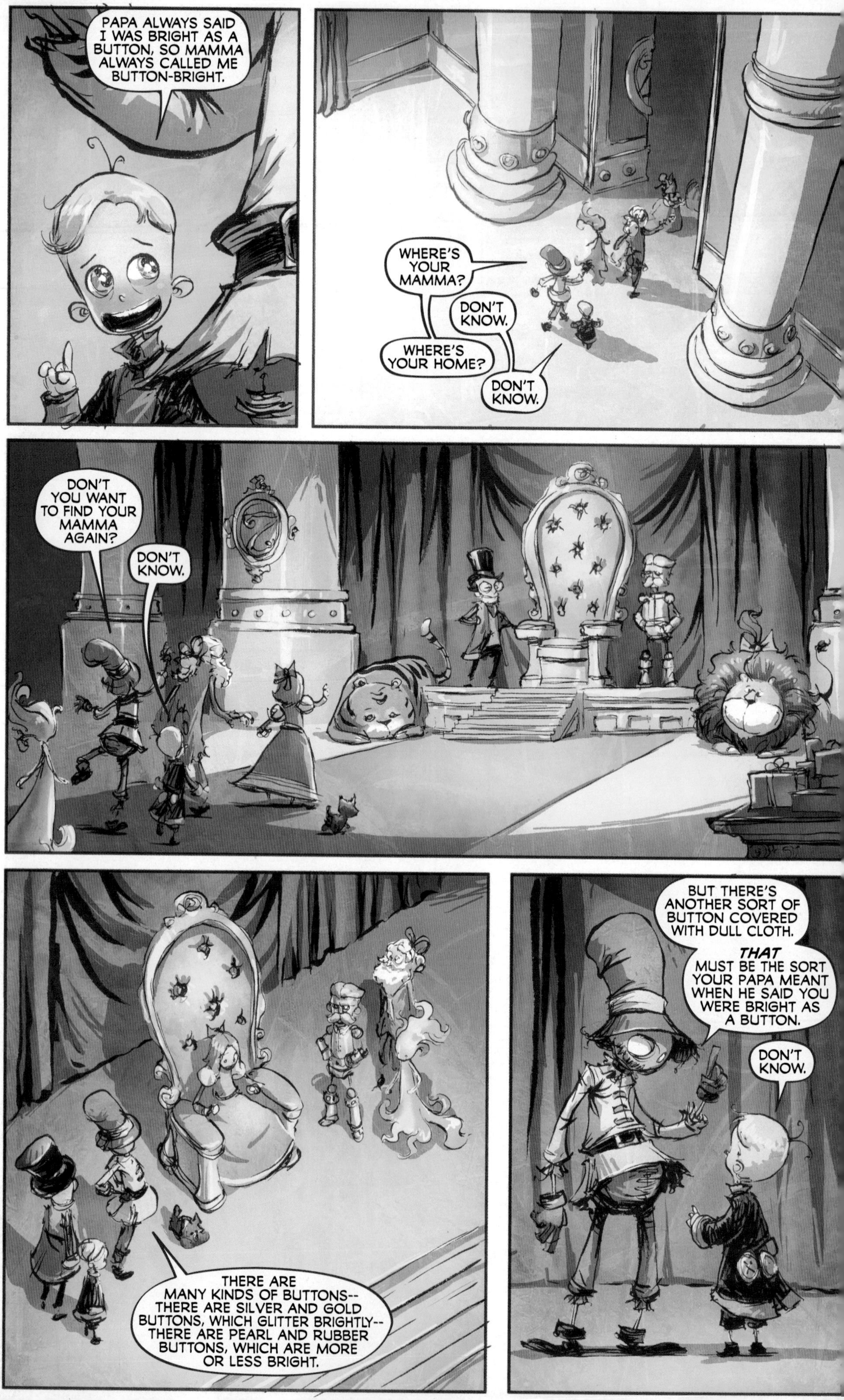
PAPA ALWAYS SAID I WAS BRIGHT AS A BUTTON, SO MAMMA ALWAYS CALLED ME BUTTON-BRIGHT.
WHERE'S YOUR MAMMA?
DON'T KNOW.
WHERE'S YOUR HOME?
DON'T KNOW.
DON'T YOU WANT TO FIND YOUR MAMMA AGAIN?
DON'T KNOW.
THERE ARE MANY KINDS OF BUTTONS-- THERE ARE SILVER AND GOLD BUTTONS, WHICH GLITTER BRIGHTLY-- THERE ARE PEARL AND RUBBER BUTTONS, WHICH ARE MORE OR LESS BRIGHT.
BUT THERE'S ANOTHER SORT OF BUTTON COVERED WITH DULL CLOTH.
THAT MUST BE THE SORT YOUR PAPA MEANT WHEN HE SAID YOU WERE BRIGHT AS A BUTTON.
DON'T KNOW.

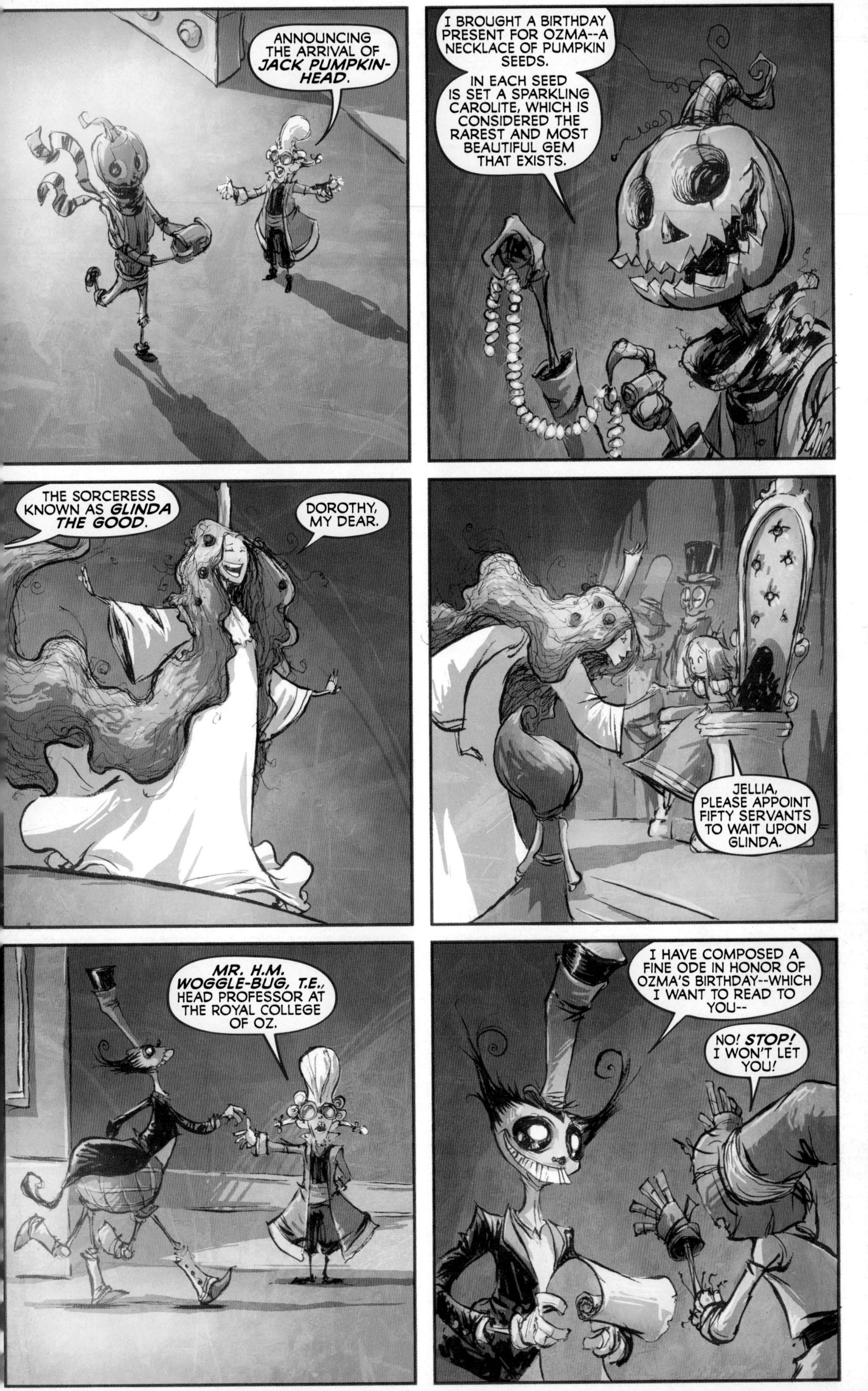
ANNOUNCING THE ARRIVAL OF ***JACK PUMPKIN-HEAD***.
I BROUGHT A BIRTHDAY PRESENT FOR OZMA--A NECKLACE OF PUMPKIN SEEDS.
IN EACH SEED IS SET A SPARKLING CAROLITE, WHICH IS CONSIDERED THE RAREST AND MOST BEAUTIFUL GEM THAT EXISTS.
THE SORCERESS KNOWN AS ***GLINDA THE GOOD***.
DOROTHY, MY DEAR.
JELLIA, PLEASE APPOINT FIFTY SERVANTS TO WAIT UPON GLINDA.
MR. H.M. WOGGLE-BUG, T.E., HEAD PROFESSOR AT THE ROYAL COLLEGE OF OZ.
I HAVE COMPOSED A FINE ODE IN HONOR OF OZMA'S BIRTHDAY--WHICH I WANT TO READ TO YOU--
NO! ***STOP!*** I WON'T LET YOU!

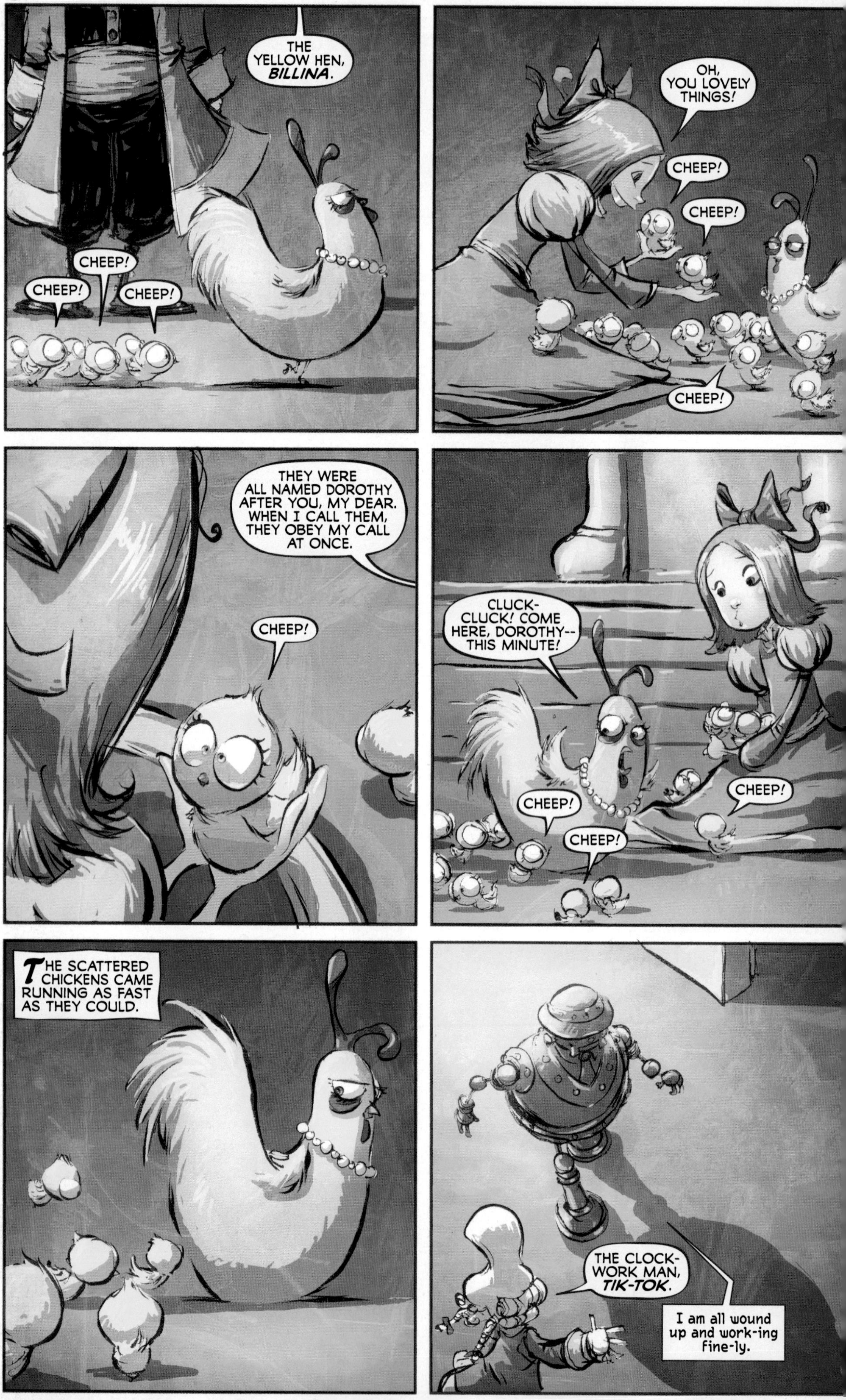
THE YELLOW HEN, ***BILLINA***.
CHEEP!
CHEEP!
CHEEP!
OH, YOU LOVELY THINGS!
CHEEP!
CHEEP!
CHEEP!
THEY WERE ALL NAMED DOROTHY AFTER YOU, MY DEAR. WHEN I CALL THEM, THEY OBEY MY CALL AT ONCE.
CHEEP!
CLUCK-CLUCK! COME HERE, DOROTHY-- THIS MINUTE!
CHEEP!
CHEEP!
CHEEP!
THE SCATTERED CHICKENS CAME RUNNING AS FAST AS THEY COULD.
THE CLOCK-WORK MAN, ***TIK-TOK***.
I am all wound up and work-ing fine-ly.

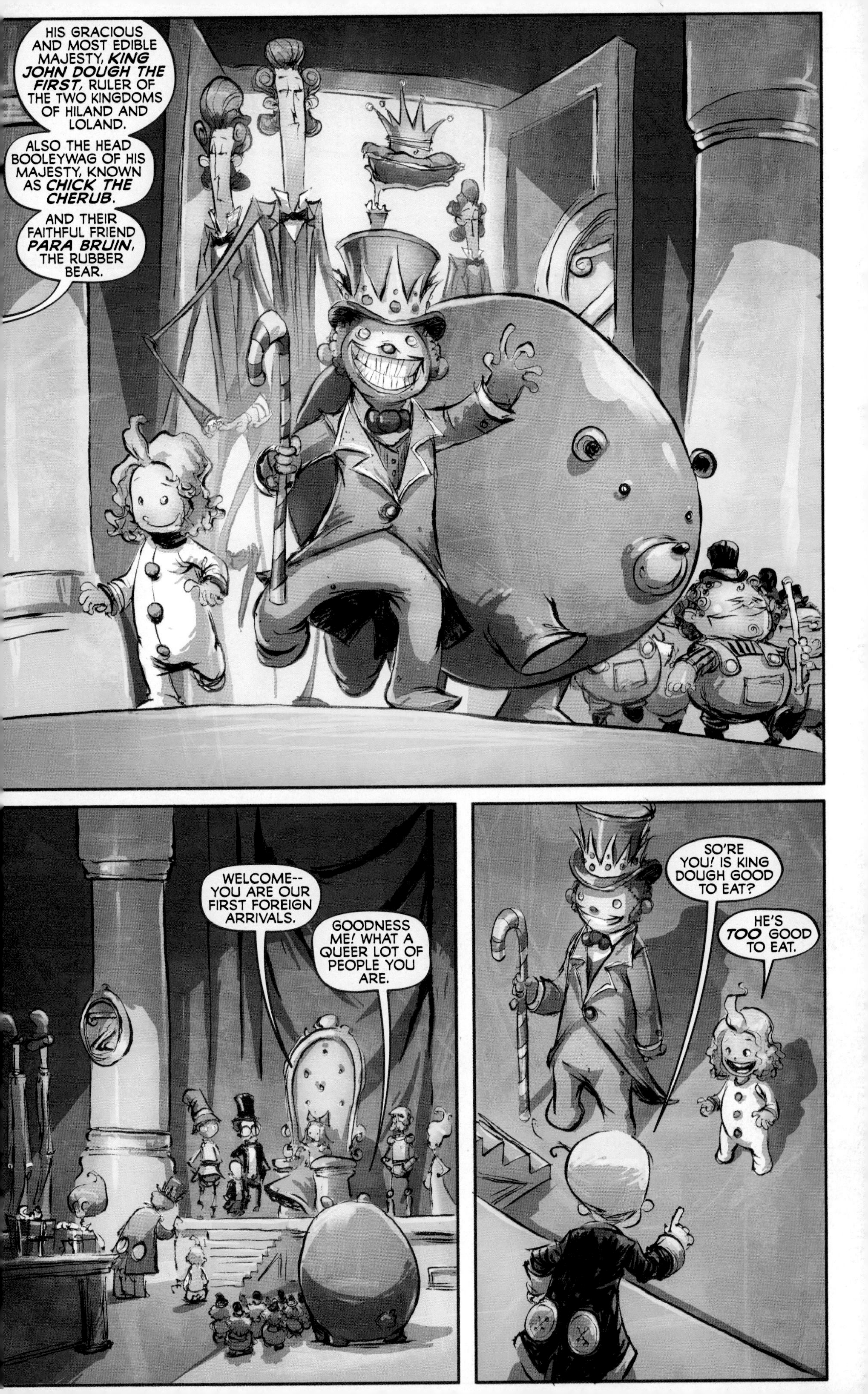
HIS GRACIOUS AND MOST EDIBLE MAJESTY, ***KING JOHN DOUGH THE FIRST***, RULER OF THE TWO KINGDOMS OF HILAND AND LOLAND.
ALSO THE HEAD BOOLEYWAG OF HIS MAJESTY, KNOWN AS ***CHICK THE CHERUB***.
AND THEIR FAITHFUL FRIEND ***PARA BRUIN***, THE RUBBER BEAR.
WELCOME-- YOU ARE OUR FIRST FOREIGN ARRIVALS.
GOODNESS ME! WHAT A QUEER LOT OF PEOPLE YOU ARE.
SO'RE YOU! IS KING DOUGH GOOD TO EAT?
HE'S ***TOO*** GOOD TO EAT.

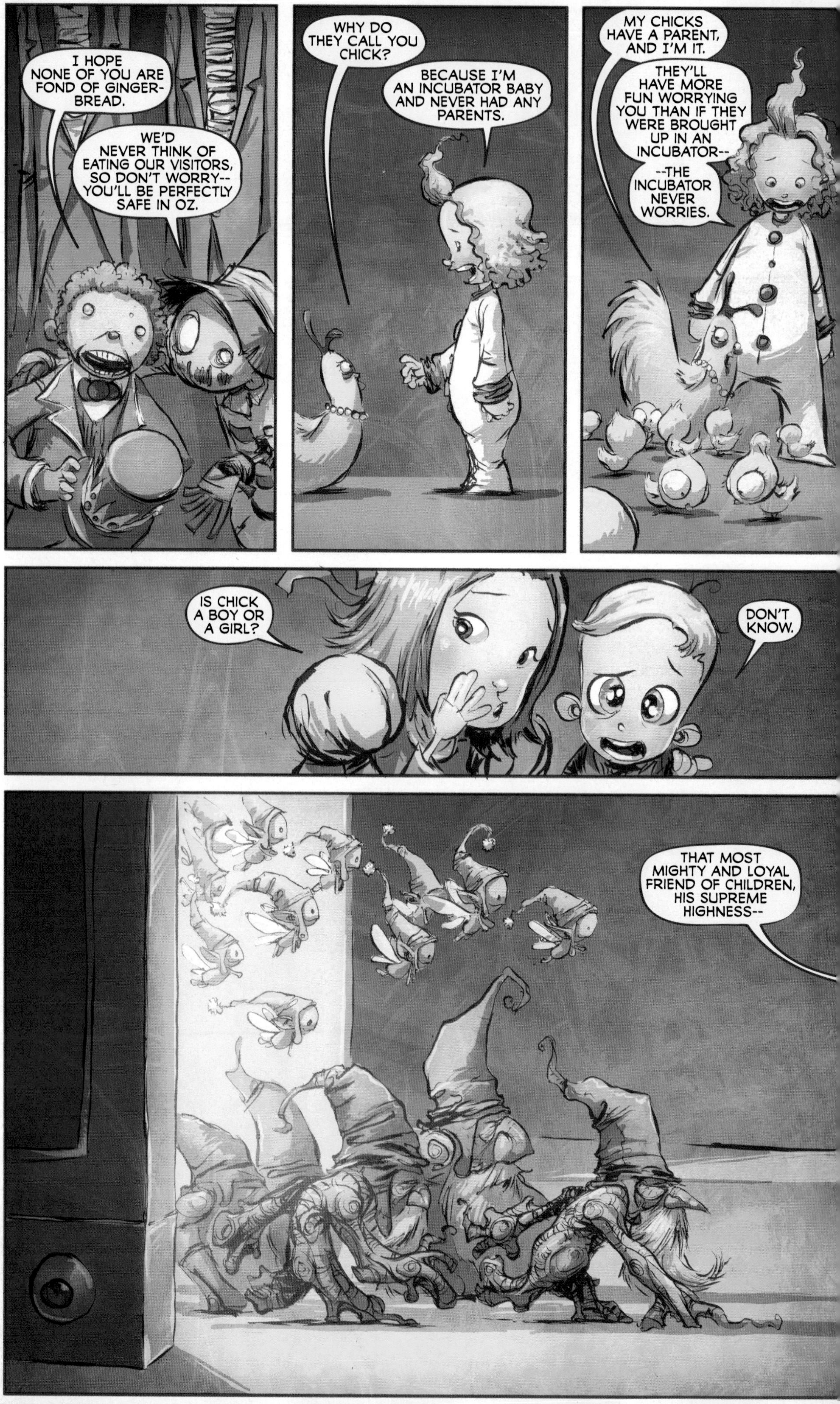
I HOPE NONE OF YOU ARE FOND OF GINGER-BREAD.
WE'D NEVER THINK OF EATING OUR VISITORS, SO DON'T WORRY-- YOU'LL BE PERFECTLY SAFE IN OZ.
WHY DO THEY CALL YOU CHICK?
BECAUSE I'M AN INCUBATOR BABY AND NEVER HAD ANY PARENTS.
MY CHICKS HAVE A PARENT, AND I'M IT.
THEY'LL HAVE MORE FUN WORRYING YOU THAN IF THEY WERE BROUGHT UP IN AN INCUBATOR--
--THE INCUBATOR NEVER WORRIES.
IS CHICK A BOY OR A GIRL?
DON'T KNOW.
THAT MOST MIGHTY AND LOYAL FRIEND OF CHILDREN, HIS SUPREME HIGHNESS--

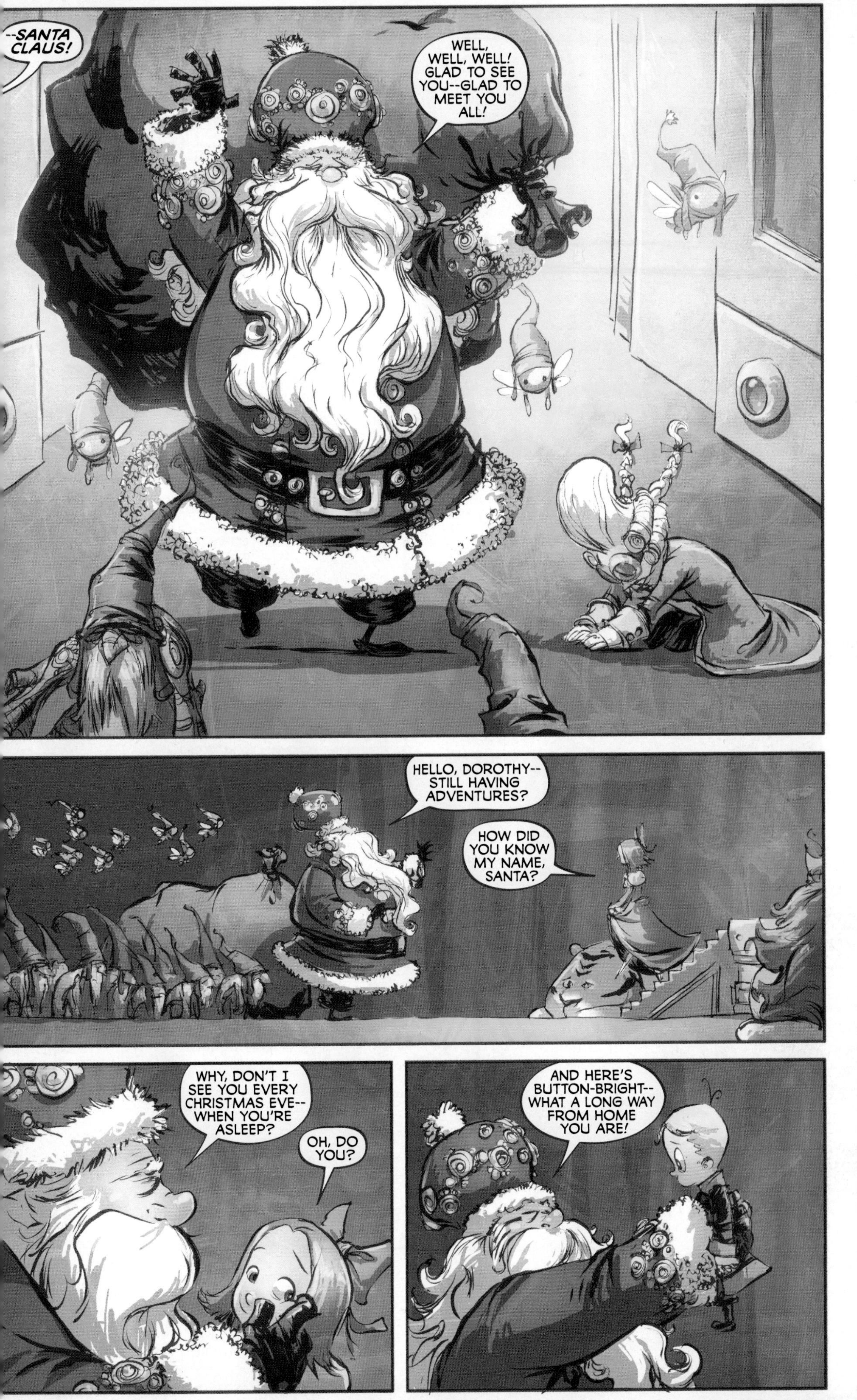
--SANTA CLAUS!
WELL, WELL, WELL! GLAD TO SEE YOU--GLAD TO MEET YOU ALL!
HELLO, DOROTHY--STILL HAVING ADVENTURES?
HOW DID YOU KNOW MY NAME, SANTA?
WHY, DON'T I SEE YOU EVERY CHRISTMAS EVE--WHEN YOU'RE ASLEEP?
OH, DO YOU?
AND HERE'S BUTTON-BRIGHT--WHAT A LONG WAY FROM HOME YOU ARE!

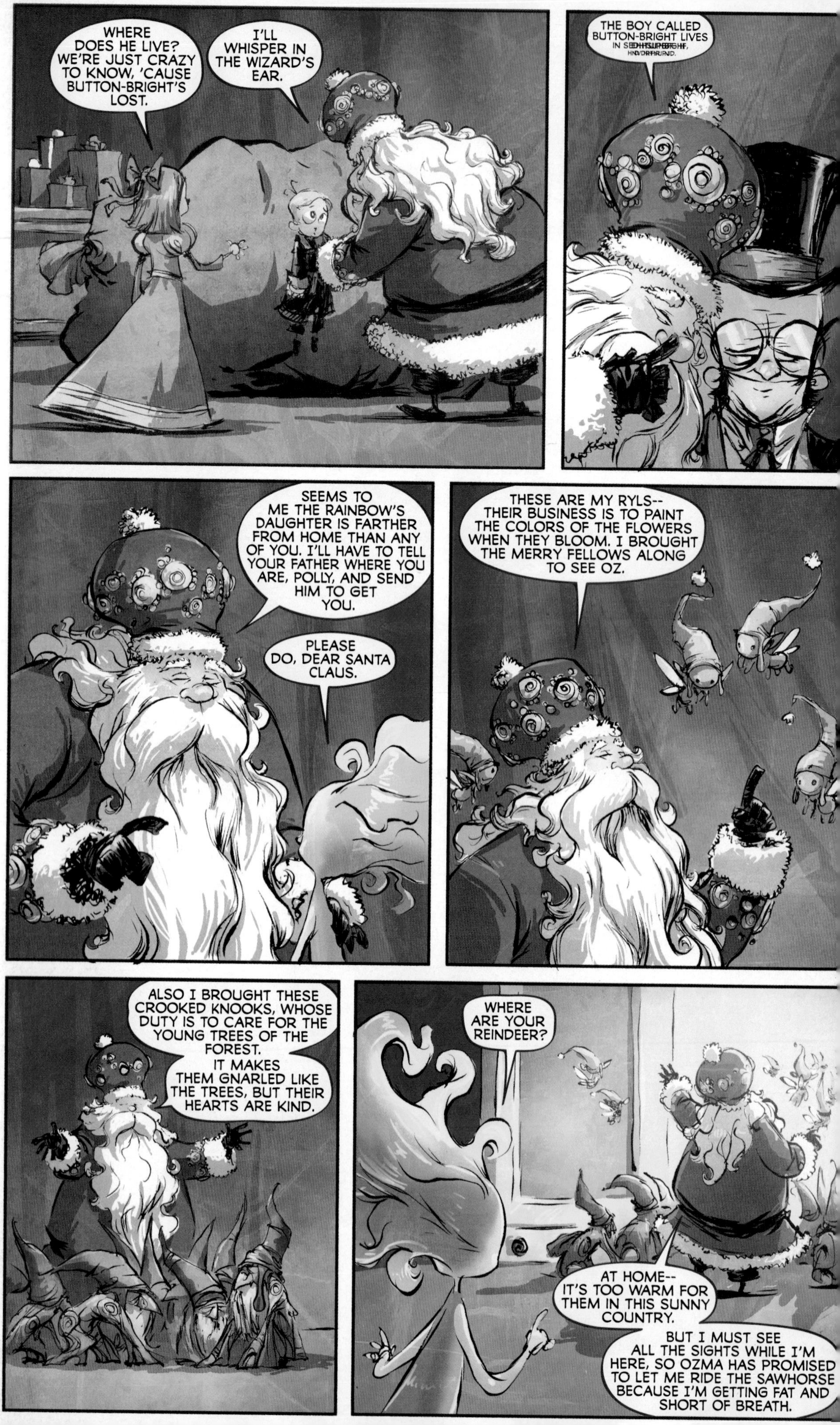
WHERE DOES HE LIVE? WE'RE JUST CRAZY TO KNOW, 'CAUSE BUTTON-BRIGHT'S LOST.
I'LL WHISPER IN THE WIZARD'S EAR.
THE BOY CALLED BUTTON-BRIGHT LIVES IN
SEEMS TO ME THE RAINBOW'S DAUGHTER IS FARTHER FROM HOME THAN ANY OF YOU. I'LL HAVE TO TELL YOUR FATHER WHERE YOU ARE, POLLY, AND SEND HIM TO GET YOU.
PLEASE DO, DEAR SANTA CLAUS.
THESE ARE MY RYLS-- THEIR BUSINESS IS TO PAINT THE COLORS OF THE FLOWERS WHEN THEY BLOOM. I BROUGHT THE MERRY FELLOWS ALONG TO SEE OZ.
ALSO I BROUGHT THESE CROOKED KNOOKS, WHOSE DUTY IS TO CARE FOR THE YOUNG TREES OF THE FOREST.
IT MAKES THEM GNARLED LIKE THE TREES, BUT THEIR HEARTS ARE KIND.
WHERE ARE YOUR REINDEER?
AT HOME-- IT'S TOO WARM FOR THEM IN THIS SUNNY COUNTRY.
BUT I MUST SEE ALL THE SIGHTS WHILE I'M HERE, SO OZMA HAS PROMISED TO LET ME RIDE THE SAWHORSE BECAUSE I'M GETTING FAT AND SHORT OF BREATH.

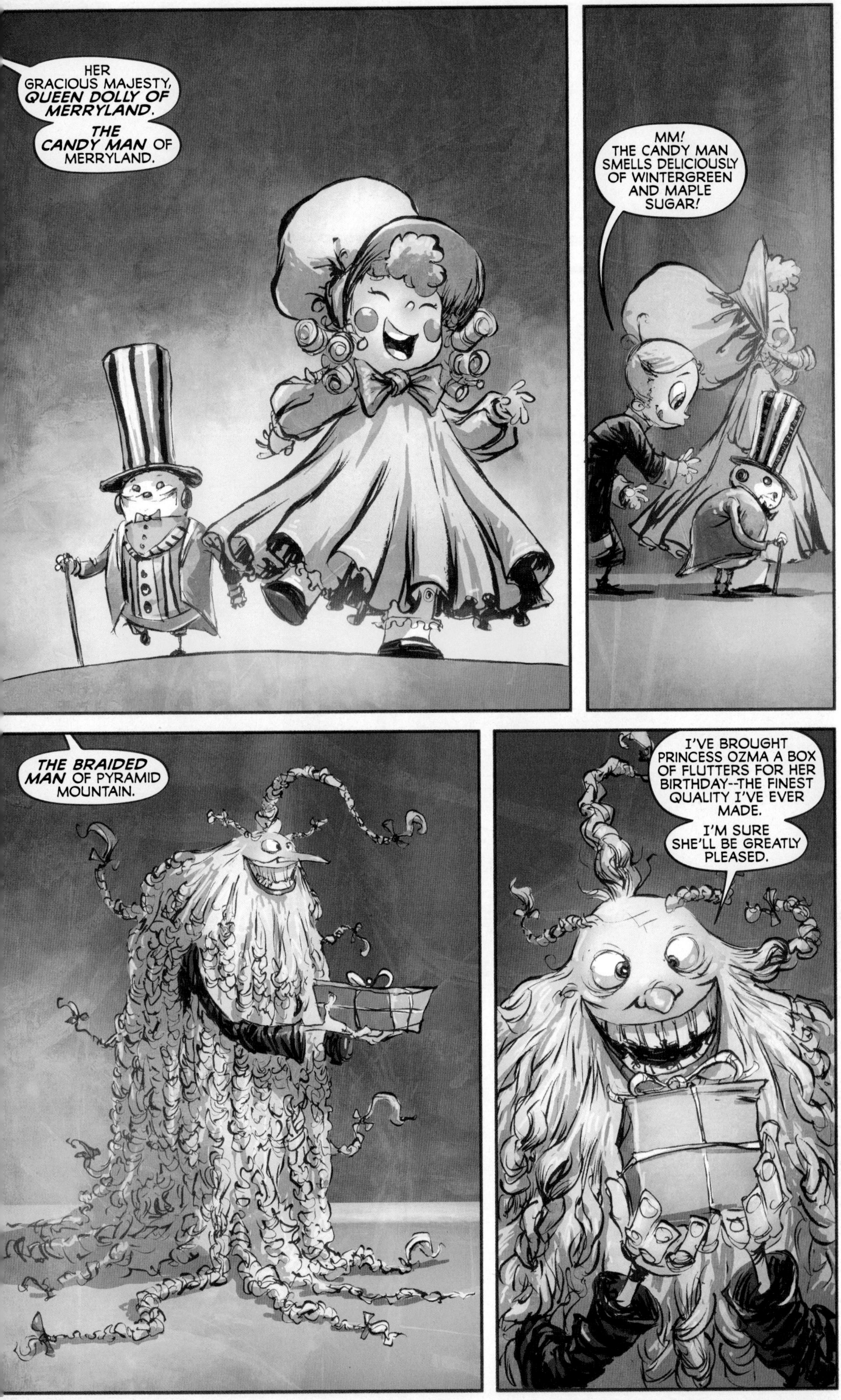
HER GRACIOUS MAJESTY, *QUEEN DOLLY OF MERRYLAND*.
THE CANDY MAN OF MERRYLAND.
MM! THE CANDY MAN SMELLS DELICIOUSLY OF WINTERGREEN AND MAPLE SUGAR!
THE BRAIDED MAN OF PYRAMID MOUNTAIN.
I'VE BROUGHT PRINCESS OZMA A BOX OF FLUTTERS FOR HER BIRTHDAY--THE FINEST QUALITY I'VE EVER MADE.
I'M SURE SHE'LL BE GREATLY PLEASED.

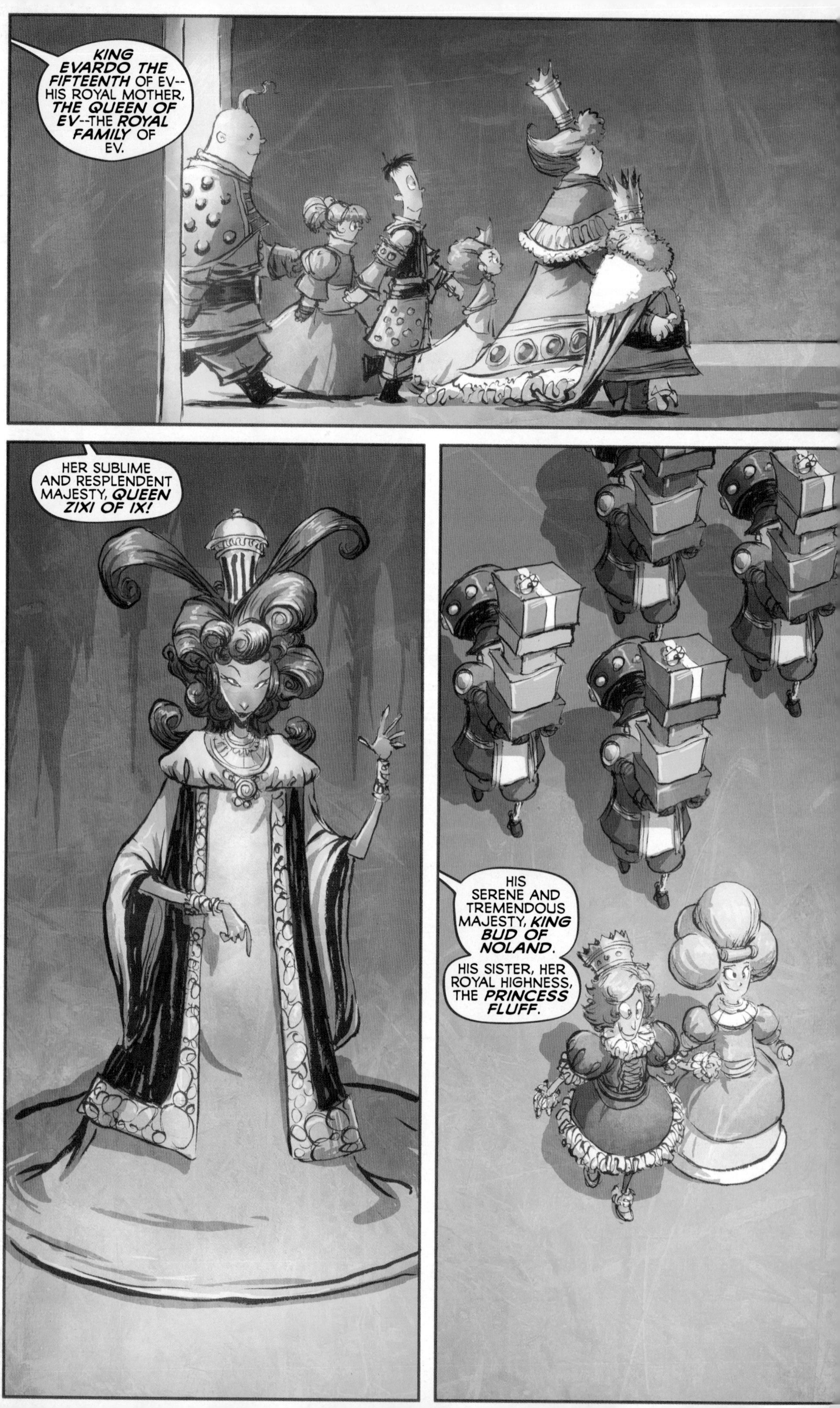
KING EVARDO THE FIFTEENTH OF EV-- HIS ROYAL MOTHER, THE QUEEN OF EV--THE ROYAL FAMILY OF EV.
HER SUBLIME AND RESPLENDENT MAJESTY, QUEEN ZIXI OF IX!
HIS SERENE AND TREMENDOUS MAJESTY, KING BUD OF NOLAND.
HIS SISTER, HER ROYAL HIGHNESS, THE PRINCESS FLUFF.

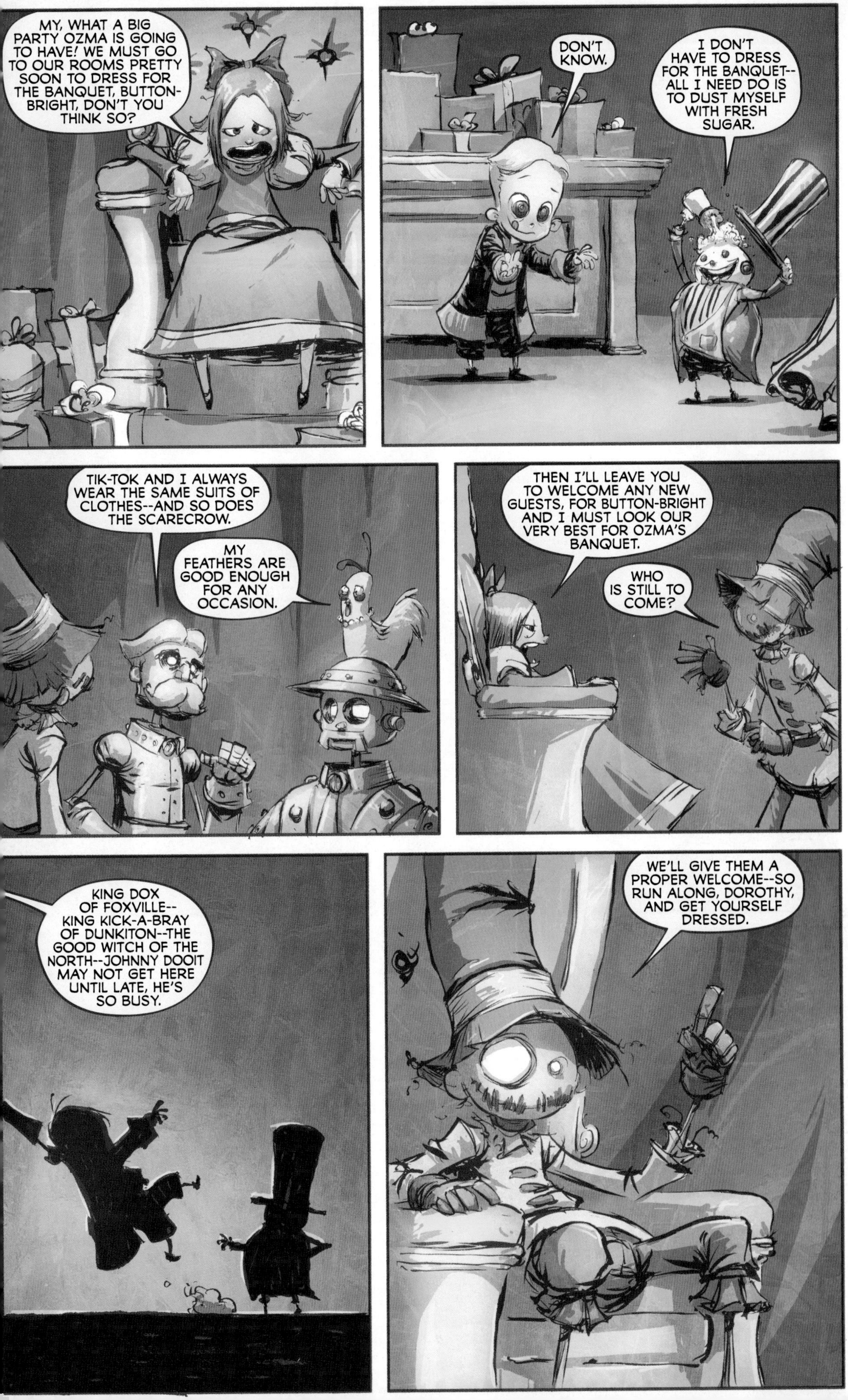
MY, WHAT A BIG PARTY OZMA IS GOING TO HAVE! WE MUST GO TO OUR ROOMS PRETTY SOON TO DRESS FOR THE BANQUET, BUTTON-BRIGHT, DON'T YOU THINK SO?
DON'T KNOW.
I DON'T HAVE TO DRESS FOR THE BANQUET--ALL I NEED DO IS TO DUST MYSELF WITH FRESH SUGAR.
TIK-TOK AND I ALWAYS WEAR THE SAME SUITS OF CLOTHES--AND SO DOES THE SCARECROW.
MY FEATHERS ARE GOOD ENOUGH FOR ANY OCCASION.
THEN I'LL LEAVE YOU TO WELCOME ANY NEW GUESTS, FOR BUTTON-BRIGHT AND I MUST LOOK OUR VERY BEST FOR OZMA'S BANQUET.
WHO IS STILL TO COME?
KING DOX OF FOXVILLE--KING KICK-A-BRAY OF DUNKITON--THE GOOD WITCH OF THE NORTH--JOHNNY DOOIT MAY NOT GET HERE UNTIL LATE, HE'S SO BUSY.
WE'LL GIVE THEM A PROPER WELCOME--SO RUN ALONG, DOROTHY, AND GET YOURSELF DRESSED.

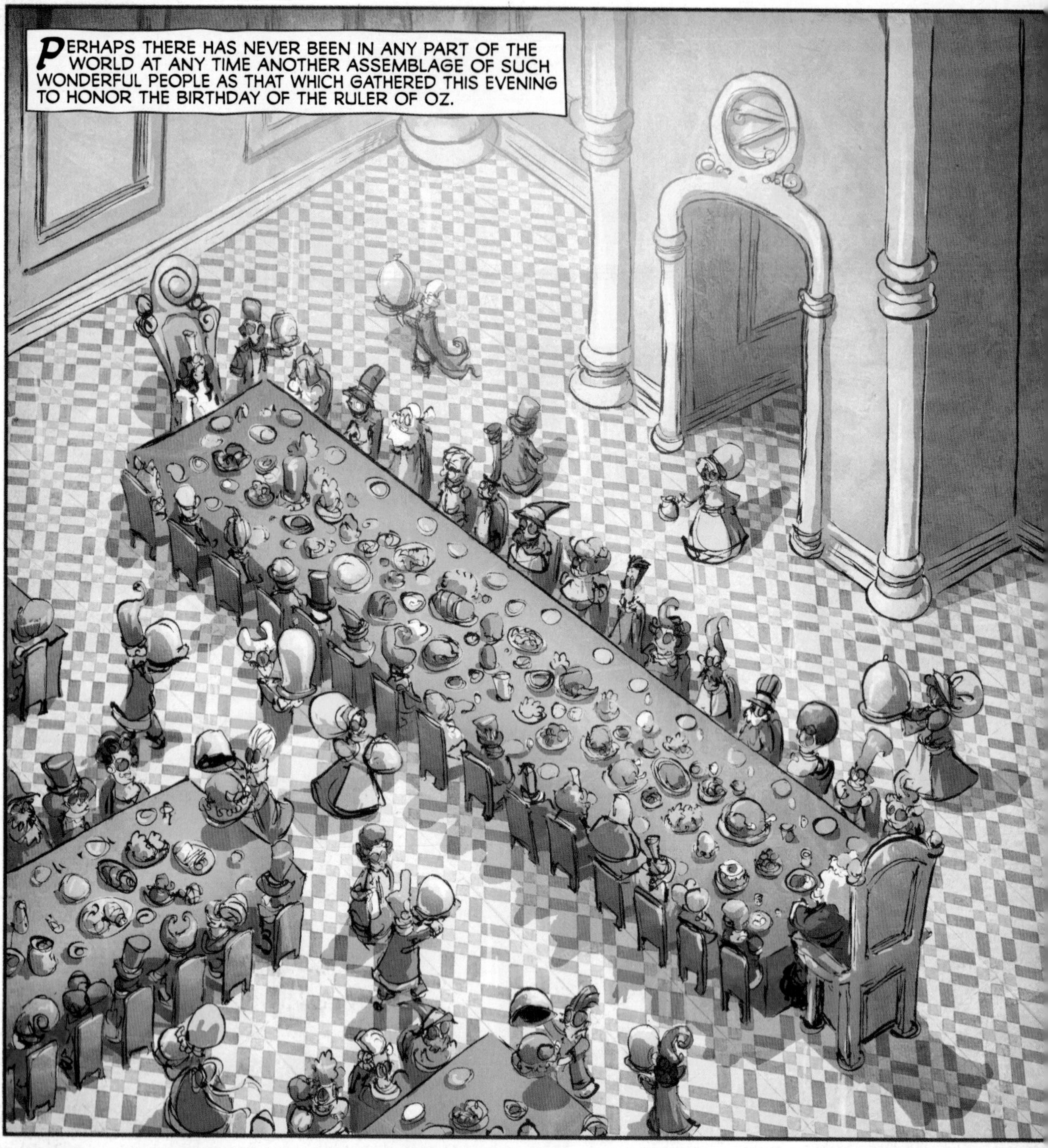
PERHAPS THERE HAS NEVER BEEN IN ANY PART OF THE WORLD AT ANY TIME ANOTHER ASSEMBLAGE OF SUCH WONDERFUL PEOPLE AS THAT WHICH GATHERED THIS EVENING TO HONOR THE BIRTHDAY OF THE RULER OF OZ.

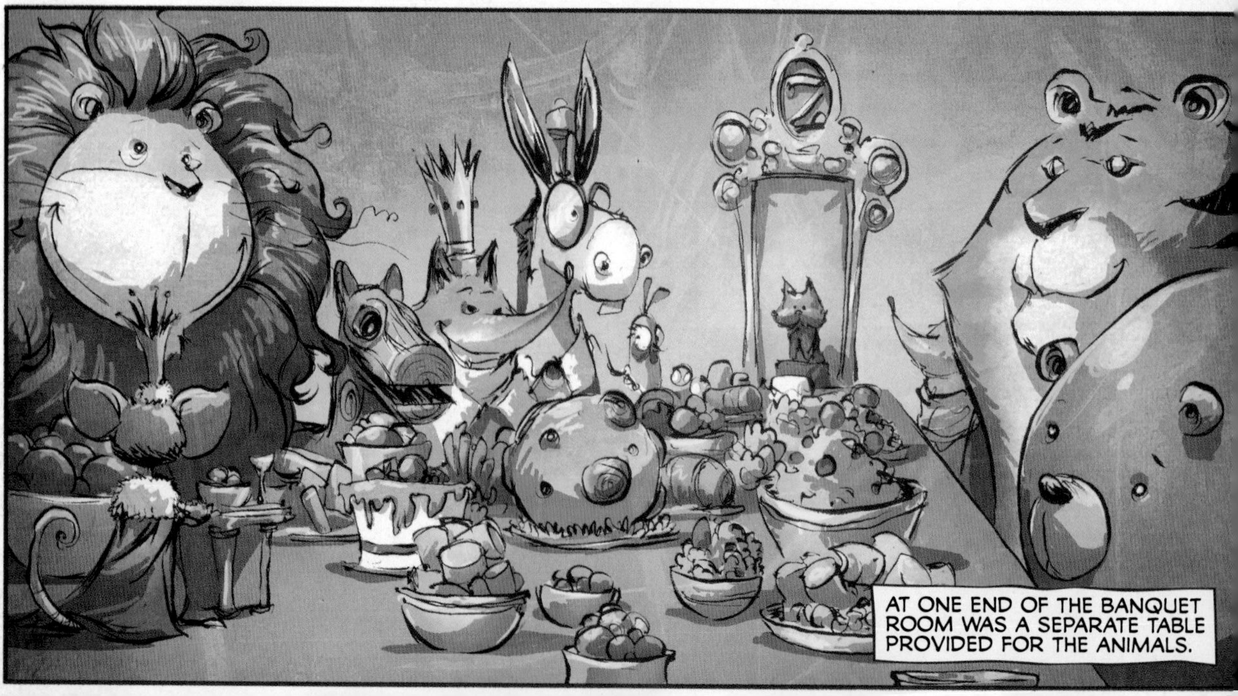
AT ONE END OF THE BANQUET ROOM WAS A SEPARATE TABLE PROVIDED FOR THE ANIMALS.

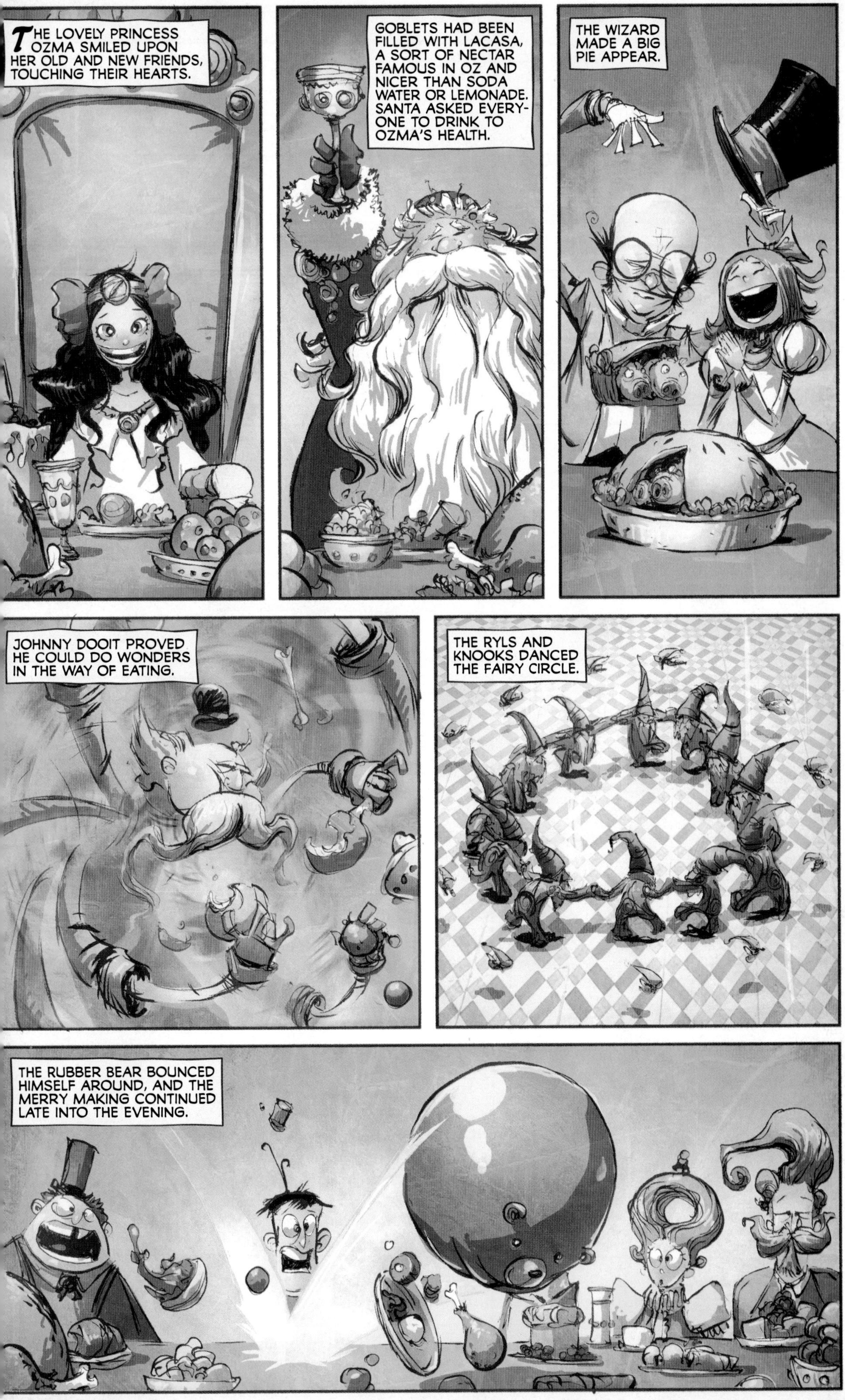
THE LOVELY PRINCESS OZMA SMILED UPON HER OLD AND NEW FRIENDS, TOUCHING THEIR HEARTS.
GOBLETS HAD BEEN FILLED WITH LACASA, A SORT OF NECTAR FAMOUS IN OZ AND NICER THAN SODA WATER OR LEMONADE. SANTA ASKED EVERY-ONE TO DRINK TO OZMA'S HEALTH.
THE WIZARD MADE A BIG PIE APPEAR.
JOHNNY DOOIT PROVED HE COULD DO WONDERS IN THE WAY OF EATING.
THE RYLS AND KNOOKS DANCED THE FAIRY CIRCLE.
THE RUBBER BEAR BOUNCED HIMSELF AROUND, AND THE MERRY MAKING CONTINUED LATE INTO THE EVENING.

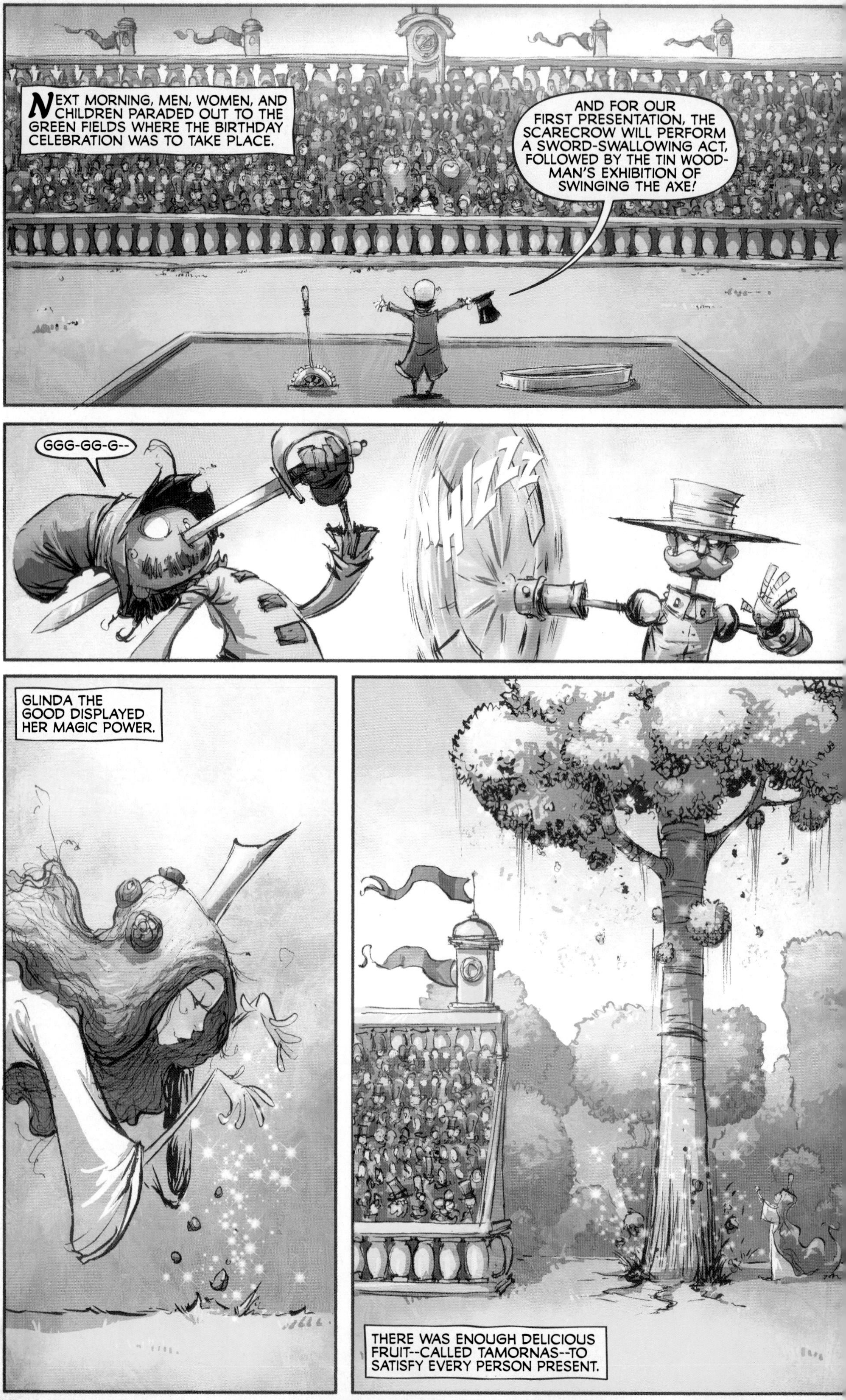
NEXT MORNING, MEN, WOMEN, AND CHILDREN PARADED OUT TO THE GREEN FIELDS WHERE THE BIRTHDAY CELEBRATION WAS TO TAKE PLACE.
AND FOR OUR FIRST PRESENTATION, THE SCARECROW WILL PERFORM A SWORD-SWALLOWING ACT, FOLLOWED BY THE TIN WOODMAN'S EXHIBITION OF SWINGING THE AXE!
GGG-GG-G--
WHIZZZ
GLINDA THE GOOD DISPLAYED HER MAGIC POWER.
THERE WAS ENOUGH DELICIOUS FRUIT--CALLED TAMORNAS--TO SATISFY EVERY PERSON PRESENT.

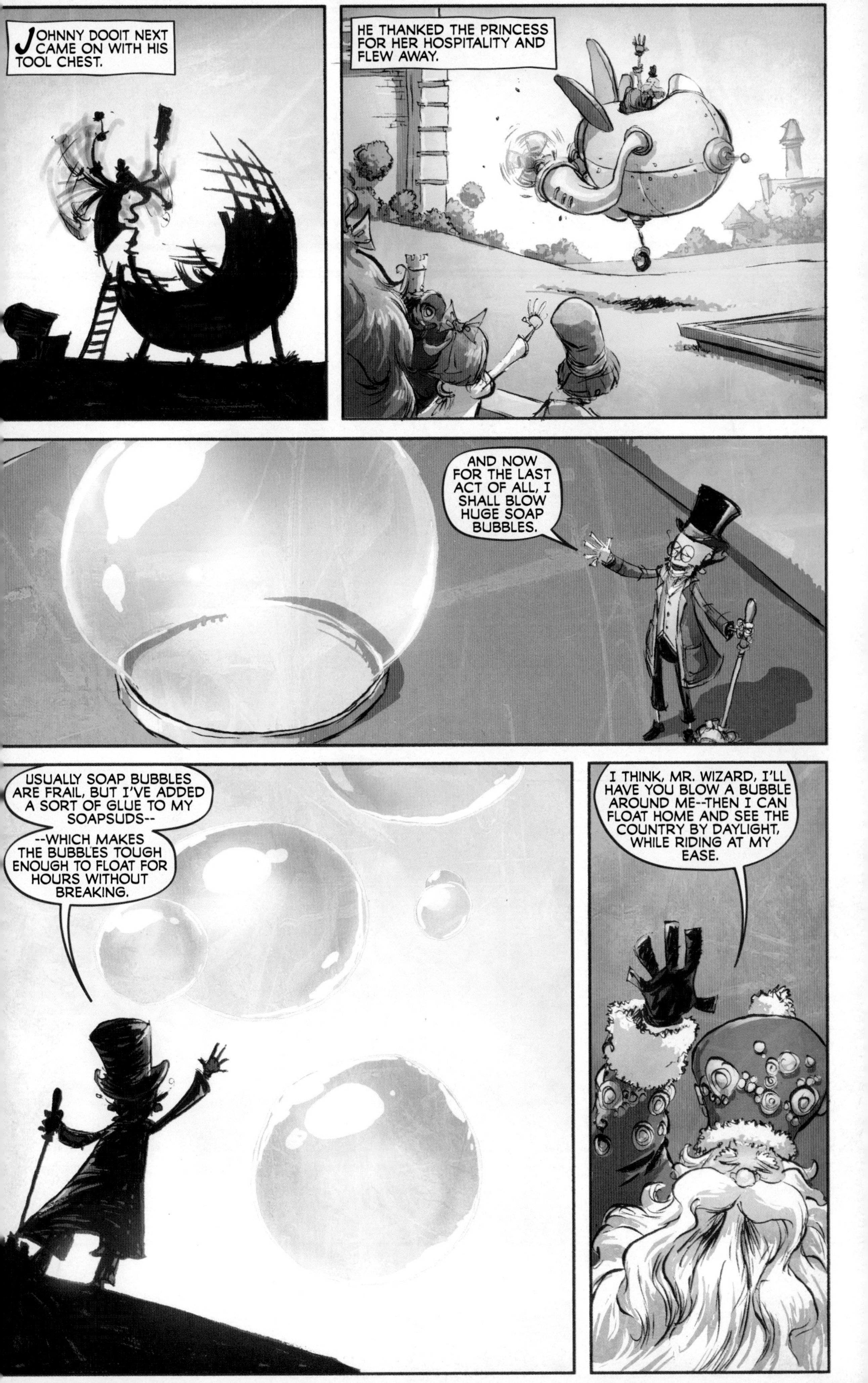
JOHNNY DOOIT NEXT CAME ON WITH HIS TOOL CHEST.
HE THANKED THE PRINCESS FOR HER HOSPITALITY AND FLEW AWAY.
AND NOW FOR THE LAST ACT OF ALL, I SHALL BLOW HUGE SOAP BUBBLES.
USUALLY SOAP BUBBLES ARE FRAIL, BUT I'VE ADDED A SORT OF GLUE TO MY SOAPSUDS--
--WHICH MAKES THE BUBBLES TOUGH ENOUGH TO FLOAT FOR HOURS WITHOUT BREAKING.
I THINK, MR. WIZARD, I'LL HAVE YOU BLOW A BUBBLE AROUND ME--THEN I CAN FLOAT HOME AND SEE THE COUNTRY BY DAYLIGHT, WHILE RIDING AT MY EASE.

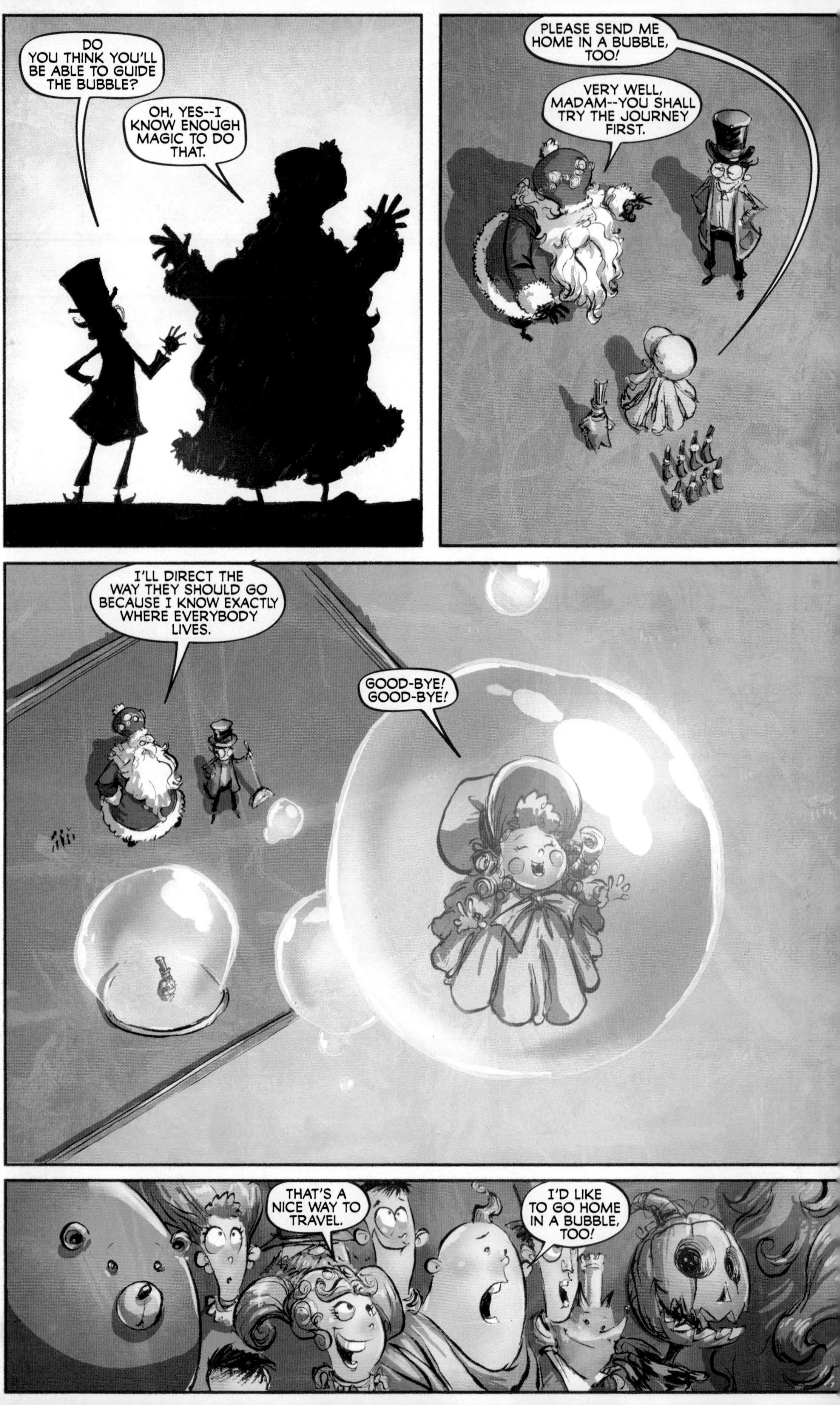
DO YOU THINK YOU'LL BE ABLE TO GUIDE THE BUBBLE?
OH, YES--I KNOW ENOUGH MAGIC TO DO THAT.
PLEASE SEND ME HOME IN A BUBBLE, TOO!
VERY WELL, MADAM--YOU SHALL TRY THE JOURNEY FIRST.
I'LL DIRECT THE WAY THEY SHOULD GO BECAUSE I KNOW EXACTLY WHERE EVERYBODY LIVES.
GOOD-BYE! GOOD-BYE!
THAT'S A NICE WAY TO TRAVEL.
I'D LIKE TO GO HOME IN A BUBBLE, TOO!

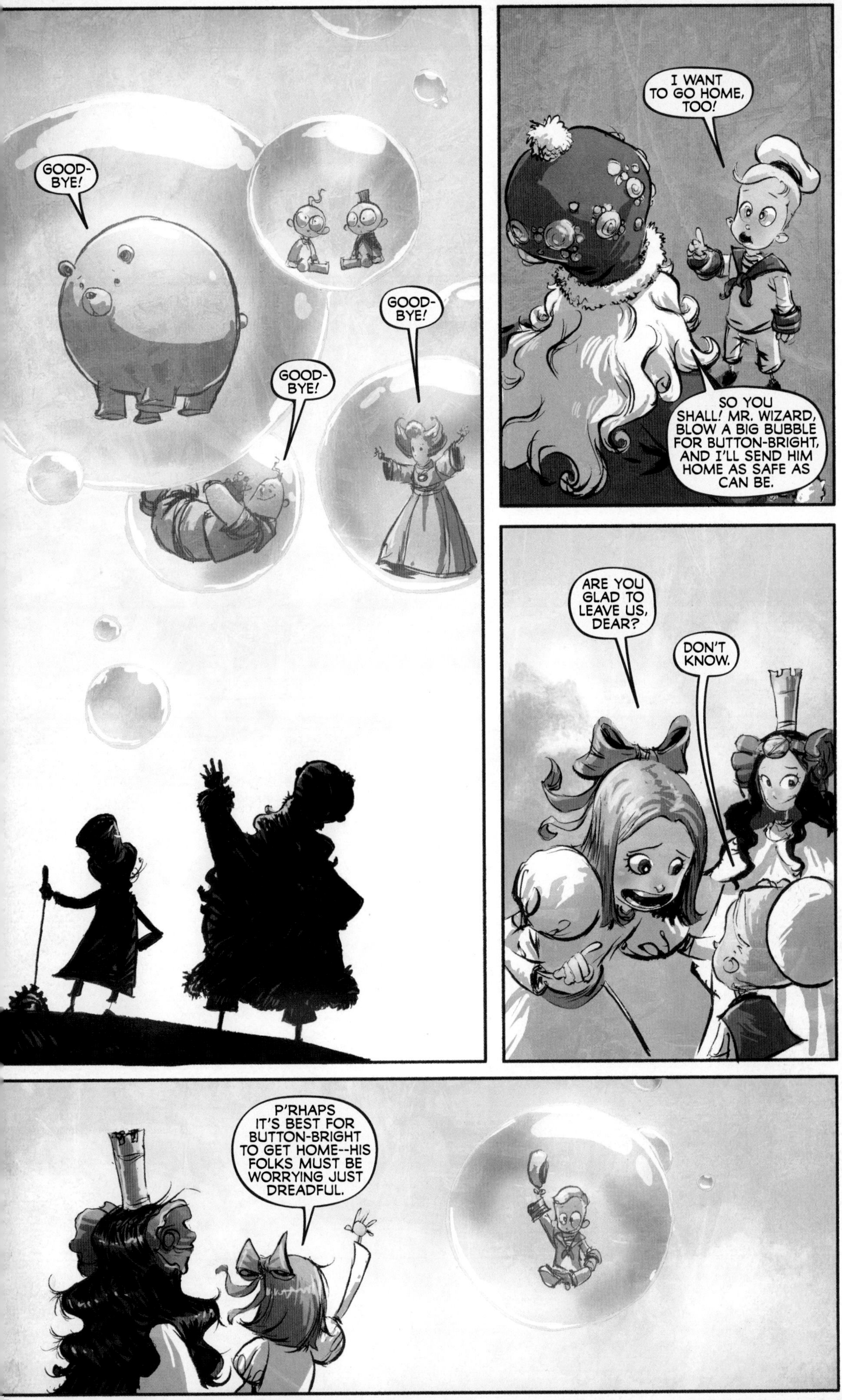
GOOD-BYE!
GOOD-BYE!
GOOD-BYE!
I WANT TO GO HOME, TOO!
SO YOU SHALL! MR. WIZARD, BLOW A BIG BUBBLE FOR BUTTON-BRIGHT, AND I'LL SEND HIM HOME AS SAFE AS CAN BE.
ARE YOU GLAD TO LEAVE US, DEAR?
DON'T KNOW.
P'RHAPS IT'S BEST FOR BUTTON-BRIGHT TO GET HOME--HIS FOLKS MUST BE WORRYING JUST DREADFUL.

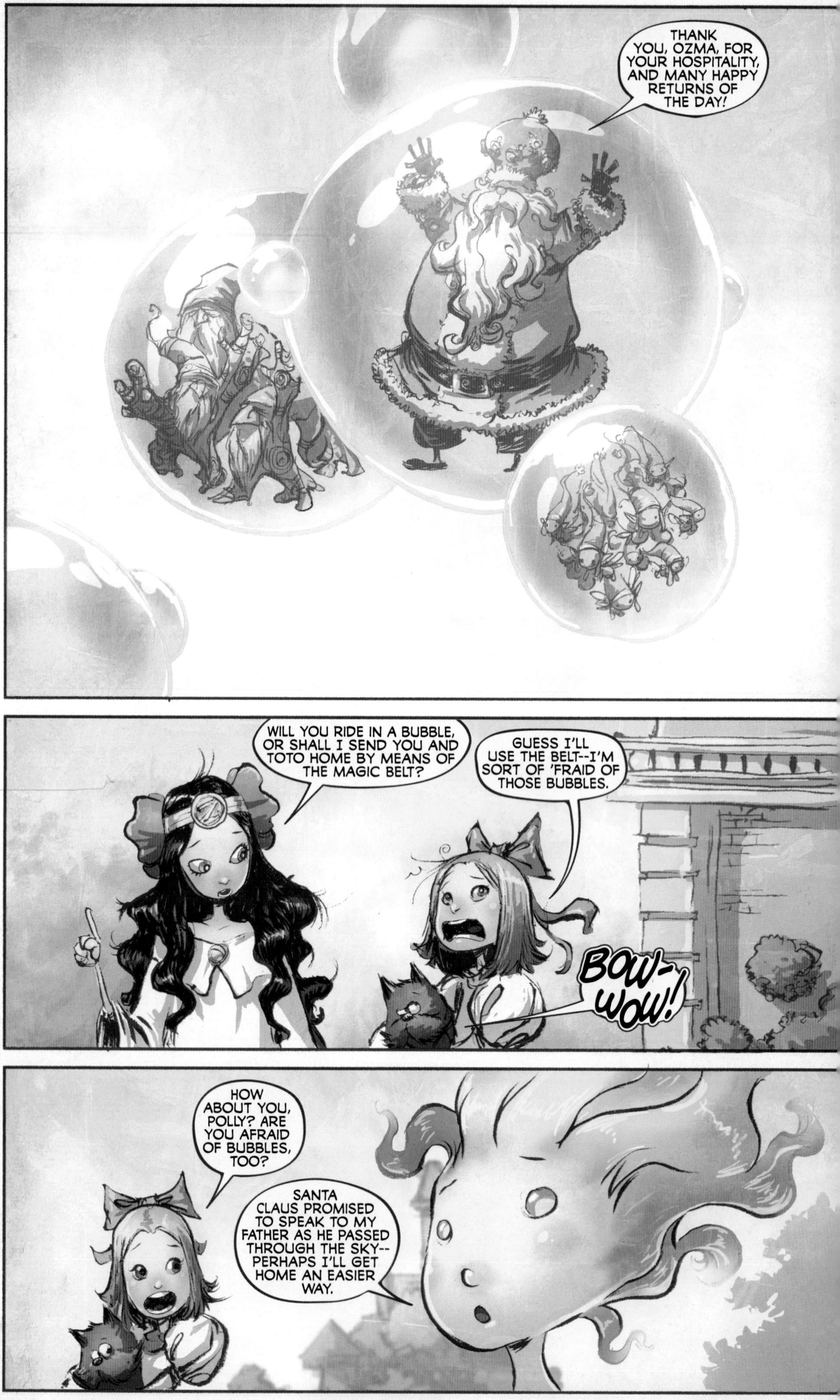
THANK YOU, OZMA, FOR YOUR HOSPITALITY, AND MANY HAPPY RETURNS OF THE DAY!
WILL YOU RIDE IN A BUBBLE, OR SHALL I SEND YOU AND TOTO HOME BY MEANS OF THE MAGIC BELT?
GUESS I'LL USE THE BELT--I'M SORT OF 'FRAID OF THOSE BUBBLES.
BOW-WOW!
HOW ABOUT YOU, POLLY? ARE YOU AFRAID OF BUBBLES, TOO?
SANTA CLAUS PROMISED TO SPEAK TO MY FATHER AS HE PASSED THROUGH THE SKY--PERHAPS I'LL GET HOME AN EASIER WAY.

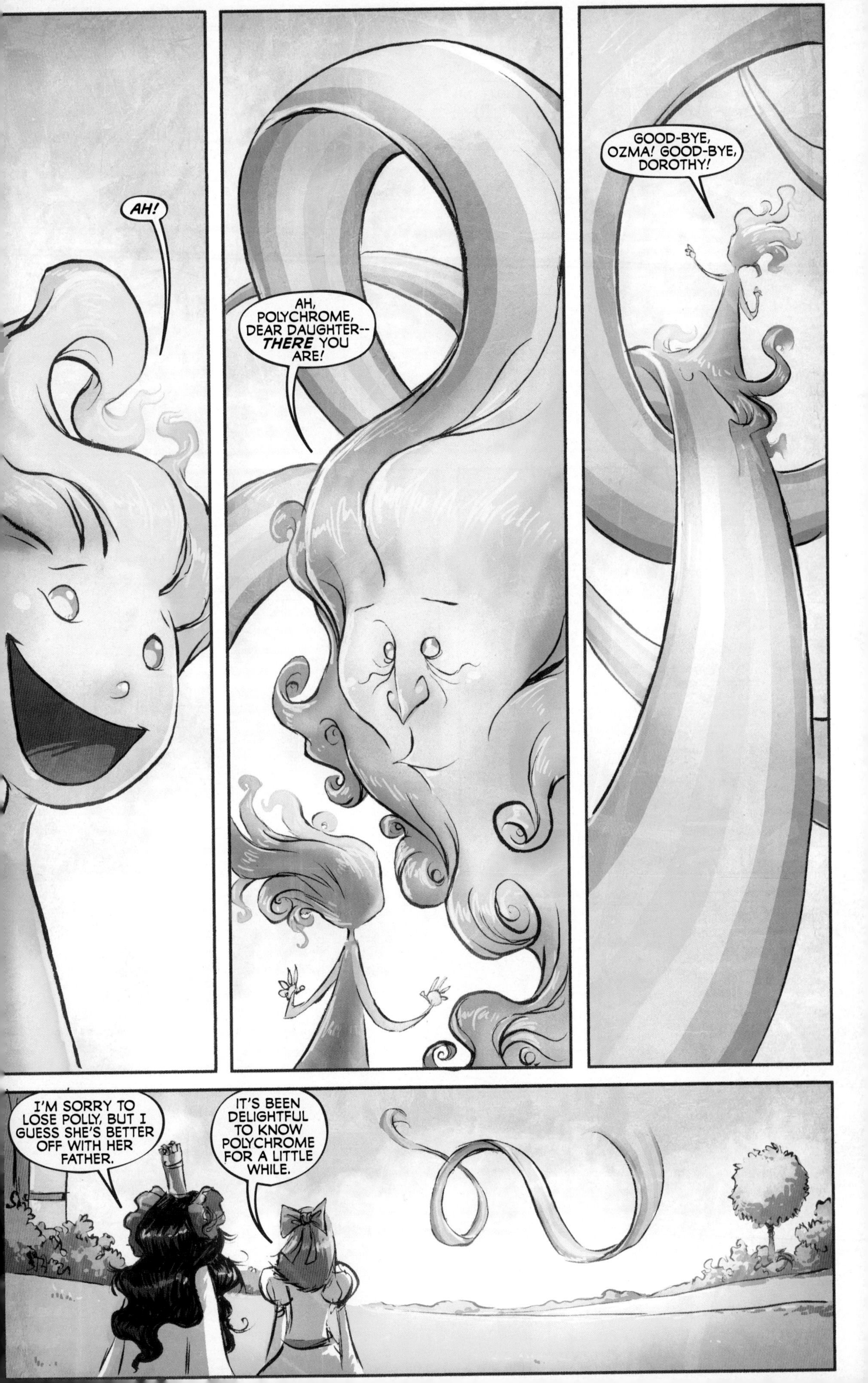
AH!
AH, POLYCHROME, DEAR DAUGHTER-- THERE YOU ARE!
GOOD-BYE, OZMA! GOOD-BYE, DOROTHY!
I'M SORRY TO LOSE POLLY, BUT I GUESS SHE'S BETTER OFF WITH HER FATHER.
IT'S BEEN DELIGHTFUL TO KNOW POLYCHROME FOR A LITTLE WHILE.

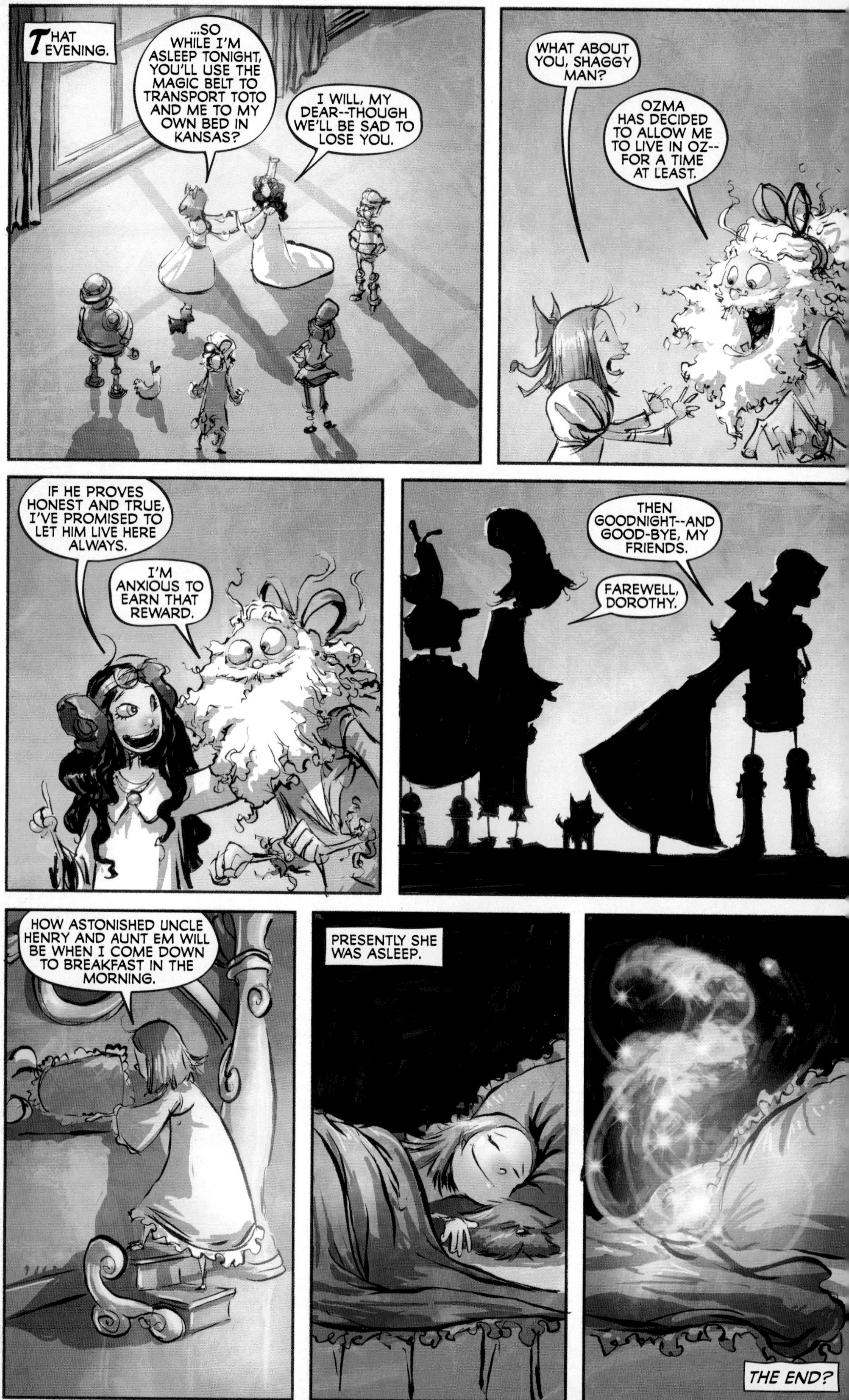
THAT EVENING.
...SO WHILE I'M ASLEEP TONIGHT, YOU'LL USE THE MAGIC BELT TO TRANSPORT TOTO AND ME TO MY OWN BED IN KANSAS?
I WILL, MY DEAR--THOUGH WE'LL BE SAD TO LOSE YOU.
WHAT ABOUT YOU, SHAGGY MAN?
OZMA HAS DECIDED TO ALLOW ME TO LIVE IN OZ-- FOR A TIME AT LEAST.
IF HE PROVES HONEST AND TRUE, I'VE PROMISED TO LET HIM LIVE HERE ALWAYS.
I'M ANXIOUS TO EARN THAT REWARD.
THEN GOODNIGHT--AND GOOD-BYE, MY FRIENDS.
FAREWELL, DOROTHY.
HOW ASTONISHED UNCLE HENRY AND AUNT EM WILL BE WHEN I COME DOWN TO BREAKFAST IN THE MORNING.
PRESENTLY SHE WAS ASLEEP.
THE END?

THE STORY CONTINUES IN...

THE EMERALD CITY OF OZ

ONE

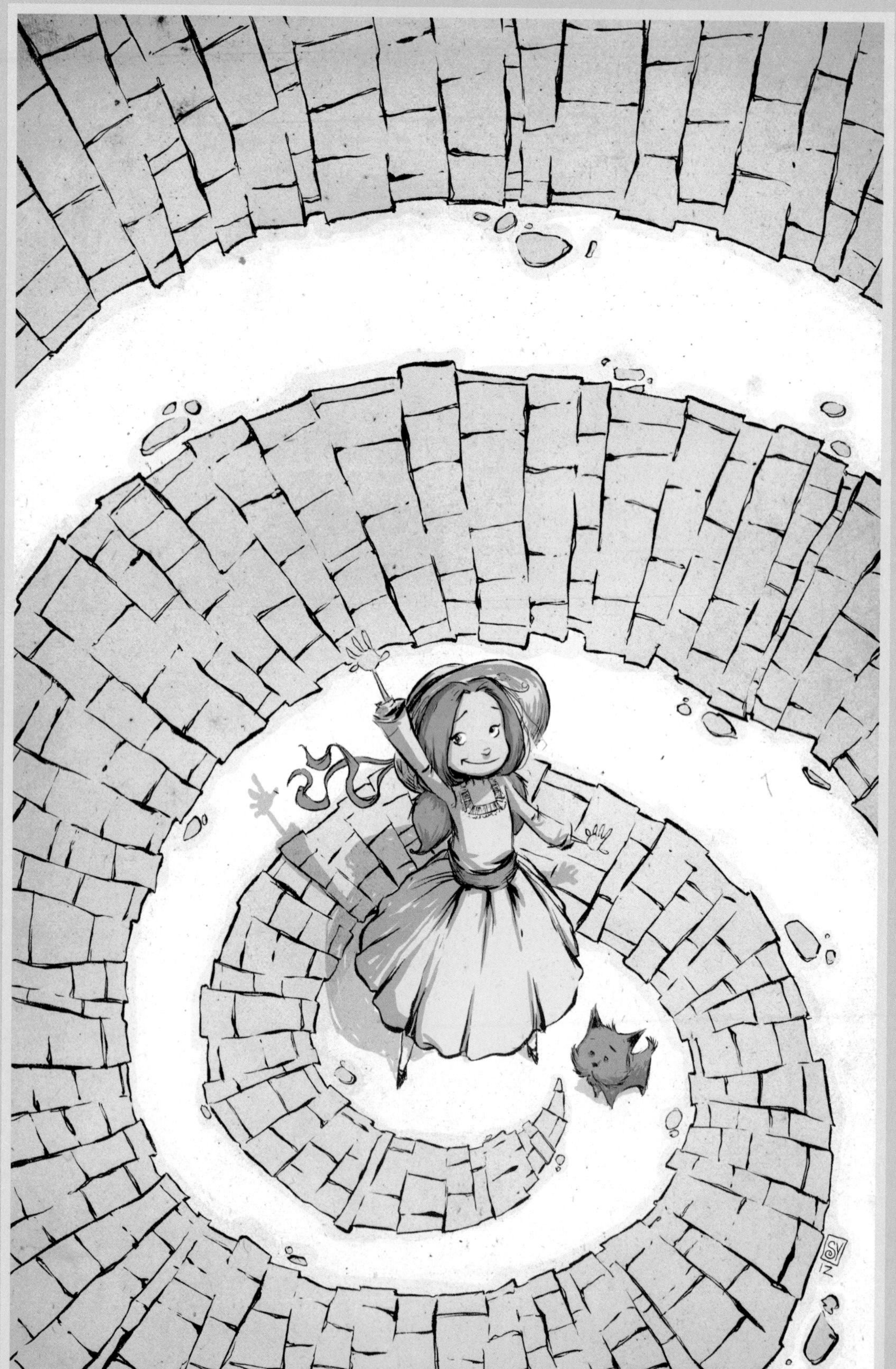

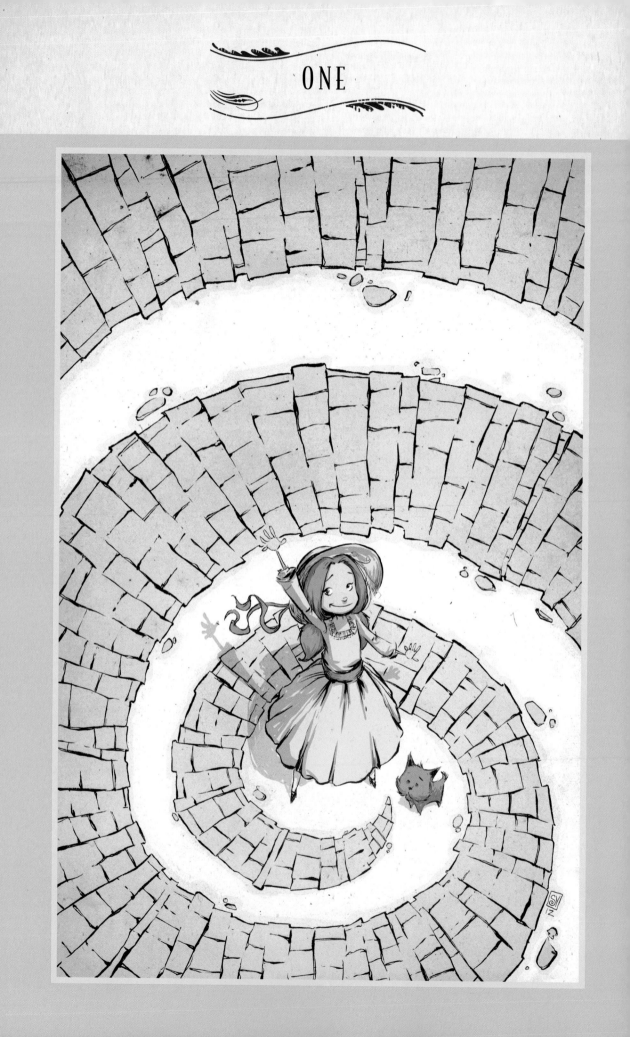

ONE

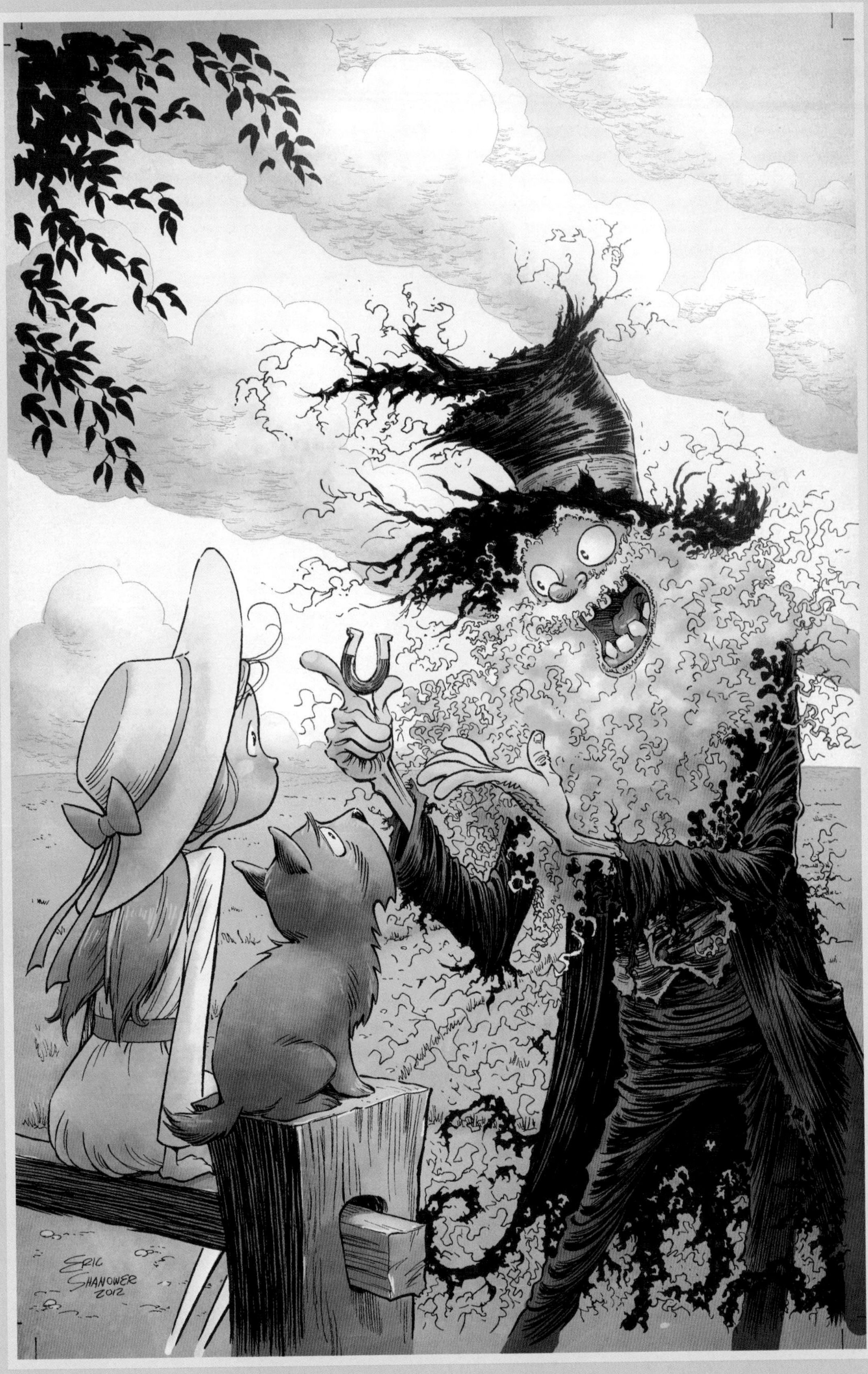
ERIC SHANOWER 2012

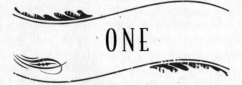

Variant Cover by Eric Shanower

ONE

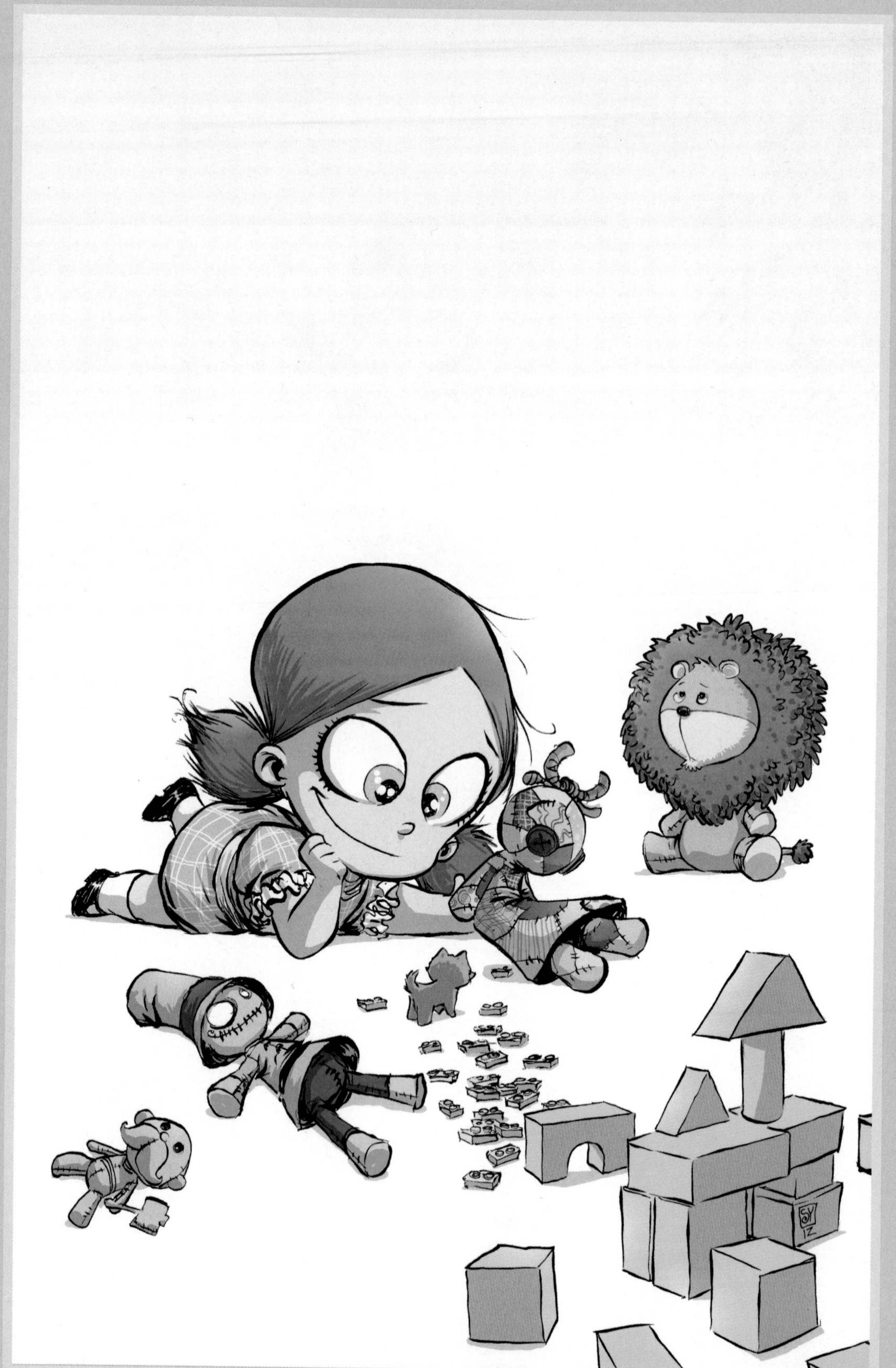

Baby Variant Cover by Skottie Young

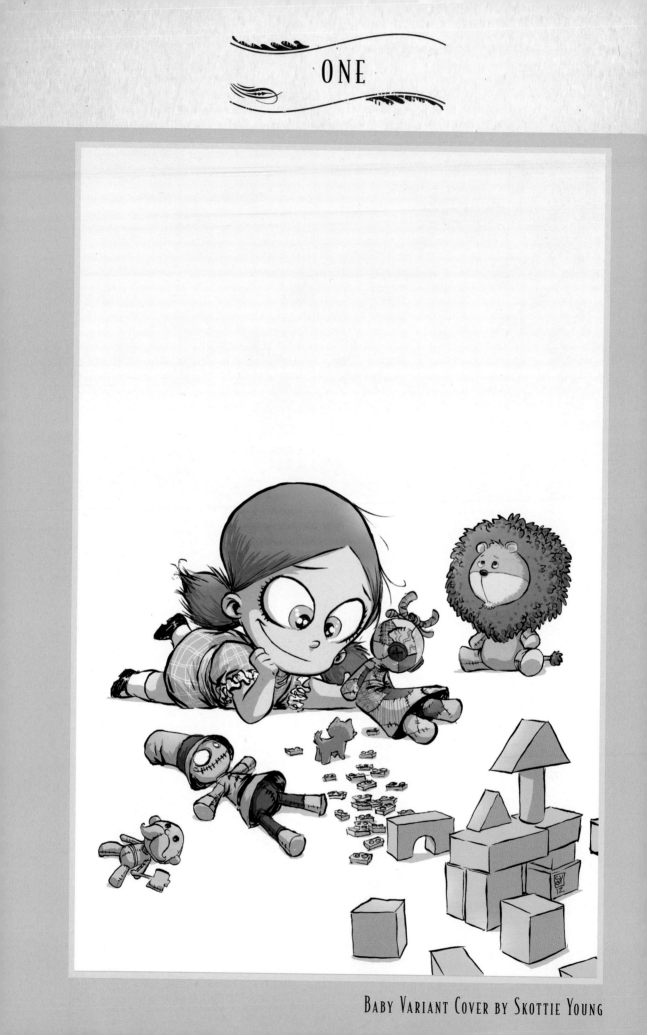

TWO

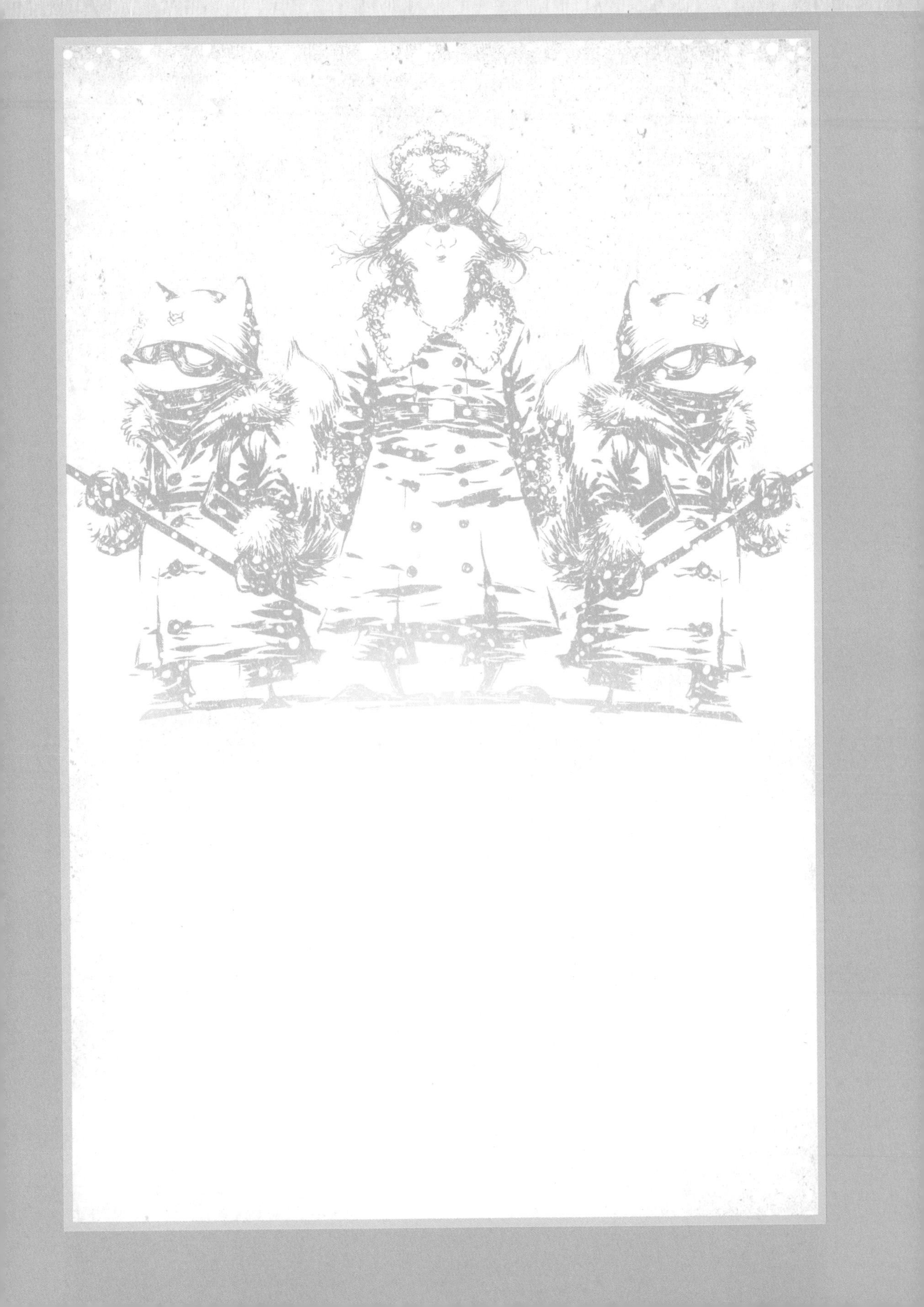

THREE

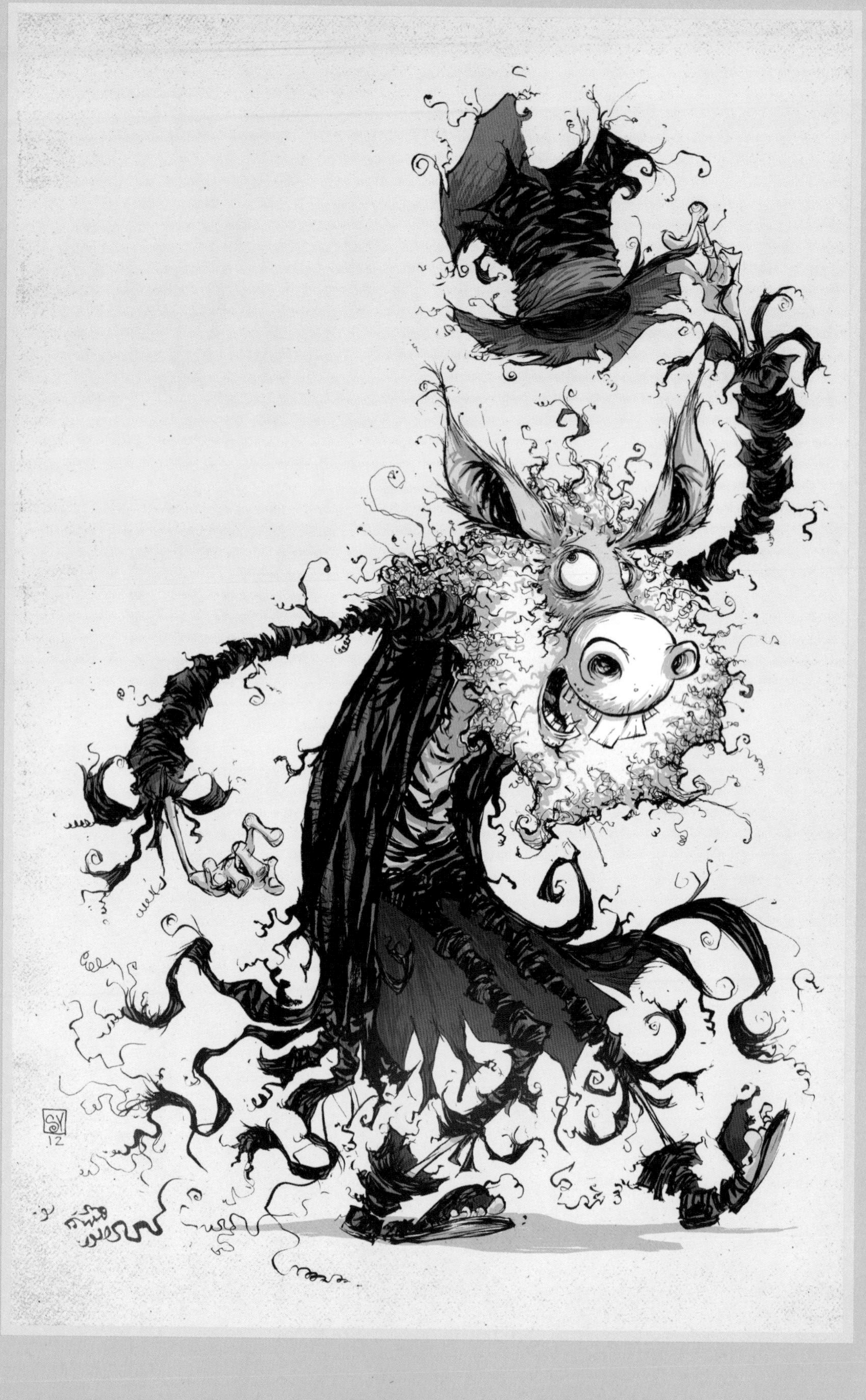

FOUR

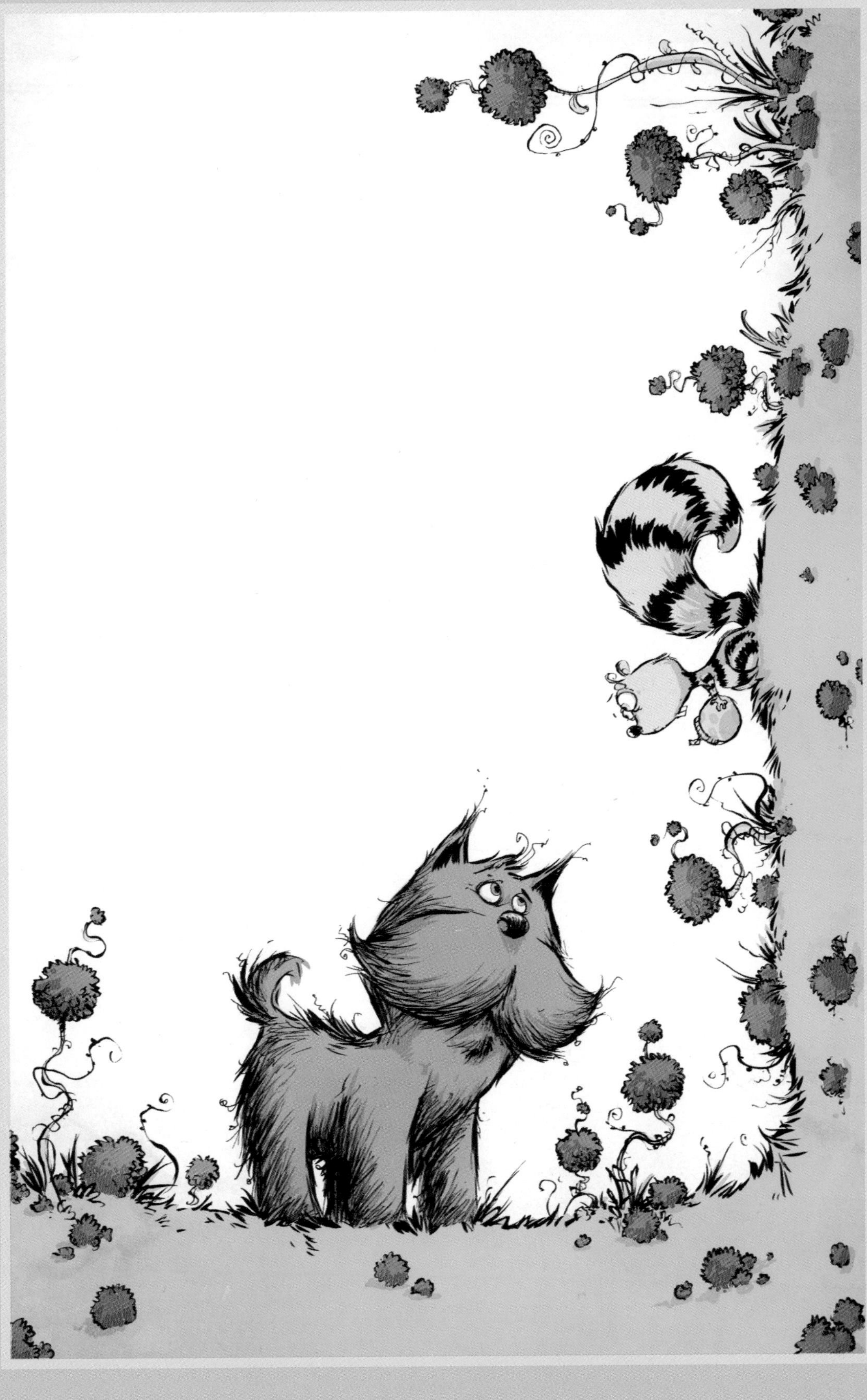

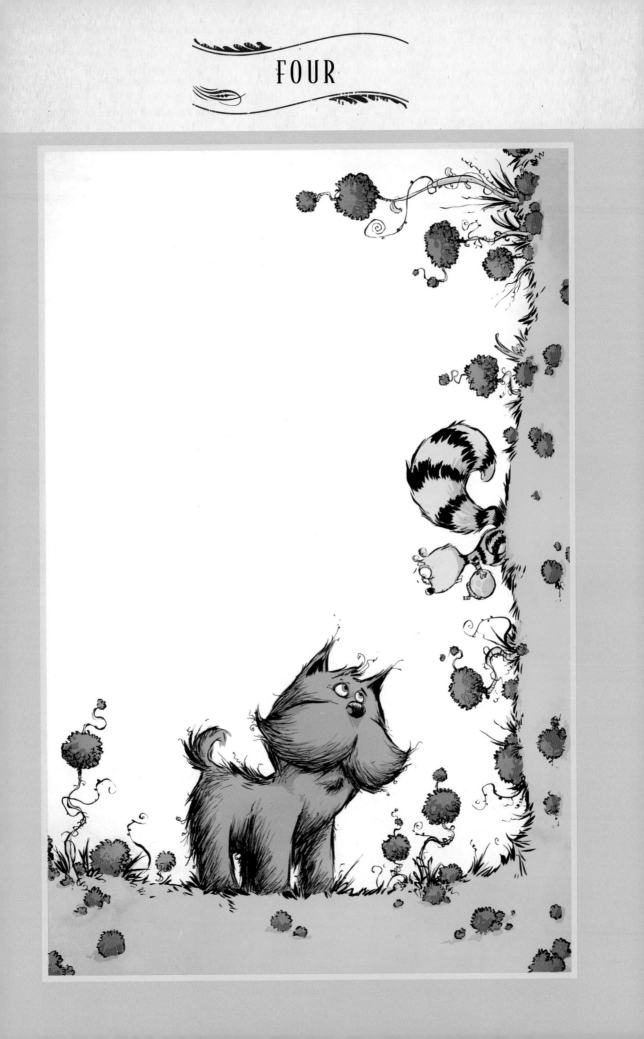

FIVE

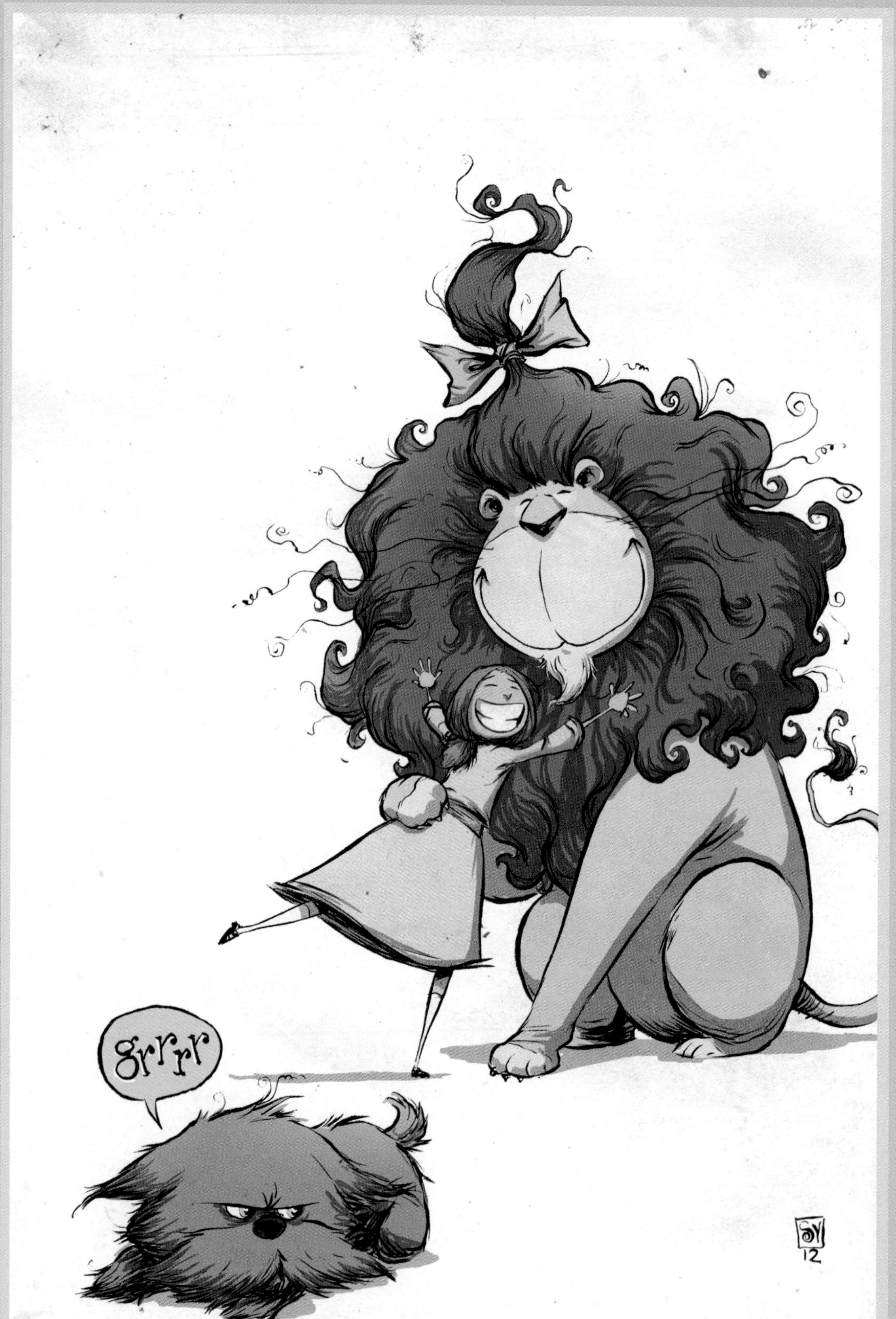
grrrr

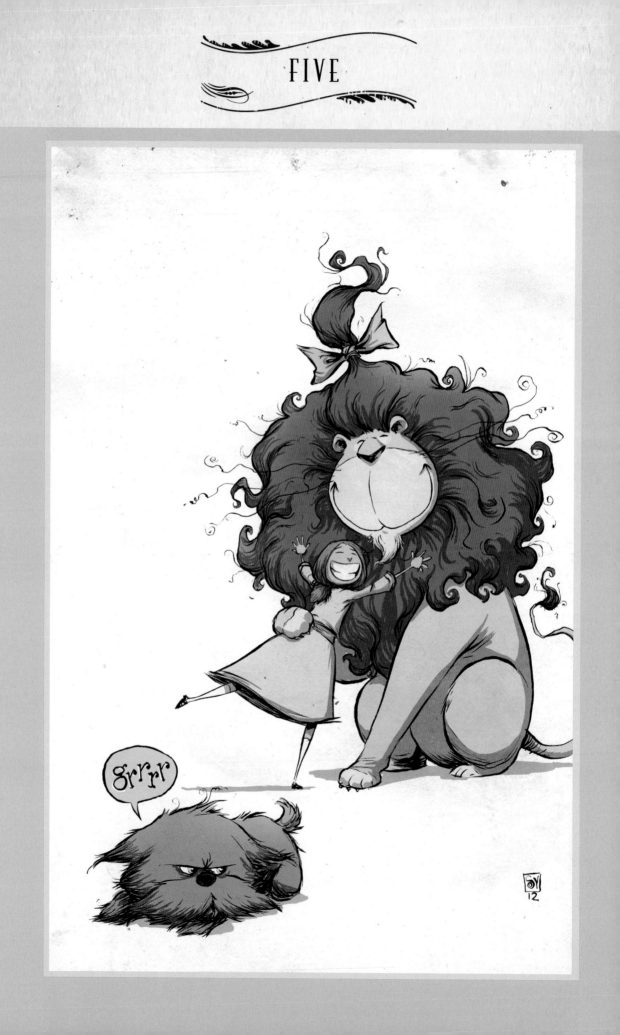

SIX

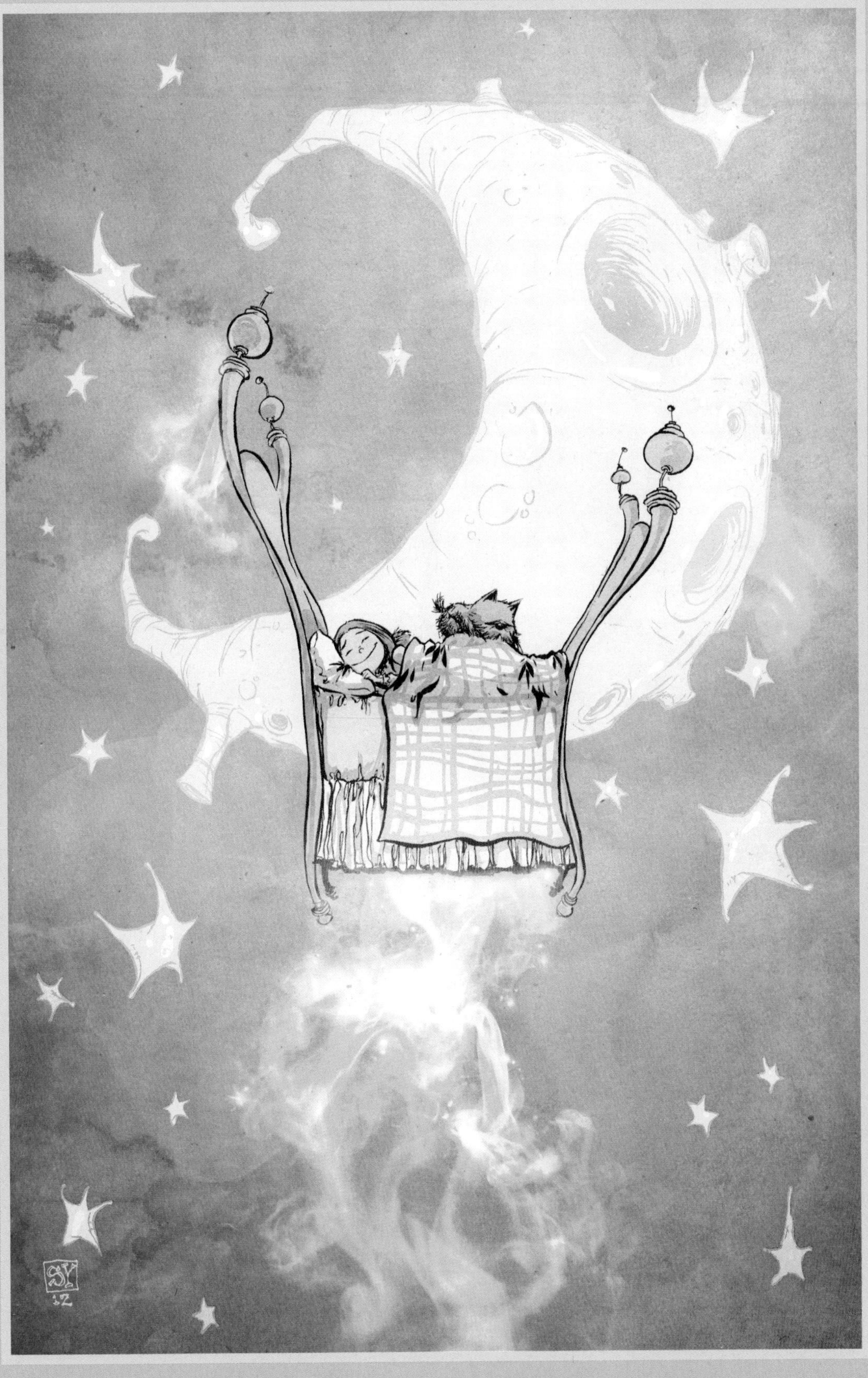